THE TRANSFORMATION OF THE
WORLD ECONOMY, 1980–93

Also by Robert Solomon

THE INTERNATIONAL MONETARY SYSTEM, 1945–1981

The Transformation of the World Economy, 1980–93

Robert Solomon
The Brookings Institution
Washington, DC

St. Martin's Press   New York

First published in the United States of America in 1994

Printed in Great Britain

ISBN 0–312–12389–2

Library of Congress Cataloging-in-Publication Data
Solomon, Robert.
The transformation of the world economy, 1980–93 / Robert Solomon.
p.   cm.
Includes index.
ISBN 0–312–12389–2
1. Economic history—1971–1990.   2. Economic history—1990–
I. Title.
HC59.S564   1994
330.9'048—dc20   94–27906
                                                          CIP

Contents

List of Tables and Figures

Tables

Figures

Preface

This book might have been entitled, less euphoniously but more accurately, *The Transformation of the World's Economies, 1980–93*. It deals not with the world economy as a unit but with the changes that have occurred in various countries and regions and with the interactions among them.

An explanation is in order regarding the amount of attention, and therefore the number of pages, devoted to different countries. They may be roughly in proportion to countries' size in the world economy, as measured by their gross domestic product (GDP). If so, that was not done deliberately. The reader will find more detail about developments and about the process of policymaking in the larger industrial countries than in most of the developing countries or the countries in transition from centrally-planned economies. The reason for that is the greater availability of information (or accessibility to me) about the policymaking process in the industrial countries. For example, I had the good luck to stumble upon Favier and Martin-Roland's *La Décennie Mitterrand*, which provides an amazing amount of detail concerning the policymaking process in France, including the discussions around the table in the Elysée between the President of the Republic and cabinet ministers.

Among countries other than those in the industrial world, the amount of space is roughly in line with the degree of transformation that has occurred since 1980. Clearly much more has happened in China than in Korea, in India than in Egypt, in Mexico than in Brazil.

I should say a word about countries that are not discussed. It was clearly impossible to cover every country. Thus I chose not to include Canada, largely because it underwent much less of a change in the past decade or so than other nations. The same is true for Italy, the Scandinavian countries, Pakistan, the Philippines, Australia and New Zealand. I have also omitted a detailed account of Spain, even though it changed greatly, simply because of the need to maintain balance in the treatment of different parts of the world.

The data used in this work come mostly from a limited and well-known number of publications: IMF, *International Financial Statistics* and *World Economic Outlook*, World Bank, *World Development Report* and OECD, *Economic Outlook*. When a source is not given for data, it can be found in one of these publications.

The writing of this book was started in Aix-en-Provence, during a month's stay as a visiting professor at the University of Aix-Marseille, thanks to Professor Gilles Nancy. It was completed at the Brookings Institution, where I have been a Guest Scholar for a number of years. I would like to thank Brookings President Bruce MacLaury for providing a most civilised and stimulating environment. One could not ask for a more congenial group of colleagues than one finds at Brookings.

I wish to express my deepest gratitude to the following friends and colleagues for reading and providing constructive comments and suggestions on various drafts of chapters of the book: Joseph Berliner, Susan Collins, Anne Cugliani, Harry Harding, Martin Kohn, Joseph Minarik, Fred Pryor, Alexis Rieffel, John Van Oudenaren (not just a friend and colleague but also my son-in-law) and Fern Solomon (not just a friend but my wife).

My thanks, finally, to Mr T.M. Farmiloe and Dr Giovanna Davitti at Macmillan for their friendly and encouraging cooperation throughout the entire process.

ROBERT SOLOMON

1 Introduction

The world has undergone dramatic changes since the end of the 1970s. This book uses a broad brush to trace the economic transformation, in its political context, that has occurred in the three areas that the globe is often divided into for economic purposes: industrial countries, former centrally-planned economies now in transition and developing countries. Actually, one of the significant changes has been a blurring of those very distinctions.

The economic transformation has several aspects. The principal one was a shift toward greater reliance on market forces in all three areas as governments became less involved in economic processes: markets were deregulated, import barriers were lowered, income taxes were reduced, state-owned enterprises were privatised and central planning, where it existed, gave way to direction by the price system. Another change was that 'globalisation' in both industry and finance was intensified. World trade continued to grow faster than world output. And there now exist 'world products': for example, a computer or an automobile may now be assembled from parts made in a number of countries. The international mobility of capital increased greatly, binding national financial markets closer together. One consequence of these developments was a heightening of the interdependence among nations and of the perception of that interdependence. That heightened perception shows up in efforts at policy co-ordination among groups of countries, in intensification of regional trading and financial arrangements – as in the European Union (formerly the European Community) and the North American Free Trade Agreement (NAFTA) – and in the completion of the negotiations in December 1993 on the GATT (General Agreement on Tariffs and Trade), the most comprehensive worldwide trade liberalisation in history.

The results of these transformations are not all favourable, but they will have lasting influence.

1

What initiated the changes? Partly the answer is a dissatis-faction with what had come earlier. The 1970s were a decade of discontent. Stagflation – an unhappy combination of too much inflation and rather stagnant economies – prevailed in industrial countries. Centrally-planned economies were less and less able to provide their citizens with rising stand-ards of living. Many developing countries had become more industrialised, often with the help of loans from banks abroad. But they were burdened with debts and often hob-bled by the heavy hand of governmental controls.

In looking for an explanation for these transformations, one has to recognise the influence of the revolution in tele-communications and computer technology. Television encouraged rising expectations, both economic and polit-ical, as people saw 'how the other half lives'. A striking instance was the series of revolutions in Eastern Europe in 1989, in which television played a significant role. In the Soviet Union, the process of economic reform 'was launched by a revolution in consumer desires and the idealization of Western consumption patterns'.[1] In China, in the throes of rapid economic reform,

> the constant refrain among urban Chinese is that they can no longer keep up with the quickened pace of life. They are confused by shifting values and outlooks on such fun-damentals as careers, as traditional beliefs clash with more modern – often Western – ideas picked up from radios and satellite dishes all over China.[2]

It is reported that hundreds of thousands of satellite dishes 'are sprouting, as the Chinese say, like bamboo shoots after a spring rain'. The result is that the Communist Party's monopoly on news is crumbling.[3]

The increase in migration from poorer to richer coun-tries, not only from developing nations to industrialised ones but within Europe, also owes something to the exist-ence of television. Actually, in present circumstances it may be said that 'a spectre is haunting Europe' – namely the possibility of mass emigration from Russia and the other republics of the former Soviet Union if political and economic instability should worsen there.

The computer has also bound the world closer together. It flashes new information around the planet instantaneously. Among other effects, it facilitates larger and faster flows of funds from country to country in response to differences in interest rates or expected changes in exchange rates.

History is also affected by the chance emergence of new political leaders at times when they can have an impact. In our period economic transformation was shaped by Margaret Thatcher, Ronald Reagan, François Mitterrand, Felipe Gonzalez, Mikhail Gorbachev, Boris Yeltsin, Lech Walesa, Vaclav Klaus, Deng Xiaoping, Carlos Salinas de Gortari, and Carlos Menem, among others. In the same period the Ayatollah Khomenei, Saddam Hussein, Mobutu Sese Seko also influenced world events but did not play a significant role in the economic transformations we are concerned with.

We owe to Isaiah Berlin the distinction between hedgehogs and foxes among statesmen (and, it must now be added, stateswomen): 'The fox knows many things, but the hedgehog knows one big thing', wrote the the Greek lyric poet Archilochus of the 7th century BC. Berlin first applied this analogy to 'writers and thinkers' in an essay on Tolstoy.[4] In his later essay on Franklin Roosevelt, Berlin, without mentioning hedgehogs and foxes, observed that there are

two contrasting types of statesmen, in each of which occasionally men of compelling stature appear. The first kind of statesman is essentially a man of single principle and fanatical vision. Possessed by his own bright, coherent dream, he usually understands neither people nor events. He has no doubts or hesitations and by concentration of will power, directness and strength he is able to ignore a great deal of what goes on outside him. This very blindness and stubborn self-absorption occasionally, in certain situations, enable him to bend events and men to his own fixed pattern....

The second type of politician possesses antennae of the greatest possible delicacy, which convey to him, in ways difficult or impossible to analyse, the perpetually changing contours of events and feelings and human activities round them – they are gifted with a peculiar, political sense fed on a capacity to take in minute impressions, to integrate a vast multitude of small evanescent unseizable detail, such as artists possess in relation to their material. Statesmen of this type know what to do and when to do it, if they are to achieve their ends, which themselves are usually not born within some private world of inner thought, or introverted feeling, but are the crystallisation, the raising to great intensity and clarity, of what a large number of their fellow citizens are thinking and feeling in some dim, inarticulate, but nevertheless persistent fashion.[5]

Among the first type of statesman I would include Thatcher and Reagan, while Mitterrand, Gorbachev and Yeltsin are more like the fox who knows many things. Vaclav Klaus appears to be a hedgehog in his determination to transform the Czech Republic into a democratic free-market economy. Mao Zedong was very much a hedgehog while Deng Xiaoping is a fox. Salinas and Menem appear to be fox-like but they have single-mindedly pursued economic reform.

The aim of this book is to bring out the transformations of the world's economies that have occurred since 1980 while these and other governmental leaders were in office. An effort is made to describe the essential changes that occurred and the interactions among nations as those changes worked themselves out. The book does not purport to be a comprehensive history. Rather its ambition is to highlight as far as can now be judged those events and developments that have had or will have a lasting impact in transforming the world economy.

It is obvious that this is an unfinished story. The world has altered considerably since the book was started and right up to the day of its completion. Needless to say that will continue.

2 The Way it was in 1980

History is a continuum, but it contains nodal points – periods of outstanding and lasting significance. The years 1979–81 brought political changes that were to have substantial impacts on economic policies and developments in many countries and would begin to transform the world economy. This narrative therefore begins with the opening of a new decade – the 1980s – one that was to contrast starkly with the 1970s. In this chapter a wide-angled snapshot view is presented of how the three segments of the world economy looked in 1980.

Many still speak or write of 'third world countries', by which is meant the developing countries of Latin America, Africa, the Middle East and Asia. The identity of the 'first' and 'second' worlds is less well-known. The first world consists of the industrial nations of North America and Western Europe plus Japan, Australia, and New Zealand. The second world countries were those with centrally-planned economies: the Soviet Union, China, and Eastern Europe, along with North Korea, and Cuba.

One of the many changes during the 1980s was the blurring of this way of categorising countries. A number of so-called less developed countries (LDCs) are industrialising rapidly and are becoming less and less distinguishable from those classified as industrial. It need hardly be mentioned that striking, historic reforms have begun in Eastern Europe, the former Soviet Union and China. Centrally-planned economies are becoming market economies, though the transition is difficult, lengthy, and one for which there is no precedent. Just as Karl Marx did not spell out how a capitalist economy was to be transformed into a socialist one, writers in the tradition of Adam Smith have not given us a blueprint for changing a command economy, in which most industry is in the hands of the government and economic decision-making is centralised, into a market economy where, broadly speaking, the 'the invisible hand'

5

does the regulating and most means of production are owned privately. Nevertheless, as the process goes on, at least some of the so-called second world nations will begin to resemble those in the first world.

Among the industrial countries too there were significant modifications in economic policy and performance in the 1980s, beginning with Margaret Thatcher's programme in the United Kingdom but also including the United States, France, Germany, Japan and others.

The decade began – purists will tell us that it started only in 1981, just as the present era began with year 1 rather than year 0 – in the midst of the second oil shock to the world economy. The fall of the Shah of Iran in 1979 led to a cessation of Iran's oil exports. The price of oil rose steeply – from about $13 per barrel in 1978 to $32 per barrel in mid-1980. As had become evident in 1974–5, when the oil price quadrupled, an increase in the price of oil has an economic effect on oil-importing countries similar to the imposition of a substantial sales tax. The price of the product goes up and consumers have less income available to spend on other goods and services. The result is a bout of inflation, at least temporarily, and sluggish economic expansion if not recession.

Thus, 1980 was not a good year for the world's economies. In the industrial countries, output, measured by gross national product (GNP) or gross domestic product (GDP), increased only 1.3 per cent, compared with an average of 4.1 per cent in the four previous years. Inflation averaged 12 per cent. The 'misery index' – the rate of unemployment plus the rate of inflation – was at a high level. In the LDCs, surprisingly, output continued to expand vigorously; the real GDP of the so-called non-oil developing countries rose 4.7 per cent in 1980, only slightly less than the average for 1970–9. But this was not to last.

Important political changes marked the opening of the era of the 1980s. In the United States, it was the last year of the less-than-successful Carter presidency. In that year, the country struggled with inflation, declining output, and an acute shortage of gasoline. Carter's difficulties were to be magnified by the seizure of American hostages in Teheran.

In November 1980, Ronald Reagan won the presidential election on a platform that promised to reduce the role of the Federal government (partly by shifting functions back to the states), to cut non-defence spending and tax rates, to balance the budget, to overcome inflation, to accelerate deregulation, and through these supply-side measures to renew economic growth.

In the United Kingdom, the political turnover came in May 1979 with a Conservative electoral victory and Mrs Thatcher's accession to 10 Downing Street as the first woman Prime Minister in Britain's history. She quickly set to work in an effort to cure the economy of some chronic ills: high inflation and low productivity growth. This was to be accomplished by firm monetary and fiscal policies, a smaller role for government, reduced power of trade unions, deregulation, and denationalisation.

In France, François Mitterrand, after two earlier unsuccessful attempts, won the presidential election in May–June 1981, replacing Valery Giscard d'Estaing. And the 'union of the left' – the Socialist and Communist Parties – achieved a majority in the National Assembly. Mitterrand's campaign was based largely on a promise to reduce unemployment, which was about $7\frac{1}{2}$ per cent in 1981, compared with less than 3 per cent in the early 1970s. Mitterrand intended to speed up the growth of the economy and shorten the working week. He was also committed to nationalising some banks and additional industries.

The political shift in Germany came in 1982, when the coalition between the Free Democrats and Helmut Schmidt's Social Democrats was dissolved and Helmut Kohl, head of the more conservative Christian Democrats, took over as Chancellor of the new coalition. Schmidt had been a towering figure on the international scene in the 1970s. He and Giscard – both former finance ministers – were largely responsible for the establishment of the European Monetary System in early 1979. This in turn created the momentum toward economic and monetary union that became evident in the later 1980s. But Schmidt faced serious domestic economic problems in 1980–82: growing unemployment, a large budget deficit, and high inflation by German standards. That is what led to the dissatisfaction of the Free Democrats and the end of their coalition with the Social Democrats.

Japan, which is completely dependent on imports for its oil supply, was hard-hit by the first oil shock. In 1980 Japan's balance of payments showed a current-account deficit of almost $11 billion. It was not evident as the decade opened that Japan would in a few years develop a massive surplus on current account and that its business and financial institutions would become major investors in the United States and elsewhere. Japan's political landscape continued to be dominated throughout the 1980s by the Liberal Democratic Party (LDP) – a party that was divided into fiercely competitive factions and was said to be neither liberal nor democratic nor a party. This gave rise to a number of political corruption scandals over the years. Oddly enough, the factional differences did not involve policy issues. They arose from the fact that political constituencies elected more than one representative to the Diet. That system was to be subject to reform after the LDP lost an election in 1993. In economic policy a move toward deregulation had begun, starting with the abolition of exchange controls in 1980.

Italy continued to experience frequent changes of government but economic policy did not change radically. In the early 1990s political scandals led to a popular decision to alter the electoral system away from proportional representation.

In Spain, an attempted military coup in February 1981 was thwarted with the help of King Juan Carlos. In December 1982 Felipe Gonzalez, a Socialist, became Prime Minister and presided over an economic renaissance as Spain undertook structural reforms and pursued policies that led to a high growth rate and attracted large amounts of capital from abroad, especially from its partners in the European Community, which Spain joined in 1986.

In Eastern Europe and the Soviet Union, too, change was in the air. In Poland, the Gdansk shipyard workers held a strike in 1980 and secured the legal right for workers to form independent unions and to strike – unprecedented in the Soviet bloc. The reforms brought a massing of Soviet troops on the common border and the threat of invasion. Lech Walesa emerged as a charismatic leader. In Hungary economic reform had been proceeding for some time. I heard Janos Kadar, in a private meeting with the Group of Thirty in Budapest in 1982, say that although he had been a Communist all his life, he had come to the conclusion that central planning did not work in a modern economy. In the Soviet Union, Leonid Brezhnev was obviously failing and would die in November 1982, to be succeeded by Yuri Andropov, who started the process of political and economic transformation.

Mao Zedong, China's paramount leader, died in 1976. At the end of 1978 Deng Xiaoping initiated a series of economic reforms in the agricultural sector and in foreign trade. In the mid-1980s the economic reform process – moving toward a market economy – was to be applied in the industrial sector and the Chinese economy was to achieve remarkably rapid growth rates.

In the third world, the oil-exporting countries, especially those in the Middle East, were once again piling up foreign exchange earnings. The current-account surplus of the OPEC nations, which had reached $68 billion in 1974, had virtually disappeared by 1978, mainly as the result of massive imports. As the oil price shot up again in 1979–80, the OPEC current-account surplus reappeared and was to reach $114 billion in 1980. Investment, both governmental and private, increased after the first oil shock and again after the second. The heightened economic activity brought with it a need for additional labour, which was satisfied by immigration. OPEC's large current-account surplus of 1979–80, like the one in 1974–5, was equal to about 1.3 per cent of the GNP of the rest of the world. The mirror image of this surplus was the combined current-account deficit of industrial and oil-importing developing countries.

The non-oil developing countries, whose terms of trade worsened in both oil shocks, consisted of at least three groups. In one group were about a dozen or so middle-income nations – mainly in Latin America. They had been

borrowing from commercial banks in the industrial countries throughout most of the 1970s, invested heavily and
grew fairly rapidly. This process was regarded as a 'recycling'
of the OPEC surpluses. As the oil exporters acquired foreign
exchange arising from their current-account surpluses, they
placed the funds in bank deposits or short-term securities in
the industrial countries. This enabled the banks to increase
their lending especially to developing countries. The latter
were then in a position to incur and finance enlarged current-account deficits. Thus, the OPEC surplus provided the
means for its own financing. What else could the OPEC
countries with large current-account surpluses do with their
accruing foreign exchange reserves but use them abroad to
make direct investments, buy securities, acquire bank deposits, or give grants to other countries? The smoothness of this
recycling process in 1974–8 refuted some of the apocalyptic
predictions made after the first oil shock.

Whether recycling would proceed so smoothly after the
second oil shock was not clear. The way it worked, most of
the lending and investing by the OPEC nations was in the
financial centres of Europe, North America, and Asia. The
funds then had to be redistributed to countries in deficit.
While some of the redistribution took the form of foreign
aid grants by industrial-country governments to low-income
LDCs and funds were available for loans by official multilateral institutions, a principal mode of recycling was extension
of credit by commercial banks in the industrial countries to
middle-income developing countries.

A major question in 1980 concerned the sustainability of
such lending by commercial banks. If it did not continue,
the recycling channels would become clogged and the
implications for both the LDCs that were heavy borrowers
and the rest of the world would be less than favourable. The
LDCs would not only have to reduce their imports, which
would have a depressive effect in the industrial countries,
but might also find it difficult to continue servicing their
debts.

Among a number of the Latin American LDCs military
governments existed in 1980. In fact Argentina, Chile,

Guatemala, Paraguay and Uruguay were condemned for human rights violations by the Council on Hemisphere Affairs. The continent was to undergo a tidal movement toward more democratic regimes in subsequent years.

Another, smaller, group of non-oil LDCs consisted of the so-called 'newly industrialised countries' (NICs) of Asia: Hong Kong, South Korea, Singapore, and Taiwan. They had been growing rapidly for some time, based on high rates of investment and strong export expansion. But they had a combined current-account deficit of $9 billion in 1980. So did most other countries in the region, except Indonesia, an oil exporter. In Korea the successful economic performance occurred under the presidency of General Park Chung Hee, who took power in a military coup in 1961. He was assassinated in October 1979, just when the second oil shock was depressing the economy and labour unrest was being expressed in demonstrations and strikes. Park was succeeded by another general, Chun Doo Hwan, and Korea remained under a military government, against which tens of thousands of students protested in 1980, followed by the imposition of martial law.

Singapore, a city state smaller than New York City, developed rapidly in the 1960s and 1970s under Prime Minister Lee Kuan Yew. Among other policies, he encouraged incoming direct investment with the result that much of Singapore's output comes from foreign-owned firms. In 1980 Singapore was in the early stages of its 'second industrial revolution' aimed at the development of high technology industries.

The third, and numerically greater, group of oil-importing developing countries – those with relatively low incomes – had to rely on official assistance from governments and multilateral institutions to help finance their enlarged deficits. These countries are in south Asia and Africa. There is a great diversity, both political and economic, among them.

In India, Indira Ghandi became prime minister for the second time in January 1980. Its economy was one of the most highly regulated outside the Communist bloc, and its growth rate in the years 1965–80 was relatively low as compared with other developing countries

Another political change early in the decade was in Egypt, where the slain Anwar Sadat was succeeded as president by Hosni Mubarak. His country was the beneficiary of heavy financial assistance from the United States, owing to Sadat's participation in the Camp David peace accord with Israel in 1979.

With the major exceptions of Gabon and Nigeria, most southern African countries were adversely affected by the rise in oil prices in 1979–80. The years ahead would not be kind to their populaces.

Our narrative begins in an atmosphere of uncertainty, political and economic, as the three areas of the world economy were being affected for a second time by a dramatic rise in the price of oil. In the OPEC countries, particularly those in the Middle East, there was a sense of economic power as the wealth came pouring in, but perhaps also an inquietude as events in Iran unfolded and its war with Iraq broke out in September 1980.

3 Changing Philosophies of Economic Policy

The 1980s began with an external shock to most economies as the world price of oil rose by about 150 per cent. The years around 1980 also witnessed numerous changes in political leadership, as was noted in the previous chapter. Many, though not all, of the political shifts brought fundamental policy modifications. In some cases – Thatcher and Reagan especially – the new leaders were hedgehogs rather than foxes and acted to impose a new ideology that was closer to orthodoxy than what it replaced. In other cases the alteration in policies – also toward greater orthodoxy – came about through the force of circumstances and under the leadership of foxes like Mitterrand in France and Gonzalez in Spain. These are four selected examples from among the industrial countries. As our story unfolds we shall encounter other instances of striking shifts away from interventionist policies based on changes in economic philosophy – sometimes carried out by ideological hedgehogs and sometimes by pragmatic foxes.

3.1 THATCHER AND REAGAN

Margaret Thatcher and Ronald Reagan, who have been called 'soul mates', are strong believers in free markets. They each initiated a series of policies that were designed to free up their economies and thereby improve economic performance by reducing the role of government. However one judges their success, there is little doubt that they had a major impact on their own countries and, very likely, on the policies of many other countries.

Even casual observation reveals a number of striking similarities between 'Thatcherism' and 'Reaganomics'. Both Thatcher and Reagan asserted primacy over the power of

13

trade unions, Reagan by breaking the air controllers' strike early in his administration and Thatcher by putting down a miners' strike in 1985. Union membership fell in both countries during their terms of office. Both emphasised supply-side policies, especially reductions in income taxes, but the favourable effects on economic growth promised by these policies are difficult to detect. Both pursued deregulation, with mixed results. Both left their successors with recessions to contend with and both were critical – Thatcher openly and Reagan by inference – of their successors. And, incidentally, both survived assassination attempts: Reagan was wounded by gunshot in 1981 and Thatcher escaped a bombing that killed five others in 1984.

In office, Thatcher and Reagan differed in many ways. She was not only a hard worker but often took on tasks that might well have been left to her ministers or staff. Reagan was above all that. He was amiable but unfocused except for a few strongly-held beliefs. She was analytical; he operated by instinct. He loved to use jokes and anecdotes; she was rather humorless. He had a soft heart; she could be hard as nails. She was a natural orator. Reagan's style, as Nigel Lawson puts it,

> was that of the actor he once was. He knew his lines perfectly, and had rehearsed and polished them endlessly, with the result that everything, from the generalizations to the anecdotes, came across with impressive fluency, obvious sincerity, and complete command. But take him off the ground covered by his script, and he often had difficulty in grasping the point.[1]

What Thatcher and Reagan shared as government leaders was a simple tenet: get the government off the backs of the people and let 'the magic of the market place' prevail.

3.2   THATCHER'S BRITAIN

The tone and substance of what was to happen in economic policy formation in many countries were foreshadowed beginning in May 1979 when Margaret Thatcher became Prime Minister. The daughter of the owner of two grocery stores who was also a local politician in Grantham, the town of her birth, Margaret Thatcher was educated at Oxford, reading chemistry and later becoming a tax attorney. She was intelligent, hard working and tough. The sobriquet 'iron lady', coined in the Soviet Union in 1976, came into wide use. But the lady is also very feminine. François Mitterrand is said to have described her as having 'the eyes of Caligula and the lips of Marilyn Monroe'.[2] Her personal qualities helped her to dominate the British government for twelve years. She was also lucky in that not long after she took office Britain became a net exporter of oil from the North Sea fields.

It is said of some people that they may be wrong but are never in doubt. Margaret Thatcher is probably in that genre. I met her a year and a half before she became Prime Minister, when she visited the Brookings Institution. I was struck by her strong-mindedness, her keen intelligence, her knowledge of economics and her ability to make her presence felt and to take charge of a meeting.

What she took charge of on entering Number 10 was an economy that had been in trouble through a good part of the 1960s and 1970s. Plagued by inflation that was aggravated by persistent upward trade-union pressure on wages and by slow productivity growth – attributable in part to 'overmanning' – Britain had been forced to devalue sterling in 1967, to leave the EC exchange-rate snake in 1972, to borrow from the IMF in 1976–7 and to put up with widespread strikes in 1979.

In September 1976, James Callaghan inadvertently paved the way for Mrs Thatcher's economic philosophy in a speech at a Labour Party Conference, where he said:

> We used to think that you could just spend your way out of a recession and increase employment by cutting taxes and boosting government spending. I tell you in all candour that that option no longer exists, and that insofar as it ever did exist, it worked by injecting inflation into the economy. And each time that happened the average level of

unemployment has risen. Higher inflation, followed by higher unemployment. That is the history of the last twenty years.[3]

At the time of the election in May 1979, the economy had been expanding at a good clip but inflation was in double digits, partly driven by wages rising by more than 15 per cent per year for most of the decade. Unemployment, though well above the levels of the first half of the 1970s, was somewhat lower than in 1976–8.

The broad economic objectives of the Thatcher government were to lower the rate of inflation and put the United Kingdom on a path of sustainable growth, to denationalise state-owned industries, to deregulate the economy and to reduce the strong influence of trade unions. In the words of Sir Alan Walters, economic adviser to Mrs Thatcher, 'The objective was to get a market economy functioning efficiently without suffocating government intervention.'[4]

The instruments for achieving these objectives were a strict monetarist policy like that espoused by Milton Friedman (he was, in fact, one of her advisers), a medium-term financial strategy to lower the budget deficit, restraint on wages, legislation to alter the way trade unions operated and a pound sterling that was appreciating under the influence of high interest rates and strong export earnings from oil.

One of the basic differences in economic philosophy between Thatcher and Reagan was that she held strongly to the need to balance the budget whereas Reagan merely paid lip-service to that principle. Ironically, Thatcher's Britain demonstrated in the later 1980s that a country can develop a large current-account deficit even when its budget is in surplus.

3.3   REAGAN'S AMERICA

Ronald Reagan took up residence in the White House about a year and a half after Margaret Thatcher came to power. While she moved into Downing Street with a coherent notion of what she wanted to accomplish as regards economic policy and how to go about it, Ronald Reagan's views were less distinct.

Part of Reagan's appeal, not only to members of his own party but also to those who had usually voted for the other party ('Reagan Democrats'), was his ability to characterise America in glowing terms, to help his countrymen 'to stand tall'. One of his favourite ways of doing this was to describe his country as 'a city upon a hill', which comes from The Gospel According to St Matthew and was used in a sermon preached in 1630 by John Winthrop, a governor of Massachusetts Bay Colony: 'For we must consider that we shall be a city upon a hill. The eyes of all people are upon us, so that if we shall deal falsely with our God in this work we have undertaken, and so cause Him to withdraw His present help from us, we shall be made a story and a byword through the world.'

Just as Thatcher's economic philosophy was anticipated by her predecessor, Reagan's approach to government was foreshadowed by President Jimmy Carter who not only initiated deregulation but declared

> we really need to realize that there is a limit to the role and the function of government. Government cannot solve our problems, it can't set our goals, it cannot define our vision. Government cannot eliminate poverty or provide a bountiful economy or reduce inflation or save our cities or cure illiteracy or provide energy. And government cannot mandate goodness.

He took some of the sting out of this surprising statement by adding: 'Only a true partnership between government and the people can ever hope to reach these goals.'[5]

Reagan's basic aims, like Thatcher's, were to lower inflation and to speed up economic growth. These were to be accomplished by reducing government spending while strengthening national defence, cutting taxes, lightening the 'burden' of Federal regulation, and encouraging 'a monetary policy on the part of the independent Federal Reserve System which is consistent with these policies'.

President Reagan's appointments to high office in his first administration reflected his lack of single-mindedness. His Treasury Secretary, Donald Regan, had been head of Merrill Lynch and was not a man with a strong ideological bent. He never received a single word of policy guidance from the President, nor had a one-on-one meeting with him as Treasury Secretary. It was taken for granted by the President that his Secretary of the Treasury had absorbed his campaign pledges.[6] Reagan's Chairman of the Council of Economic Advisers, Murray Wiedenbaum, was – and is – a well-known economist who is certainly not an ideologue. David Stockman, Director of the Office of Management and Budget, appeared to be idiosyncratic in both his behaviour and his policy views. He too has reported that Reagan 'gave no orders, no commands; asked for no information; expressed no urgency'.[7] But three Treasury appointees were men with burning convictions. The Under Secretary for Monetary affairs, Beryl Sprinkel, was known as a single-minded monetarist, a faithful disciple of Milton Friedman. The Under Secretary for Tax Policy, Norman Ture, and the Assistant Secretary for Economic Policy, Paul Craig Roberts, are both orthodox supply siders.

Although this diffusion existed in the early days of the Reagan tenure, the supply-side philosophy had a powerful influence on the President, on his team, and on a number of members of Congress – most notably Representative Jack Kemp of upstate New York. Outside the administration, Arthur Laffer and Jude Wanniski used their well-honed talents for publicity to popularise the supply-side view, as did George Gilder in his book *Wealth and Poverty*.[8]

What is the supply-side view all about? Its main thesis is that what drives economies are incentives to engage in economic activity – incentives felt by workers, by savers, and by investors. The way to strengthen these incentives is to reduce marginal tax rates.

No economist will disagree with the proposition that incentives are important. What distinguished the small but vociferous band of supply siders in and around the first Reagan Administration was their rejection of the mainstream belief held by both Keynesians and monetarists that aggregate demand is a major – if not the major – determinant of output, income, employment, and prices. This rejection was spelled out in a confused way in a book by *The Wall Street Journal* editorial page editor Robert Bartley.[9]

The supply siders claimed that cutting marginal tax rates would lead to large increases in employment, in saving, and in investment while also reducing the rate of inflation. All that seemed to matter was tax rates. Even the budget deficit could be ignored, either because of a Laffer curve effect – the view propounded by economist Arthur Laffer that tax cuts would induce such a large increase in incomes that growth of tax revenues would rise despite the lower tax rates – or the Paul Craig Roberts argument that issuing bonds is equivalent to taxing the public as a way of financing the budget deficit.[10] The latter argument, it may be noted, must have been reconsidered; it does not appear in a book that Roberts published after he left office.[11]

While supply siders tended to ignore the budget deficit, they were not alone. Other conservative thinkers were also tolerant, if not welcoming, of the budgetary imbalance on the grounds that deficits create persistent political pressure to reduce government spending. Olivier Blanchard, of the Massachusetts Institute of Technology, identifies this as the 'centerpiece' of the Reagan conservative strategy, distinguishing it 'from its European counterparts and their strategy of fiscal austerity'.[12]

One of the many oddities in the case put forward by the supply siders was a surprising neglect of the role of corporations in capital formation. Reductions in marginal tax rates were supposed to lead to greater investment. The bulk of investment in the United States, and other industrial countries, is carried out by corporate business. But the supply siders were concerned almost entirely with cutting the taxes paid by individuals.

It is difficult to determine how seriously this group of ideologues was taken at higher levels of the administration. There was a good deal of in-fighting among the White House, the Office of Management and Budget, and the

Treasury, as is described in detail in Craig Roberts's book. And the supply siders were not fully united; Roberts rejected Laffer's curve and regarded Wanniski as a bull in a china shop. What is clear is that the supply siders helped to engineer the massive tax cut enacted in 1981 – the so-called Kemp–Roth legislation. That the ideology had influence at a high level is illustrated by a hyperbolic statement in a speech by Treasury Secretary Regan in early 1981 to the effect that supply-side economics is a new economic paradigm comparable to Sir Isaac Newton's approach to physics, which 'changed mankind's understanding of the universe'.[13]

The failure of the Reagan tax cuts to produce the results promised by the supply siders induced two types of rationalisation. One was to blame the Federal Reserve's restrictive monetary policy – especially Chairman Paul Volcker, who became Paul Craig Roberts's favourite whipping boy – for repressing the economy. This argument was, of course, inconsistent with the supply-side view that aggregate demand is unimportant. The other response was to claim that the promised results were realised. For example, Jude Wanniski wrote in 1991 that the Reagan tax cuts were responsible for making the US economy one-third bigger than a decade earlier.[14] What he failed to point out is that the economy grew even faster in the two previous decades. Robert Bartley goes even further in exaggeration; he measures economic expansion from the bottom of the 1981–2 recession to the peak in 1990 and compares that with the growth rate from the peak year 1973 to the recession year 1982, thereby claiming to demonstrate the beneficial effects of supply-side policies.[15]

In general, the promised effects on investment and saving are impossible to discern in the available statistics. Some increase in labour supply occurred but much of it was due to factors other than tax reform.[16]

While Ronald Reagan was anxious to lighten the tax burden on the American public, he was also eager to strengthen the country's defences against what he was later to call 'the evil empire'. The result was that Federal defence expenditures rose from 22.7 per cent to 27.6 per cent of total budget outlays in the eight Reagan years.

The growing budget deficits that resulted from the combination of tax cuts and rising military outlays were to have major effects on the US economy, on the dollar's exchange rates, on the balance of payments and on America's trade partners in both the industrial and developing worlds. From 1980 to early 1985, the average value of the dollar in terms of the currencies of other industrial countries rose by 80 per cent. Can one imagine any other country putting up with that? Such a large currency appreciation would probably have toppled a government more sensitive to the foreign trade position and less addicted to the belief that markets are always right. That view was to change in 1985 when James Baker became Secretary of the Treasury.

Deregulation was another significant plank in the Reagan platform, though it started under President Carter in the oil and airline industries. The deregulation of saving and loan associations – widening their scope to invest well beyond their traditional field of residential housing – has been assigned some of the blame for the crisis that afflicted those institutions in the latter part of the 1980s. But other aspects of deregulation have been widely applauded – for example, liberalisation in telecommunications and natural gas.

In line with reducing the role of government in the economy, Treasury Under Secretary Sprinkel made it known in May 1981 that the United States would henceforth intervene in foreign exchange markets 'only when necessary to counter conditions of disorder in the market'. This decision was based on the view that

> markets have become more efficient in evaluating and adjusting to new information. Significant and frequent intervention by governments assumes that a relatively few officials know better where exchange rates should (or shouldn't) be than a large number of decision makers in the market, and that public funds should be put at risk on the basis of that assumption.[17]

In general, then, both Thatcher and Reagan tried to take the government 'off the backs' of their populaces. While in both cases the move toward more market-oriented economies succeeded, the macroeconomic policies left something to be desired, as we shall see in the next chapter.

It is difficult to discern an economic philosophy during the four years of the presidency of George Bush, aside from his campaign pledge, 'Read my lips: no new taxes.' In a four-part survey of economic policymaking in the Bush years, published just before the election of 1992, *The Washington Post* reported that

> President Bush' s top economic advisers have worked for nearly four years without agreeing on an overall philosophy or plan and have been divided by personal animosity and turf fights that are fierce even by Washington standards, according to more than two dozen sources inside and outside the administration.

The same report tells us that Treasury Secretary Nicholas Brady was 'muddled', Office of Management and Budget Director Richard Darman was brilliant, had an 'acid tongue' and was in conflict with other members of the administration; and Council of Economic Advisers Chairman Michael Boskin was often left out of the policymaking circuit. The President is said to have complained that 'it is hard at times to sort out or make sense of the advice he receives from his economic team ....'[18]

The election of William J. Clinton in 1992 ushered in a very different approach to government. Clinton ran for office on a programme calling for 'change' and he lost no time, after assuming office, in proposing a reduction in the budget deficit and starting the process of reforming the health care system of the United States. In economic policy, his first year featured passage by Congress of his proposal to reduce the budget deficit modestly – from 4 per cent to 3 per cent of GDP over a five year period and passage of the North America Free Trade Agreement (NAFTA).

3.4   MITTERRAND'S FRANCE

François Mitterrand, who had unsuccessfully run for the Presidency of the Republic against de Gaulle in 1965 and Giscard in 1974, finally came to power in the elections of May–June 1981, along with a Socialist majority in the National Assembly. The first Mitterrand government, under Prime Minister Pierre Mauroy, included four Communist ministers. This political upheaval, while it may have shocked some of the chanceries of the world, oddly enough was greeted by Washington and Moscow in almost identical language. The official statements from Reagan's White House and Brezhnev's Kremlin both dwelt on the traditional ties between their countries and France and expressed assurance of continued good relations. 'Brezhnev could have signed Reagan's message and vice versa.'[19]

In contrast to the consistency over time of Thatcher and Reagan, Mitterrand came into office with one economic philosophy but within a year was forced to switch to another. He and his government had to move toward the right, adopting a policy of *rigueur.* Ten years later, French economic policy was not very different from that in Great Britain and the United States.

But at the outset the Mitterrand Government moved in the opposite direction from Thatcher and Reagan. In fact, Thatcher began a programme of privatisation while the French National Assembly was debating the Mitterrand nationalisation proposals. President Mitterrand presented several justifications for the nationalisations. In a press conference in September 1981, he declared that nationalised industries play a pilot role in industrial policy, noting that since 1976 public investments had increased more than 50 per cent compared with only 1 per cent in the private sector. Also, nationalised industries are an arm of defence of French production comparable with de Gaulle's nuclear strategy: a French *force de frappe.* In a more nationalistic mode, Mitterrand said that nationalisation would keep French companies from coming under 'international control'. He went on to state: 'I am opposed to an international division of labour and production, a division decided not from our shores and obeying interests that are not our own.' Thus, 'for us nationalisation is a weapon to protect France's production apparatus'.

This statement was reminiscent of French policy in the 1960s when Charles de Gaulle, as President of the Republic, opposed foreign direct investment in France. He had to abandon that policy as new foreign plants were established in neighbouring countries from which they could ship their products to France under the rules of the Common Market.

While the nationalisations were being debated in the Parliament, the French franc was devalued in the EMS (4 October, 1981) by 3 per cent and the Deutschemark was revalued by 5.5 per cent. This was a warning shot across the bows of the Mitterrand Socialist armada, whether or not it was realised at the time.

Other policy changes introduced by the new government were an increase in the minimum wage and higher family and housing allowances, a one-year 10 per cent surtax on high incomes (affecting about 2 million out of 15 million taxpayers), and a bitterly-resented tax on wealth over 3 million francs (affecting about 200 000 taxpayers).

While the economic philosophies of the Reagan and Mitterrand governments could not have been more different, they both adopted measures that increased the budget deficit substantially.

Another action of the Mitterrand government was to try to reduce unemployment by cutting the work week, lowering the age of retirement to 60 years, providing a fifth week of paid vacations, among other measures that Prime Minister Mauroy characterised as 'social advances'. The work week was initially cut to 39 hours but the aim was to go all the way to 35 hours by 1985.

This combination of policies was hardly designed to strengthen the foreign exchange value of the franc. France already had a current-account deficit in 1980, which increased in 1981–82, reaching $12 billion. The franc suffered periodic bouts of weakness, which caused concern to Minister of Finance Jacques Delors. The weak franc and the balance-of-payments deficit were to be the Achilles' heel of Mitterrand's initial policies and were to lead to a complete turnaround.

3.5 JAPAN

Policies changed in Japan in the course of the 1980s but less dramatically than in Britain, the United States, and France. And alterations in the basic philosophy of policy were slight. Still Japan moved toward a less-regulated and less export-oriented economy. Exchange controls were removed in 1980. Partly under pressure from the United States, Japan liberalised its financial markets and institutions. A number of administrative reforms lightened the heavy hand of government on the economy. And some privatisation, including the giant Nippon Telephone and Telegraph Company (NTT), took place. Prime Minister Nakasone (1982–7) is said to have been influenced by Margaret Thatcher.

In the 1970s, Japan had the highest growth rate among the major industrial countries. The economy slowed along with others in the early 1980s. Yet, Japan's fiscal policy moved toward restraint ('fiscal consolidation') at that time in a reaction against large budget deficits.

Japan had a temporary current-account deficit as the decade began, under the impact of the steep rise in the price of oil. A current-account surplus reappeared as early as 1981 and grew to large proportions as the decade wore on. As a result, Japanese financial institutions and other investors became major capital exporters, especially to the United States. These investments included some conspicuous acquisitions – notably the Rockefeller Center in New York – that aroused some resentment among Americans, most of whom had forgotten that their fellow-countrymen had done something quite similar in Europe in the 1950s and 1960s.

By 1987 Japan's current-account had become embarrassingly large. That was one reason for a shift in focus to the domestic economy. The Mayekawa report, published in

1986, recommended that Japan shift its priorities to encouraging domestic demand and solving some of its problems at home. A substantial programme of domestic spending was inaugurated in 1987. Together with a stimulative monetary policy, it set off the boom – the bubble economy – that Japan experienced in the next few years. That gave way in the early 1990s to a falling stock market, a drop in property values, and the most severe recession in Japan's post-war history.

At the same time a series of political scandals involving bribery and other forms of corruption led to the defeat of the Liberal Democratic Party, which had been in power for 38 years. A coalition government under Prime Minister Hosokawa began a process of political reform and deregulation in the latter part of 1993.

3.6   GERMANY

Germany at the beginning of the new decade found itself with a stagnant economy, too much inflation, higher unemployment and a larger budget deficit than it was accustomed to. The Kohl government, when it took over in October 1982, was determined to improve this situation. Emphasis was placed on reducing the budget deficit ('consolidating' was the popular word for this) by holding down expenditures, on reforming the tax system so as to encourage private investment and on stimulating housing construction.

Yet as two German scholars wrote:

> in contrast to both the UK and US experience, the change in government in 1982 did not represent a *complete* break with the past. The Schmidt government had already been pledged to a policy of fiscal consolidation, which was then more forcefully pursued by its successor. The main difference was that the Kohl government was less hamstrung by internal divisions, and from the very beginning its fiscal policies appeared to be more decisive than those that the Schmidt government pursued in 1982.[20]

It is fair to say, therefore, that the switch from Schmidt to Kohl did not have anything like the earth-shaking effects on economic policies that occurred in Britain, the United States, and France. The big change in the West German economy came only with unification with what was East Germany.

3.7 COUNTRIES IN TRANSITION

It goes without saying that the philosophy of economic policy has changed radically in the former Soviet Union, Eastern Europe and China. Mikhail Gorbachev started the process with *glasnost* and *perestroika* but his heart was not in thoroughgoing economic reform. Boris Yeltsin is struggling to bring it about. The countries of Eastern Europe differ in the extent to which they have succeeded in reforming their economies. China has undergone tremendous economic changes since 1978 without explicitly abandoning communism. In one way or another these countries are abandoning central planning and shifting towards market-based systems. The transition is difficult and painful, at least in Eastern Europe and the former Soviet Union. But it is clearly of historic importance.

3.8 DEVELOPING COUNTRIES

The many so-called third world countries are in different stages of development, ranging from the high income Asian 'tigers' (Korea, Hong Kong, Taiwan and Singapore) to some very poor countries in Africa. In the early decades after World War II, many developing countries, reacting to colonialism and anxious for economic progress, adopted socialist philosophies, established state-owned enterprises, discouraged direct investment from abroad and pursued import substitution behind high tariff walls and quantitative import controls. The period since 1980 brought a basic change in orientation towards free-market economies in east Asia, India and much of Latin America. The policy of import substitution gave way to more open trade. Beyond that, numerous developing countries launched themselves on a process of more basic reform involving less state intervention in their economies. This may help to account for the fact that in the recession of the early 1990s the industrial countries were given a boost in demand as developing countries as a group maintained rapid growth rates and rapid import expansion.

4 Reaganomics and Thatcherism

This chapter and the following one trace developments – both macroeconomic and structural – in a number of major industrial countries from 1980 on. Chapter 6 will be devoted to the interactions among these economies. The purpose is not to review history comprehensively but to bring out the more lasting impacts of the events of 1980–93 – the legacies of Margaret Thatcher, Ronald Reagan, François Mitterrand, and other national leaders. The initial focus is on the United States since it is the largest economy with the greatest impact on other countries.

4.1   UNITED STATES

Developments in the United States since 1980 have been strongly affected by fiscal policy that produced a large and persistent budget deficit.

Macroeconomic Evolution

The combination of the tax reductions enacted in 1981 and the build-up of defence outlays produced a budget deficit that increased from $74 billion in fiscal year 1980, the last year of the Carter presidency, to $185 billion in 1984 when recovery from the recession of 1981–2 was well under way. The structural, or cyclically-adjusted budget deficit – which abstracts from the effects of recession – increased from 1.8 per cent of GDP in 1980 to 3.6 per cent in 1984. The structural deficit remained at roughly this level during the following eight years.

Meanwhile the Federal Reserve System, under the chairmanship of Paul Volcker, had begun in 1979 to combat inflation with a highly restrictive monetary policy. Inflation in the United States had crept up in the late 1970s, partly under the influence of substantial wage increases in the automobile and steel industries. But inflation accelerated with the advent of the second oil shock. Consumer price advances exceeded 11 per cent in 1979 and 13 per cent in 1980, the highest rate of inflation since 1947, with the single exception of the year 1974, when the previous oil shock had its effect.

Paul Volcker, who was hardly a monetarist, was shrewd enough to persuade his policymaking colleagues at the Federal Reserve to adopt a quantitative approach to the implementation of monetary policy, based on target growth rates for the monetary aggregates. While interest rates soared – the Treasury bill rate was above 15 per cent and the prime rate on bank loans reached 20.5 per cent in the summer of 1981 – the Federal Reserve was able to minimise the political heat by sticking to its announced money supply targets.[1]

The oil-price increase and tight money created, or at least contributed to, the recession in which real GDP fell by more than 2 per cent and unemployment reached 9.7 per cent in 1982. That recession carried the US economy to its lowest point in post-war history in terms of idle labour and unused industrial capacity.

It is also noteworthy that more than one-third of the reduction of GDP in 1982 was accounted for by the fall-off of exports. While Americans had ample reasons to become aware of international interdependence after the two oil shocks, this experience added another dimension. The decline of US exports was the result not of arbitrary action by OPEC but of three other factors: appreciation of the dollar by some 36 per cent from 1980 to late 1982, the slashing of imports by Latin American countries owing to the debt crisis which erupted in the summer of 1982, and the slowdown in economic activity and therefore in imports in other industrial countries. The trough of the recession came in the third quarter of 1982. The Reagan tax reductions – embodied in the Economic Recovery and Tax Act of 1981 (ERTA) – provided for cuts in marginal tax rates of individuals and families by 5 per cent in 1981, 10 per cent in 1982, and another 10 per cent in 1983, cumulating to 23 per cent. The maximum marginal rate was reduced from 70 to 50 per cent. For corporations, depreciation allowances were liberalised (this was partly reversed in 1982) and the investment tax credit was extended to cover additional types of equipment.

The Federal Reserve began to ease monetary policy around the middle of 1982 and interest rates came down sharply from their record high levels as the growth rate of the money supply doubled. The prime rate on bank loans fell from 16.5 per cent at midyear to 11.5 per cent in December and the yield on long-term Treasury bonds declined from 13 to 10 per cent, bringing with it a drop in mortgage interest rates.

With both fiscal and monetary policy shifting toward stimulus, consumers and businesses stepped up their spending. Housing starts rose and automobile sales increased sharply in the latter part of 1982.

The recovery was also aided by a significant reduction in the rate of inflation. Consumer prices, which had risen in double digits in 1980 and 1981, advanced only 1.2 per cent in the second half of 1982. To some extent, the price rise was bound to taper off. What the United States and other oil-importing countries were experiencing was a jump in the price of oil, not a continuing advance. As long as wages did not respond fully to the sharp upswing in consumer prices – and they did not – there was no reason for prices to continue to climb rapidly. In addition, the appreciation of the dollar (lowering the cost of imports) and the recession itself helped to bring about the deceleration of inflation.

The economy recovered vigorously in 1983–4 and maintained a satisfactory rate of growth during the next five years, when GDP increased on average by 3.1 per cent per year. The rate of inflation averaged 3.6 per cent annually in the years 1985–9, with an upward trend during the period.

The economic expansion that began in 1982 brought with it some financial and economic excesses. That was the 'go, go' era of speculative construction of office buildings based on readily supplied credit, of mergers and acquisitions, of

Figure 4.1   Growth and inflation, 1980–93

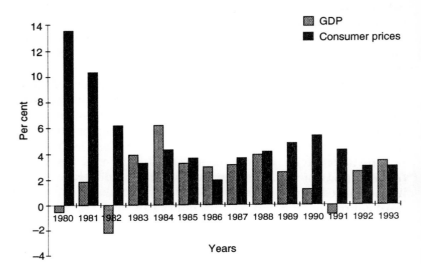

leveraged buyouts and hostile takeovers of corporations, of
'junk bonds', of computerised trading in stocks, of illegal
stock market transactions that sent several notorious opera-
tors to gaol and of a rapid run-up in stock prices. From 1982
to mid-1987, stock prices tripled as measured by the Dow
Jones industrial average. In the first eight months of 1987,
they rose 40 per cent . The ratio of prices to earnings, which
had been about 17 in the 1960s and 11 in the 1970s, rose
sharply in the 1980s to a peak above 23 in August 1987. Part
of the explanation lay in the issuance of large amounts of
debt – especially bonds – by corporations, some of the proceeds of which were used to buy up outstanding shares of
their common stock – to the extent of about $100 billion per
year in 1984–9.

It is clear that what was going on in the stock market was a
speculative bubble: a market in which each investor knew
that the inflated price of stocks was unsustainable but hoped
to be able to sell before the predictable downturn. This phenomenon is also known as 'the greater fool theory'. The day

of reckoning came on 19 October 1987 – Black Monday – when stock prices fell 23 per cent in a near panic.

What brought on the sharp drop? The main explanation is that the market rose too steeply and a reversal was inevitable. But other forces were also at work. Interest rates in the United States had risen sharply in 1987; the yield on 10-year US Government bonds went up from $7\frac{1}{4}$ per cent in March to over 10 per cent in mid-October. A rise in interest rates tends to depress stock prices for two reasons: corporate earnings are adversely affected and investors are attracted away from stocks to bonds.

The advance in interest rates in turn can be attributed to expectations of a further depreciation of the dollar. As is discussed in Chapter 6, the Group of Seven finance ministers and central bank governors agreed in early 1987 – at a meeting at the Louvre – to stabilise exchange rates; in particular, to reverse the policy initiated at their meeting at the Plaza Hotel in New York in 1985 and put a stop to the decline of the dollar. As events unfolded in 1987, this new policy became less and less credible. To sustain it, central banks had to intervene heavily in foreign exchange markets buying dollars. When market participants expect a currency to depreciate, they will also sell fixed-interest securities denominated in that currency. Hence the rise in US interest rates.

The stock market 'crash' turned out not to have serious macroeconomic repercussions either in the United States or abroad, where stock prices had also fallen. US stock prices recovered and surpassed their 1987 peak in late 1989.

The economy continued to expand briskly during Ronald Reagan's final years in office. George Bush was less fortunate. In the spring quarter of 1989, following his inauguration, the economy grew only 1 per cent , and it was flat in the third quarter. After a moderate rebound, economic activity turned down in the summer of 1990 and declined 1.4 per cent through the first quarter of 1991. This was followed by a sluggish and uncertain recovery – the slowest since World War II. As a result, by the summer of 1992, during the election campaign, real GDP was only 4.6 per cent above the level just before Bush became president. And unemployment had risen from 5.3 to 7.5 per cent . These were the main reasons for the plunge in Bush's popularity from its extraordinarily high level after the war against Iraq and it contributed to Clinton's victory over Bush at the polls in November 1992.

Bush took a step toward containing the budget deficit. His administration negotiated with the Congress a large cut in the deficit from what it would have been by imposing ceilings on spending, higher tax rates on upper incomes and new excise taxes.

President Clinton's main accomplishment in domestic economic policy in his first year was to present and persuade Congress to adopt a deficit reduction package, involving higher taxes mainly on high-income groups and ceilings on expenditures. The result is projected to be a decline in the deficit from about $275 billion in 1993 to less than $200 billion in 1998 but, in light of the growth of the economy, that will represent a substantial fall-off in the deficit as a proportion of GDP. The OECD estimates that the structural budget deficit will drop from 4.0 per cent of GDP in 1992 to 2.2 per cent in 1995.

Balance of Payments and Exchange Rates

While interest rates came down from their elevated levels of 1980–81, real interest rates remained unusually high in the 1980s. If we measure real interest rates as inflation-adjusted rates, subtracting the rate of consumer price inflation within each year from the rate of interest, we find that the real rate on 3-month Treasury bills was, on average, 3.7 per cent in 1983-9 compared with 1.4 per cent in the 1960s and a negative 1.3 per cent in the 1970s; similarly, the real rate on 10-year US government bonds was 4.9 per cent in 1983–9, compared with 2 per cent in 1961–9 and near zero in 1971–9.

With real interest rates relatively high and the budget deficit continuing to swell, the dollar appreciated further in 1983 and 1984, and turned down only in early 1985. The result was a growing deficit on current account.

We shall use virtually no equations in this book. But one equation – really an identity – helps to portray the relationship between domestic macroeconomic variables and the balance of payments:

$$(I - S) + (G - T) = (M - X)$$

where I is gross private domestic investment, S is gross private domestic saving (of businesses and households), G is total government spending, T is total tax revenue, M is imports of goods and services, and X is exports of goods and services. Thus, $(G - T)$ is the budget deficit (or surplus if T exceeds G) and $(M - X)$ is the current-account deficit (or surplus if X is greater than M). What the relationship tells us, basically, is that if a country is a net dissaver – because its investment outruns its saving, including net government saving via a budget deficit or surplus – it borrows saving from abroad in the form of a net capital inflow that finances a current-account deficit. Similarly, if a country is a net saver, it makes those savings available to the rest of the world by means of net capital outflow and a current-account surplus.

In the United States after 1982, $(I - S)$ increased as business investment and residential construction advanced and private saving declined. Moreover, as noted, $(G - T)$ rose. The inevitable result was a growing current-account deficit.

At the same time, the dollar was appreciating. Differing explanations for the rising dollar were advanced, depending upon ideology or theoretical preconception. Some members, or defenders, of the Reagan administration argued that the admirable policies pursued by the United States, especially the tax cuts enacted in 1981, were influencing investors abroad to place their funds in the United States. Others leaned on interest-rate differences. Still others saw the explanation in terms of expectations about interest rates as the US economy was likely to recover ahead of Europe and Japan.

By February 1985, the dollar's average value relative to the currencies of ten industrial countries had gained no less than 80 per cent . In real terms, taking account of price movements in the various countries, the appreciation amounted to 72 per cent . This was without doubt the largest *real* change in the exchange rate of a major currency in modern history.

In Chapter 6 we consider the repercussions abroad and internationally-coordinated actions to deal with exchange rates. The effects of the dollar's appreciation on the US economy were mixed. Export growth was very slow as American producers lost market share in many countries. On the other hand, the appreciating dollar lowered the cost of imports, thereby contributing to the deceleration of inflation while also speeding up the entry of goods and services from abroad. Total imports appear to have risen about in line with GDP, but non-oil imports increased much faster than GDP while the sharp drop in the world price of oil held down growth in the total value of imports.

The combination of a rising dollar and a growing current-account deficit was rather unusual. Normally, a country moving into larger external deficit finds its currency weakening. In this case, the advance of the dollar – pulled up by relatively high interest rates – was part of the mechanism by which the budget deficit and the private-saving deficiency translated themselves into the current-account deficit called for by our equation. If the dollar had not appreciated – because, say, the Federal Reserve had pursued a less restrictive monetary policy – inflation in the United States would have been greater. That would have discouraged exports and encouraged imports, thereby pushing the current account into deficit in any event. That deficit rose year by year from $11 billion in 1982 to $164 billion in 1987, when it amounted to 3.6 per cent of GDP.

A final burst of appreciation occurred in late 1984 and early 1985. This was regarded as a 'speculative bubble' – a rise in the market driven by speculators each of whom knew that it could not last but hoped to sell before the downturn. The dollar did turn down in February. It declined irregularly to September 1985, when it was given an additional downward push by the finance ministers and central bank governors of the five largest industrial countries (France, Germany, Japan, United Kingdom and United States) meeting at the Plaza Hotel in New York.

The dollar did not react precipitously to the Plaza agreement. Except for a brief period in 1987, the decline was orderly. My explanation at the time for the somewhat hesitant downward movement of the dollar, which was widely believed to be seriously overvalued, was that after each decline market participants were uncertain about whether the next move would be up or down. Therefore they were hesitant to take bearish positions on the dollar.

It took a while for the depreciation of the dollar to have a visible effect on the US trade balance. In testimony before Congressional committees in 1986 and 1987, a number of us carefully explained the so-called J-curve: exchange-rate changes have their effects only with a lag; the initial effect is to raise the domestic cost of imports, and until the volume of imports declines, the total value of imports increases, worsening the trade balance.

Sure enough, the trade balance did eventually respond, but only beginning in 1987. The current-account deficit reached its peak in the third quarter of 1987, more than two years after the dollar turned down. By 1991, the deficit had been reduced by more than 40 per cent, from 3.6 to 1.6 per cent of GDP.

The reversal of the dollar's steep appreciation of 1980–85 led to an impressive increase in American exports. From 1986 to 1991, the dollar value of merchandise exports soared by 86 per cent . The volume of exports rose 68 per cent while the volume of world trade increased 31 per cent . In other words, the share of US exports in world markets went up substantially during this period. Moreover, the increase in exports of goods and services accounted for almost half of the growth of American GDP in those five years. The rapid advance of exports from 1986 to 1991 more than compensated for the slowdown of US export growth in the first half of the decade. By 1991, US exports of goods and services in constant dollars were 68 per cent higher than in 1980 while real GDP was up a little less than 28 per cent and world trade had increased 55 per cent .

It appears that the widespread talk about a loss of American competitiveness is not borne out by the facts. It may be that

American automobile producers were unable to compete with their counterparts in Japan but they were apparently not representative of American industry in general.

Referring back to the equation on page 35, we may ask how the US current-account deficit could decrease when the budget deficit remained high. Does the equation still hold? The answer is yes, because private saving increased and investment decreased. The current-account deficit (excluding official transfers, which were strongly affected in 1991 by payments to the United States in connection with the Gulf war) fell by $125 billion from 1987 to 1991. Over the same period, total private saving, personal and business, increased by $199 billion while gross private domestic investment decreased by $12 billion. Thus $(I - S)$ decreased by $211 billion. The deficit of all levels of government $(G - T)$ went up by $84 billion. Therefore the sum of $(I - S)$ and $(G - T)$ declined by $127 billion. The tiny difference ($2 billion) between this sum and the reduction in the current-account deficit can be attributed to that bane of analysts, the statistical discrepancy in the national income and product accounts.

One of the effects of the string of current-account deficits starting in 1982 was an alteration in the net international investment position of the United States. Up to that time, America was the foremost creditor nation – that is, its assets abroad exceeded its liabilities by an amount that was larger than the net asset position of any other country. The cumulative current-account deficit from 1982 to 1992 reached more than $1 trillion. Concurrently, American investment abroad, mainly direct corporate investment and purchases of foreign securities, came to more than $700 billion. To finance the current-account deficits as well as the outflows of American capital, the United States relied on inflows of foreign capital in a variety of forms: direct investment, purchases of US Government securities by both private investors and monetary authorities abroad, and deposits in banks in the United States. Acquisitions of American assets by Japanese investors attracted a lot of attention, partly because they chose some conspicuous properties. But British and Dutch holdings in the United States exceeded those of Japan.

As it turned out, US investments abroad tended to yield higher earnings than foreign holdings of American assets. Thus even though the raw figures showed the United States to be a net debtor – to the extent of more than $500 billion at the end of 1992 – its current investment income exceeded its payments of such income to the rest of the world.

Structural Developments

In addition to the tax reductions of 1981, a major reform of the tax system was enacted by the Congress in 1986, under the leadership of Secretary of the Treasury James Baker. In general, the tax reform aimed at eliminating loopholes and tax preferences, broadening the tax base, and reducing tax rates – all in a 'revenue neutral' manner. Marginal tax rates for individuals and families were lowered and the number of rates was reduced from five to three: 15, 28, and 33 per cent. But various exemptions and deductions were dropped or became less generous. For corporations, the tax rate was reduced, but the investment tax credit was eliminated and depreciation allowances were made less favourable. On balance the tax reform lowered the share of personal taxes and increased that of corporations in total tax payments.

A question that has given rise to political controversy is whether the enlarged budget deficits were the result of the Reagan tax cuts or of higher government spending. Defenders of the Reagan policies point out that total Federal tax revenues did not go down as a proportion of GDP during the 1980s, but expenditures rose. What they ignore is that tax revenues would have risen were it not for the Reagan tax cuts. Reforms of the social security system undertaken in the 1970s and 1980s provided for increases in payroll taxes designed not only to finance current outlays but to create a surplus in the social security trust fund. Thus, income taxes fell and indirect taxes rose, relative to GDP, in the 1980s. The growth of expenditures, also relative to GDP, was fully accounted for by defence, health care, and interest

payments on the growing Federal debt. Other civilian outlays, including grants to state and local governments, fell
substantially as a share of GDP.

In addition to the increase in government dissaving – in
the form of budget deficits – in the 1980s, private saving
declined significantly, continuing a trend that became evident in the mid-1970s. (Private saving decreased in most
industrial countries.) Saving by both businesses and
households fell off. The result was lower net private
domestic investment in terms of GDP and a larger current-account deficit. As a by-product, the real income of
Americans grew more slowly. Real per capita income after
taxes rose by only 1.7 per cent annually in the 1980s compared with more than 3 per cent in the 1960s. Even that
lower rate of income growth owed much to the fact that
an increasing proportion of the population joined the
labour force. In particular, the participation rate of
women rose from 51 per cent in 1979 to 58 per cent in
1992.

The slowdown in the growth of Americans' incomes
cannot be blamed totally on Mr Reagan's policies. The fact
is that the advance in US productivity – on which the growth
of incomes ultimately depends – began to decelerate in the
early 1970s. Moreover, productivity advance and economic
growth also slowed in other industrial countries.

There is a silver lining in this cloudy picture. While productivity in the entire non-farm business sector of the US
economy rose by only about 1 per cent per year in the 1970s
and 1980s compared with 2.4 per cent in the 1960s, productivity growth in manufacturing did much better. Output per
hour of work in manufacturing rose almost 3 per cent annually from 1980 to 1990, half again as much as in the 1970s
and about the same as in the 1960s.

It was in the service industries that productivity growth
lagged. While employment in services accounted for virtually all of the new jobs in the American economy in the
1980s, the recession that began in 1990 appears to have led
to a slimming down of employment in the service industries.
Another silver lining may be in the making: a pickup in pro-

ductivity growth in the service industries and therefore in the whole economy.

Related to the more rapid rise in manufacturing productivity has been a shrinkage of employment in that sector relative to total employment. In 1991 manufacturing accounted for only 17 per cent of total jobs in the US economy, down from 31 per cent in 1960 and 22 per cent in 1980. This change has led some observers to the conclusion that manufacturing output has also declined as a share of total output. This is not so. The production of goods has been virtually unchanged as a proportion of GDP since 1980 and is down by a minuscule amount from 1970.

Trade union membership continued to decline, from 25 per cent of the work force in 1980 to 16 per cent in 1992. And the unions became less militant. The number of working days lost to strikes fell to little more than one-third of what it was in the 1970s. And the unions did not press for large wage gains. Moreover, there was a change in worker diligence. In the 1970s, it was commonly believed that one should not buy a car that came off the assembly line on a Monday or a Friday because it was likely to have been sloppily put together. That is no longer true.

Finally, it is not surprising that these structural changes brought an alteration in income distribution toward greater inequality – another trend that goes back to the early 1970s but accelerated in the 1980s. Income inequality among American families increased for a number of reasons. The demand for labour shifted toward those with more education and more advanced skills. Many additional women in higher income groups entered the labour force and their earnings rose much faster than those of women in less affluent families, whereas in the 1950s and 1960s it was women in lower income groups who entered the labour force in large numbers. Contrary to what may be commonly believed, the increase in single-parent families did not accelerate in the 1980s and explains only a little of the greater income inequality. Finally the tax system became less progressive.[2]

The Reagan–Bush Legacy

The principal and best known outcome of the twelve-year incumbency of Presidents Reagan and Bush is the large budget deficit of the Federal government. Despite two major efforts to do something about it – the Gramm–Rudman legislation of 1985 and the budgetary agreement of 1990, which followed President Bush's disavowal of his 'read my lips' statement pledging not to raise taxes – the outsized budget deficits persisted. As noted, President Clinton succeeded in getting Congress to pass legislation that should reduce the deficit moderately.

The chronic budget deficits initiated in the early 1980s will have long-lasting effects, lowering the real incomes of Americans and their children and grandchildren below what would otherwise have been expected. Sustained budget deficits reduce the incomes of future generations either by crowding out domestic investment or by inducing a current-account deficit or by some combination of the two. Lower domestic investment means a smaller rate of future growth of the economy and therefore less income to go around. A cumulative current-account deficit requires net borrowing from abroad and the necessity to pay out, as interest and dividends, a part of the income produced by future generations.

Despite Ronald Reagan's contagious optimism, Americans now have a less hopeful outlook than in the past. The sharp slowdown in the growth of incomes has led to a distinct alteration in expectations. Whereas in the past most young adults anticipated that they would be better off than their parents, that is no longer so.

Another part of the legacy – attributable in part to the Congress – is the insolvency of many Federally-insured savings and loan associations and the required 'bailout' by the government. These institutions were hurt by the sharp rise of interest rates beginning in 1979. While they held mostly fixed-rate mortgages, they had to raise the rates they paid on deposits in order to retain them. Later, after legislation gave them greater freedom to invest, many of their real estate loans went sour as the construction boom came to an end. Numerous associations became insolvent and the US Government had to pay off depositors one way or another. Part of the explanation for this débâcle was lax supervision of these institutions.

While the supply-side tax cuts of 1981 failed to produce the promised favourable effects on saving, investment, and work effort – as was discussed in the previous chapter – the election campaign of 1992 featured attention to the supply side of the economy: to the need to improve worker training and education in general, to the desirability of increasing research and development, to the broad question of how to encourage productivity advances, and to infrastructure needs, some of which have become pressing because they were neglected during the Reagan–Bush years.

A positive accomplishment during Mr Reagan's presidency was the tax reform of 1986, which left the United States with a somewhat simplified and somewhat more equitable tax system.

Perhaps another aspect of the legacy is the change in the Democratic Party. Its Congressional leaders are now more pragmatic and less ideological and certainly less influenced by the views of labour leaders. And President Clinton is more oriented to the well-being of business enterprises than most of his Democratic predecessors. As we shall see, a similar change occurred in Britain.

Finally, we pose the question: is America in decline? Some of the developments noted above gave rise to a debate between 'declinists' and those who reject their thesis. The debate was highlighted by the publication in 1987 of Professor Paul Kennedy's *The Rise and Fall of the Great Powers*.[3] This massive book traces the evolution of empires over the centuries and attributes their decline mainly to 'imperial overstretch' or 'strategical overextension' – especially the diversion of resources from wealth creation to military purposes. Actually Kennedy's thesis, in so far as it applies to the United States, may have been rendered nugatory by the ending of the Cold War. If military rivalry, and therefore the arms race, between America and Russia is a thing of the past, what is left of Kennedy's thesis?

One may still ask whether or not America's influence on the course of world events is decreasing as the result of its economic performance in the past decade or so – specifically its budget and current-account deficits and its lower productivity growth.

There is no doubt that the twin deficits affect the present and future income and wealth of Americans. The relevant question is: can these deficits be corrected? The Clinton administration has made a start. Much more is needed.

As to productivity, the United States still has the highest absolute output per person in the world, just as Americans have the highest per capita income when it is properly measured, which Professor Kennedy fails to do. What has been happening for many years is a 'catching up' of other industrial countries with the United States. According to William Baumol and his colleagues, a process of convergence takes place in which technology is transferred from the most advanced countries to those less advanced. The 'catching up' permits nations with lower productivity to achieve faster increases in output per worker or per unit of input generally.[4]

Will this process lessen American influence on world events? Joseph Nye and Henry Nau have written books that answer in the negative and refute the Kennedy thesis.[5]

One may also ask, if the United States is to become a second rate power, which countries will be in the ascension? While Japan's economic performance is impressive, it has been characterised as a 'one-dimensional' power. According to *The Wall Street Journal* editor Karen Eliot House: 'Its economic might isn't bolstered by either military, political, or ideological clout, elements that have always been essential for a nation to shape international events'.[6]

Germany, like Japan, is burdened by its history. Besides, even with the addition of east Germany, it only a little larger than Oregon. But the European Community as a unit has a population one-third larger than the United States and, in 1987, a combined GNP about seven-eighths that of the

United States. The EC, whether or not it moves to Economic and Monetary Union, is a formidable economic power. The obvious shortcoming, from the viewpoint of its potential for global leadership, is the absence of political unification. At present, that appears far in the future.

Thus the judgement seems warranted that America will not soon follow the fate of the earlier dominant powers that Kennedy regards as exemplars. Partly because its present weaknesses are not fatal and partly because there exists no obvious successor – as Kennedy acknowledges late in his book (pp. 534–5) – the United States is likely to remain not necessarily dominant but the most important country on the political spectrum in terms of influence over world affairs.

Toward the end of 1993 and the beginning of 1994 two happenings tended to support this judgement. The US economy appeared to be the most vibrant among those of the larger industrial countries. Economic activity picked up speed in the latter part of 1993, unemployment fell to the lowest level in three years, and inflation subsided further. At the same time the prospects were dim for early revival of economic momentum in continental Europe and Japan. The second factor was President Clinton's trip to Europe and the former Soviet Union. In Brussels, Prague, Moscow and Geneva he was clearly exerting international leadership in a way that none of the other heads of government were willing or able to do. Both observations were short-term phenomena, but they looked relevant at the time.

4.2 THE UNITED KINGDOM

The Thatcher government, which came into office in May 1979, wasted no time in introducing what Nigel (now Lord) Lawson, initially Financial Secretary to the Treasury and later Chancellor of the Exchequer, calls an 'enterprise culture'. As he puts it, the new government was seeking 'not simply to remove various controls and impositions, but by so doing to change the entire culture of a nation from anti-profits, anti-business, government-dependent lassitude and defeatism, to a pro-profit, pro-business, robustly independent vigour and optimism.'[7]

In its early months the government abolished exchange controls. A year later, it lifted the regulation limiting the interest rates banks could pay on deposits (known as 'the corset'), thereby allowing banks to compete freely for interest-bearing funds.

In the initial budget, introduced in June 1979 by Mrs Thatcher's first Chancellor of the Exchequer, Geoffrey Howe, income taxes were lowered and indirect taxes were raised. Specifically, the value-added tax (VAT) went up from 10–12 per cent to 15 per cent while the standard income tax was reduced from 33 to 30 per cent and the top income tax rate came down from 83 to 60 per cent (and in 1988 to 40 per cent). On balance, the budget provided for a small decrease in the deficit.

Monetary policy was tightened. In November 1979, the minimum lending rate (akin to the discount rate elsewhere) was raised by an unprecedented three percentage points, to 17 per cent . While interest rates advanced, the targeted money aggregate (M3) was exceeded, perhaps because of the removal of the corset. Meanwhile the foreign exchange value of sterling rose under the influence of high interest rates and the strong balance of payments. Oil exports exceeded oil imports beginning in 1980. The oil surplus reached a peak of £8.1 billion ($10.5 billion) in 1985.

The shift from direct to indirect taxes was designed to strengthen incentives for growth. The rationale for this and other policies bore some resemblance to the views of the supply siders in the United States. In particular, Nigel Lawson argued that growth was to be achieved by microeconomic policies while the function of macro policies was to prevent inflation. Although Lawson publicly proclaimed this view with vigour in a lecture in 1984, in his published memoirs he states: 'In reality, the distinction may not always be quite as clear-cut as this. In certain circumstances, which history suggests do not occur very often, macroeconomic policy could also play a role in supporting economic activity.'[8]

The 1980 budget incorporated a small increase in taxes despite the budget forecast of a decline of GDP of more than 2 per cent . At the same time, the Medium Term Financial Strategy was introduced, fathered by Nigel Lawson. It provided for a steady reduction in both monetary expansion and the budget deficit with the aim of bringing down inflation. As the strategy was originally conceived, 'a declining PSBR [public sector borrowing requirement] would enable our monetary objectives to be reached without 'excessive reliance on high interest rates'.[9] Milton Friedman is reported to have been astounded to learn that a Treasury paper gave as the main reason for tightening fiscal policy the need to exercise control of the money supply.[10]

In March 1981, a much more stringent budget was introduced. It increased indirect tax rates on items of general consumption: petrol, beer, wine, and other 'spirits', tobacco and vehicles. It also raised taxes on oil production and placed a one-time tax on bank deposits. The latter seemed inconsistent with the economic philosophy of the Thatcher government. In addition, the budget withdrew an allowance that adjusted personal income taxes for bracket creep owing to inflation. The only relief offered was a two percentage point reduction, to 12 per cent, in the Bank of England's minimum lending rate, which was then suspended. Thereafter, changes in officially-determined interest rates were measured by base rates – those on which banks base their interest charges to borrowers.

Thus the mix of fiscal and monetary policies was switched – in the opposite direction from the mix in America – as fiscal policy was tightened and monetary policy was eased.

As I wrote then: 'This is probably the first time in half a century that a major industrial country has tightened fiscal policy significantly while its output and employment were falling.'[11] Why was fiscal policy tightened? According to Lawson, the Treasury was worried about the ballooning budget deficit. The PSBR 'was running well ahead' of the target set in the previous budget. Lawson concedes that 'roughly half of the overrun could be attributed to the recession'.[12]

The budget evoked a letter to *The Times* from 364 British economists protesting the restrictive fiscal policy. Others have argued that deficit reduction was necessary in order to 'engender long-run credibility for money growth limitation' and hence for anti-inflation policy.[13]

As it happens, control over the money supply turned out not to be very effective. The target range for the growth of broad money (sterling M3) was 7–11 per cent in 1980–81 and 6–10 per cent in 1981–2, but actual expansion of this monetary aggregate was almost twice as great as the targets. Part of the explanation for the overshooting was an increase in 'intermediation' through the banks after removal of the corset. If one judges the tightness of monetary policy from interest rates and the growth of narrower monetary aggregates – not to mention what was happening to output and employment – it becomes clear that the economy was being subjected to monetary restraint.[14] Britain was not the only country that was to have difficulty in the 1980s adhering to a monetary policy based on targets for monetary aggregates.

While the complaints about the 1981 budget may have seemed justified at the time, the fact is that the economy apparently hit bottom in the first quarter of 1981 as marked by the rise of GDP by 1.8 per cent over the next four quarters. Economic growth speeded up to 3.2 per cent per year in 1983–6. As in the United States, this favourable performance after 1981 reflected in part its starting point: a rather deep recession. In 1987–8 the economy grew by more than $4\frac{1}{2}$ per cent per year and became overheated.

The economic recovery did not quickly reduce unemployment. It rose from $4\frac{1}{2}$ per cent in 1979 year by year to a peak of 11.8 per cent in 1986 and then fell to just under 6 per cent in 1990. On the other hand the early Thatcher policy of squeezing the economy brought a distinct deceleration of inflation. By 1983, consumer prices were rising only 4.6 per cent, compared with an average increase of 13 per cent in 1979–82. This price performance was broadly maintained until 1988, when inflation began to creep up, averaging 8.6 per cent in 1989–90.

The second half of the 1980s witnessed a boom in consumer spending and residential and commercial construction – the so-called 'bubble economy' – reflecting in part financial deregulation including the abolition of restrictions on hire purchase (instalment credit). Consumer spending was also encouraged by income tax cuts in 1987 and 1988 (when Lawson announced an income tax reform that reduced the maximum marginal rate to 40 per cent). Spending by consumers increased 6.3 per cent per year in 1986–8 in an economy that was growing 4.1 per cent per year. Expenditure on housing rose 20 per cent in real terms from 1984–5 to 1987–8. The counterpart of the spending spree was a sharp drop in personal saving as a proportion of income and a reversal of the current account from surplus to large deficit. Again we observe a similarity to events in the United States. In both countries, the reduction in income taxes, which was supposed to provide an incentive to save and invest, mainly fuelled a surge in consumer spending.

The boom in the latter part of the 1980s also owes something to the monetary policy pursued. Chancellor Lawson, dissatisfied with the various money supply targets, shifted to an exchange-rate target in early 1987 by 'shadowing the D-mark'. Lawson had for some time been recommending that Britain join the ERM, but Mrs Thatcher would not agree. Moreover, in a speech in April 1986 he expressed his misgivings about the various definitions of the money supply and went on to assert: 'In the right circumstances membership of a formal fixed exchange rate system can itself provide a very effective framework for monetary policy.'[15]

In his memoir Lawson tells us that Mrs Thatcher frequently complained about the D-mark-shadowing policy. In her memoirs, she writes: 'Extraordinarily enough, I only learned that Nigel had been shadowing the deutschmark when I was interviewed by journalists from the *Financial Times* on Friday, 20 November 1987.'[16] We may leave it to the historians to sort this one out.

The new policy aimed at keeping sterling between about 2.8 and 3 D-marks. Sterling had declined from a peak above 5 D-marks to less than 3 D-marks between early 1981 and early 1987. It began to recover strength just as the shadowing policy was adopted. As a result, that policy required heavy exchange-market intervention in the form of Bank of England purchases of foreign exchange as sterling tended to rise above 3 D-marks. Published foreign exchange reserves, measured in dollars, almost tripled from the end of 1986 to the end of 1988. While these purchases of foreign exchange were sterilised, by equal sales of government securities to the market, it is not clear what was guiding monetary policy. Interest rates were brought down substantially in 1987–8 – the base rate fell from a peak of 11 per cent in the autumn of 1986 to a low of $7\frac{1}{2}$ per cent in May 1988 (except for a brief reversal in the autumn of 1987) – as was called for by a monetary policy guided by a pegged exchange rate that was tending to rise. But the monetary aggregates increased rapidly as did the supply of credit to the economy. This credit expansion, along with cuts in income taxes in March 1988, helped finance the boom of the late 1980s.

Martin Wolf wrote in September 1992 that 'several senior officials in the Treasury and the Bank of England viewed the ERM as no more than a second-best method of running monetary policy. But Mr Lawson's erratic monetary policies convinced officials that a first-rate monetary policy – one run by themselves – would never be allowed to happen. Along with others, they concluded that monetary policy was far too important to be entrusted to politicians.'[17] The implication is that these officials preferred targeting the D-mark – in or out of the ERM – to letting the Chancellor make decisions about monetary policy. Unfortunately, Mr Wolf does not tell us what method of 'running monetary policy' the officials would have employed.

As the boom developed and the current-account deficit increased, Lawson began to raise interest rates again. Between May 1988 (when base rates were lowered at Mrs Thatcher's suggestion) and the end of the year, base rates were increased from $7\frac{1}{2}$ to 13 per cent. Sterling, which had been 'uncapped' in early 1988, rose above 3.2 D-marks in early 1989 and then declined.

In any event, the boom gave way to slow growth in 1989 and to falling GDP beginning in mid-1990, shortly before Lawson's resignation as Chancellor (about which more below). Real GDP fell more than 4 per cent from the second quarter of 1990 to the same period of 1992. With the recession came a bursting of the bubble, including declines in house prices that left many new homeowners with negative equity and threatened with repossession. And unemployment rose from its low point of 5.9 per cent in 1990 to above 10 per cent in 1992. That is the economic condition that John Major inherited.

Balance of Payments, Exchange Rates and Monetary Policy

In its early years, the Thatcher government enjoyed a luxury denied to most of its predecessors. It did not have to worry about the balance of payments – at least not until near the end of her time as Prime Minister. The combination of oil exports and the recession-induced fall-off of imports produced a current-account surplus of nearly $7 billion in 1980 and $14 billion (2.7 per cent of GDP) in 1981. In 1982–5, the surplus averaged almost $5 billion per year.

Tracking movements in the exchange rate is complicated by the wide swings in the dollar against all currencies in the 1980s. While the pound changed little in terms of dollars from 1978 to 1981, its effective exchange rate – that is, its trade-weighted average value – rose almost 18 per cent; its rate in terms of the Deutschemark went up by about the same amount. As interest rates came down in 1982–5, sterling's foreign exchange value also decreased. By 1985 its D-mark value was back roughly to where it had been in 1979.

Britain's current-account surplus disappeared in 1986 – owing in part to the sharp drop in world oil prices – and turned to a rapidly growing deficit, reaching more than $33 billion in 1989. Although the inflation rate remained relatively stable, the effective exchange rate of sterling declined 10 per cent from 1985 to 1987 and its D-mark value went

Figure 4.2   DM value of sterling

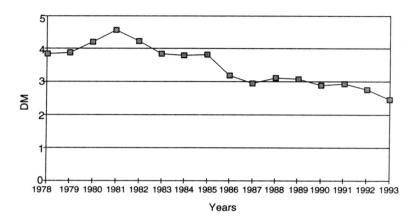

down by about 23 per cent. As noted above sterling strengthened again beginning in 1987.

We have observed that Lawson's policy of shadowing the D-mark and consequently engaging in heavy intervention in foreign exchange markets was a basis for disagreement between the Prime Minister and her Chancellor of the Exchequer. She was presumably receiving advice from Sir Alan Walters, either in London or from across the Atlantic in Washington. By March 1988, the disagreement between Thatcher and Lawson was out in the open both in the House of Commons and in the press. According to Lawson, 'It was conspicuous how, during her last three years in office, she was always eager to claim that her Ministers agreed with her, but found it extraordinarily difficult to say that she agreed with her Ministers.'[18]

Through much of Mrs Thatcher's time in office, debate about entry into the ERM raged in the inner circles of policymaking. Sir Alan Walters's book, *Britain's Economic Renaissance*, published in 1986 with a preface dated October 1985, contains a strong criticism of the EMS. One gets the impression that, in this part of the book, Sir Alan drew on memoranda he had written for the Prime Minister. His opponents in the inner debate were Chancellor Lawson and Foreign Secretary Geoffrey Howe.

The simmering disagreement between Lawson and Walters had a dramatic denouement. On 26 October 1989, Nigel Lawson abruptly left office, stating in his letter of resignation that 'the successful conduct of economic policy is possible only if there is, and is seen to be, full agreement between the Prime Minister and Chancellor of the Exchequer. Recent events have confirmed that this essential requirement cannot be satisfied so long as Alan Walters remains your personal economic adviser'. On the same day John Major was appointed Chancellor and Walters resigned.

Mrs Thatcher is of the opinion that the Alan Walters question was merely Lawson's pretext for resigning, which she seems to believe he wished to do in any case, for reasons that she does not explain.[19]

Lawson, in addition to pushing for membership in the ERM, had proposed that the Bank of England become an independent central bank.[20] It is doubtful that Sir Alan disagreed with that proposal. What he strongly opposed was the EMS, which he had characterised in print as 'half baked'. One of his criticisms, which came to be known as the 'Walters critique', was that under the fixed exchange rates of the EMS nominal interest rates among its members would equalise so that those with higher rates of inflation would have lower real interest rates than those with less inflation. In fact, this did not happen. Short-term interest rates in Italy exceeded those in Germany by several percentage points while the lira was in the ERM.

Lawson's initial motivation for wanting Britain in the ERM was that it would impose financial discipline by forcing a restrictive monetary policy on Britain in the face of political opposition to tight money. Later, he became disenchanted with the monetary aggregates as guides to monetary policy. Geoffrey Howe, as Chancellor, rejected Lawson's recommendation concerning ERM membership partly on the basis that it might conflict with domestic monetary policy. Only when he became Foreign Secretary did Howe begin to advocate ERM membership.

The *Economist* for 4 November 1989 offered the view that 'Mr Lawson's resignation may one day be seen as the moment that Mrs Thatcher's term of office started to draw to its close' (p.69).

Just under a year later Mrs Thatcher reluctantly agreed to British entry to the ERM. Many of us believed, and wrote, that this was done at too high an exchange rate (2.95 D-marks) and recalled that Winston Churchill, as Chancellor of the Exchequer, had restored Britain's pre-war exchange-rate parity in 1925, leading Keynes to attack the move in a book entitled *The Economic Consequences of Mr. Churchill.* The consequences of Mrs Thatcher's decision became evident in September 1992, when Britain was forced to drop out of the ERM. Over the next six weeks sterling depreciated against the D-mark by almost 15 per cent.

A month after the decision to join the ERM, Mrs Thatcher resigned. Her standing with the public had been eroded not only by the Lawson–Walters episode and her views about Britain's role in Europe, but, more importantly, by her insistence on the adoption of a poll tax, which Nigel Lawson identifies as 'the greatest single political blunder of the Thatcher years'. This regressive form of taxation, which was euphemistically dubbed a 'community charge', was substituted for the local property tax on residences. It was highly unpopular.

Structural Developments

Privatisation – a term that came into much more common use during the Thatcher era – was pursued both in the field of residential housing and nationalised industry.

Publicly-owned rental housing was sold to occupants with the aid of mortgage interest relief. From 1979 to 1989 the proportion of houses that were owner-occupied increased from 55 to 67 per cent.

The privatisation of nationalised industries took the form of sales to the public either of shares in those companies or of the physical assets. Among the companies privatised, in whole or in part, were many in the energy field (oil and gas), airlines, automobiles (Jaguar and Rolls-Royce), steel, and telecommunications.

The total proceeds from the sale of shares and physical assets came to £61 billion in the years 1979–90. These receipts financed almost 60 per cent of the fiscal deficit. The number of shareowners in Britain rose from 2 million in 1979 to 12 million in 1989 and the public sector's share in the nation's capital stock fell from 44 to 31 per cent.

Some of the privatised companies were natural monopolies – such as public utilities. The case for their privatisation was problematical. In some industries, a procedure for regulation was established.

The *Economist* saw fit to comment as follows on the process:

It was once the popular mainspring of Thatcherism, but privatisation now threatens to become a political liability
.... Public unease about privatisation has been growing for months, and needs no encouragement from Labour. Few people are persuaded that water and electricity should be sold, and the extravagant efforts of the advertising industry have served only to reinforce their doubts.

This is a pity. Privatisation has been a powerful force for good in Margaret Thatcher's Britain. The sale since 1979 of 54 state-owned companies into the private sector has been a remarkable feat of political will, in the face of hostile vested interests.[21]

The combination of privatisation, deregulation, legislation to curb the power of trade unions, and an overvalued exchange rate led to a pickup in productivity growth, especially in manufacturing. Output per worker increased at a rate of 2.4 per cent per year in 1980–88, compared with 1.5 per cent in the 1970s. In manufacturing, output per worker advanced 4.6 per cent annually in the 1980s as against 1.5 per cent in the previous decade. 'Overmanning' was cut back, but at a cost, perhaps inevitable: unemployment averaged more than 10 per cent in 1980–87.

As might be expected, the changes in taxation during the Thatcher years led, as in the United States, to a relative decrease in the weight of income taxes and a corresponding rise in indirect tax revenues. As a proportion of total taxes collected, income taxes declined from 33 per cent in 1978 to 26.5 per cent in 1989. Also, as in the United States, income distribution became more unequal.

The Thatcher Legacy

Mrs Thatcher's growing unpopularity led to what some have called a 'palace coup' by the powers that be in her party and to her resignation in November 1990, the longest serving Prime Minister in this century.

Somewhat earlier *The Economist* summed up her legacy as follows:

> Mrs Thatcher's departure might be good for Britain. Some of the challenges facing the country are ones on which she is ill-equipped to give a lead. She is instinctively unhappy with the thought of spending a lot more on education, particularly at secondary schools. She is temperamentally opposed to some of the things the government ought to do to revive the inner cities, because she has persuaded herself that most local government is bad government.
>
> ... Mrs Thatcher's achievement – and it has been a great one – has been to articulate a few simple but necessary rules for British politics, when all around her were speaking in the conditional. The rules include a commitment to an open, market economy; a recognition that wealth creation is more important than redistribution, because without it there is precious little to distribute; a clear-eyed understanding that the world is a risky place, where military defences remain necessary; a determination to challenge the corruption of vested interests; perhaps above all, the incessant repetition that people must bear the consequences of their actions.[22]

We have also observed that the Thatcher revolution left Britain's economy less 'overmanned' and therefore more productive, less subject to governmental controls and more responsive to the price system, less dominated by trade unions and less nationalised.

But it also has to be said that macroeconomic policy left something to be desired. Although inflation was brought down by 1987 to its lowest level in two decades, it was reignited by the boom of the late 1980s, reaching 9.5 per cent in 1990. The current-account deficit also increased markedly. The boom gave way inevitably to recession.

Finally, as in the case of Reagan's America, the Thatcher revolution had a profound effect on the terms of political debate as reflected in the positions taken by the opposition party. Britain's Labour Party has become much less Socialist and much more accepting of the market mechanism.

Although Margaret Thatcher deserves credit for this change, it is useful to recall that its seeds existed long before she came along. As far back as 1951 Denis (now Lord) Healey, later to become Defence Minister and Chancellor of the Exchequer in Labour governments, wrote these words (in an obituary article on Ernest Bevin):

> The Labour Party may hope to carry the Welfare State and planning further than the Tories, but for a long time physical and psychological factors will fix rigid limits. Further 'soaking the rich' will no longer benefit the poor to any noticeable extent. Further nationalisation no longer attracts more than a tiny fringe of the Labour Party itself; it positively repels the electorate as a whole. Even among Labour economists there is a growing revolt against physical controls in favour of the price mechanism. A policy based on class war cannot have a wide appeal when the difference between the classes is so small as Labour has made it.[23]

Britain after Thatcher

John Major inherited an economy in recession and suffering from a high rate of inflation. While the inflation rate came down in 1991–2, unemployment rose to $10\frac{1}{2}$ per cent of the labour force at the end of 1992. And, of course, the foreign exchange trauma of September 1992 (next chapter) was still haunting the government.

Although a recovery started in mid-1992, unemployment decreased only slowly and Major's popularity rating, like that of Bush, Mitterrand, and Kohl, fell to a low level after his party won a surprising victory in a general election in April 1992. Britain was not a happy place. Anthony Sampson was quoted as saying 'Britain is going through a period of self-examination and self-doubt and self-humiliation that is greater now than at any time I can remember over the last 30 years'.[24] Maybe so.

The question is, how different is the British economy from what it was in 1979? Apart from the structural changes such as privatisation of industry and housing, which prevail, inflation is back down again but the structural budget deficit is up, almost as high as when Mrs Thatcher entered office. On the other hand, there is little labour unrest and wages are increasing only moderately. Productivity is rising some-what faster in the overall economy than in the 1970s and much faster in manufacturing. What was called the 'British disease' is not very evident, whatever the other causes of discontent.

5 Adjusting to Shocks in France, Germany and Japan

Each in its own way, France, Germany and Japan have had to make substantial adjustments in economic policy and political orientation in the years since 1980. France shifted away from Mitterrand's socialist electoral programme of 1981 towards the policies of Thatcher and Reagan. Germany had to adjust to the economic shock of unification and absorption of the former East Germany. Japan became a major capital exporter but in the late 1980s went on a speculative spree at home that gave way to its most severe recession since before World War II while also undergoing a political upheaval.

5.1 MITTERRAND'S FRANCE

François Mitterrand was born in 1916 in the Cognac region of France to a relatively prosperous family that was conservative, religious and nationalistic. He studied law and political science. Nothing in his background or early life pointed to his assumption of the leadership of the Socialist Party in the 1970s.

Mitterrand served in the French army and was wounded and taken prisoner by the Germans in 1940. After two failed attempts, he escaped and joined the Resistance. This led him into politics in the post-war period and to his first ministerial post: Overseas Territories in the government of René Pleven in 1950–1. He held eleven ministerial positions under the Fourth Republic.

Mitterrand opposed de Gaulle's return to power in 1958 and lost his seat in the National Assembly. After some time in the Senate he was returned as a deputy in 1962 and joined the opposition to de Gaulle. He ran against de Gaulle in the presidential election of 1965, leading a centre-left coalition including the Communists.

In 1971 he participated in the regeneration of the Socialist Party and was chosen as its First Secretary. His rhetoric then became more 'socialist', even revolutionary – calling, among other things, for 'the appropriation of the great means of production'. As Guy Mollet, former Socialist prime minister, put it, 'M. Mitterrand has learned to speak socialist'.[1]

He lost the election of 1974, by a narrow margin, to Giscard d'Estaing. Finally, in 1981, he led the left wing coalition to victory.

Having based its election campaign heavily on the need to reduce unemployment, the Mitterrand government, on entering office in May 1981, increased the budget deficit it inherited from 29 billion to 52 billion francs by raising family allowances, housing subsidies, aid to industry including capital contributions to nationalised industries, and by enlarging public employment. In addition, the minimum wage was immediately increased by 10 per cent and from June 1981 to March 1983 by 38 per cent.

The first full-fledged budget under the new government – prepared by the young Budget Minister, Laurent Fabius – was aimed at economic recovery. Two features are noteworthy from our point of view. The budget has been described as Keynesian: an effort to encourage economic expansion by adding to aggregate demand through fiscal policy. The second feature is that, in hindsight, France appeared to be 'going it alone' with expansionary measures while some of its neighbours were pursuing contractionary – or at best neutral – policies. Yet, in July 1981, the OECD was forecasting that the industrial countries would show a growth rate of GDP of 2 per cent in 1982, whereas there turned out to be a contraction of 0.4 per cent. Expecting other economies to expand, the French policymakers did not deliberately 'go it alone'.

In any event, the budget for 1982 called for a 27 per cent increase in expenditures and a deficit of 95 billion francs or 2.6 per cent of GDP. The budget also included some tax increases presented as a means of financing the battle against unemployment but aimed, in addition, at 'taxing the rich'. The tax on individual incomes was raised and a ceiling was placed on family exemptions above certain levels of income. What incited the greatest outcry was a new tax on wealth. Above 3 million francs (about $450 000 in 1982), an annual tax between 0.5 and 1.5 per cent was levied. Works of art were exempt for fear that they would be exported to escape the tax. This 'tax on large fortunes', which Mitterrand had proposed in his election campaign, brought in 3 billion francs in 1982 as only half of the estimated 200 000 eligible taxpayers made declarations of their wealth above the taxed minimum.

While François Mitterrand and Ronald Reagan could not have differed more in basic philosophy, both adopted what looked like expansionary Keynesian policies – via deliberate increases in budget deficits – in the midst of recession in 1981–82, although Reagan's programme went under the title of 'supply-side' economics. In addition to stimulating demand, Mitterrand's actions increased unit labour costs. Less than five months after the new government took office, the franc was subject to its first devaluation in the EMS – by 3 per cent while the D-mark went up by 5.5 per cent.

Meanwhile the new government's nationalisation law found its way through the parliament. It involved the public takeover, with compensation of stockholders, of five industrial groups, 39 additional banks (several major banks had been nationalised immediately after World War II under General de Gaulle's first government), and two financial institutions. Added were two large steel companies, a maker of military aircraft, and a conglomerate that produced armaments, computers, and a variety of other products. After the nationalisations of 1982, state-owned firms were responsible for one-fourth of value-added in industry, about 10 per cent of total employment, and 80 per cent of banking activity.

A result of the shift in macroeconomic policy was that the French economy grew by 2.5 per cent in 1982 as domestic demand rose by 3.5 per cent, while many other industrial countries were undergoing contractions in demand and output. Other results were an acceleration of inflation in France to nearly 12 per cent and a more than doubling of the current-account deficit to $12.1 billion in 1982. The latter change together with capital flight led to a reduction in the foreign exchange reserves by one-fifth in 1981 and an additional one-fourth in 1982.

In light of these developments, the government began to reconsider its economic policies in the spring of 1982. It turned toward the views of Finance Minister Jacques Delors who had for some time argued for a 'pause' in the pace of Socialist reforms. Then the party in power did badly in the cantonal elections of March 1982. A plan for an abrupt policy change was worked out by the Prime Minister's office and officials in Delors' Treasury. Shortly after the 7-nation economic summit meeting that Mitterrand hosted at Versailles in early June, he held his second large press conference at the Elysée. He spoke in very general terms about the economic difficulties and, in a new departure, stressed the need to reconstitute savings, develop risk capital, give priority to investment, control the budget deficit and combat inflation. For the first time, he put the battle against inflation on the same footing as the fight against unemployment.

What motivated Mitterrand to accept Mauroy's recommended turnaround was the prospect that 'the left' would fail again as it had under Leon Blum in France in 1936 and under Harold Wilson in Britain in 1964–7. It would fail partly because France could not successfully pursue an expansionary policy when the other major countries were mainly concerned with inflation and were therefore in a deflationary mode. Mitterrand learned this at the Versailles summit if he did not already know it.

President Mitterrand left the specifics of the new policy to be made public by Prime Minister Mauroy, but only after an early June weekend meeting of European finance ministers and central bank governors at Brussels had agreed on another devaluation of the French franc, by $5\frac{3}{4}$ per cent, and another revaluation of the Deutschemark, by $4\frac{1}{4}$ per cent.

With the objective of reducing inflation in 1983 to 8 per cent, Mauroy announced that, accompanying the latest franc devaluation, wages and prices would be frozen for four months and the budget deficit would be limited to 3 per cent of GDP. In a vote of confidence on these measures in the National Assembly, the Communists supported the government.

Thus France turned to '*rigueur*' in order to deal with its high rate of inflation and menacing external deficit. The decision was based, in large part, on the realisation by the government that it existed in a world of interdependence.

As Favier and Martin-Roland put it, both Mauroy and Mitterrand were motivated by the necessity to change policy if they were to 'endure'. To endure they had to show that they knew how to lead, to manage.

On 1 November 1982 the wage and price freeze came to an end but the government succeeded in getting the unions to accept, or at least tolerate, an end to the indexing of wages to prices. This historic change was made possible by the participation of four Communist ministers in the government.

Even so, inflation in France was higher than in many other industrial countries. The trade deficit was large and France's foreign exchange reserves were running low. In the early months of 1983, debate went on within the government concerning the foreign exchange problem. The alternatives were either to drop out of the EMS or to tighten the screws on the economy once again with a further dose of rigour. But as the debate proceeded, it became clear that these were not realistic alternatives. Dropping out of the EMS would lead to a brusque decline of the franc on foreign exchange markets, which in turn would raise the domestic cost of imports. To support the franc, either interest rates would have to be hiked steeply – which would be a form of rigour – or France would have to adopt highly restrictive import controls, which would run counter to its EC obligations.

Another weekend meeting at Brussels, 19–20 March 1983, resulted in France's third devaluation in less than two years. The franc went down an additional $2\frac{1}{2}$ per cent and the D-mark was revalued by $5\frac{1}{2}$ per cent. Then Mitterrand addressed the nation. He defended the decision to remain in the EMS and stressed that France must now do battle against unemployment, inflation, and the trade deficit. The decision to remain in the EMS was widely interpreted as historic: France confirmed its commitment to the European Community.

Once again, Mitterrand left it to Prime Minister Mauroy to announce the details of the new economic programme. The measures, aimed mainly at reducing the trade deficit, included, among others, a further 20 billion franc cut in the budget deficit by means of new taxes, 'forced saving' in the form of advance payments of income and wealth taxes, and a decrease in foreign exchange outlays via a limitation on travel allowances for French tourists going abroad. It was estimated that the new measures would lower GDP growth by 2 per cent.

Some of these decisions were hard for the Communist ministers to swallow, and they began to distance themselves from the government while continuing to support it in the parliament.

Thus Mitterrand's France moved from rigour to austerity. This was reinforced by the budget for 1984 prepared in Delors's ministry and characterised as the most stringent since the Liberation. It was proposed that receipts rise by 8.4 per cent while outlays would increase by only 6.3 per cent.

Public agitation against rising taxes became evident in the summer of 1983. Mitterrand shocked his ministers in September by announcing that this tendency would be reversed beginning in 1985. What worried Mitterrand, as always, were the politics. The French Socialists were becoming the party of high taxes while the right, as represented by Thatcher and Reagan abroad and Jacques Chirac at home, were for tax reduction.

While Mitterrand's rhetoric was designed to keep a distance between his economic policies and those of Thatcher and Reagan, in practice he shifted economic policy in the liberal direction. Income tax rates and social contributions were reduced in the budget for 1985. Tax revenues, which had risen from 38.5 per cent of GDP in 1970 to 42.7 per cent in 1979, reached a peak of 47.6 per cent in 1985 before falling slightly.

As the result of the budgetary decisions of 1982 and 1983, French fiscal policy had became more restrictive. According to the OECD's measure of the cyclically-adjusted budget balance, the budget moved towards restraint by 0.4 per cent of GDP in 1984 and by 0.6 per cent in 1985.

Economic growth remained sluggish in 1983–4, averaging only 1 per cent per year, but picked up in the following years. The unemployment rate continued to creep up, reaching 9.8 per cent in 1984, and peaking at 10.5 per cent in 1987. But the rate of inflation came down from 13.4 per cent in 1981 to 5.8 per cent in 1985 and only 2.5 per cent in 1986 when both the dollar and the oil price declined. And the balance-of-payments improved greatly. The current-account deficit virtually disappeared by 1985. In 1986 there was a surplus of $2.4 billion. With this improvement in the external position, the franc was revalued (by 2 per cent) along with the D-mark and other ERM currencies against the lira in July 1985.

The continued rise of unemployment was the result not only of slow growth but also of another basic reform aimed at industrial modernisation: ending subsidies to inefficient firms and helping those sectors on the frontier of technology. There followed massive lay-offs in a number of industries, particularly steel and coal, and numerous demonstrations by unemployed workers. One is reminded of the policies of Margaret Thatcher.

In July 1984 Mauroy was succeeded by Fabius, who, at just under 38, became the youngest Prime Minister in the history of Republican France. The four Communist ministers left the government, and Pierre Beregovoy became finance minister when Jacques Delors assumed the presidency of the European Commission.

Fabius's role was to continue to reconcile his Socialist government with the French business community by emphasising 'the importance of profit, and of individual or private initiative as motors of investment and therefore of the creation of employment'. His new finance minister pursued deregulation by abolishing quantitative credit controls and liberalising financial and foreign exchange markets.

First Cohabitation – 1986–8

The legislative elections of March 1986 gave a bare majority to the rightist parties in the National Assembly and required Mitterrand to appoint a prime minister of a different party from his own. He chose Jacques Chirac, and this led to a period of 'cohabitation' for the first time in the Fifth Republic under the constitution that Charles de Gaulle had fashioned.

The Socialists lost their majority even though, as Favier and Martin-Roland put it, they 'had succeeded where one least expected it. Disinflation, de-indexation [of wages], recovery of profit margins of enterprises, industrial modernisation, and, on the plane of behaviour, a reduction in the ideological antagonism between labour and capital.'[2]

One of the early actions of the Chirac government was to devalue the franc by 3 per cent in the EMS, while the D-mark was revalued by the same amount. The aim was to encourage exports, but Mitterrand advised against it and the Socialists in the National Assembly were also critical. That turned out to be the last French devaluation in the EMS until its near demise in the summer of 1993.

There was considerable political disagreement between Chirac and Mitterrand. A law was passed authorising privatisation, and the government proceeded to sell shares in a number of large firms. The plan was to privatise 65 enterprises in five years. In 18 months, 40 per cent of the programme was accomplished. After the stock market decline of October 1987, the privatisation effort was suspended.

The Chirac government also repealed the tax on large fortunes and reduced the top marginal tax rate from 65 to 58 per cent.

In the two years of cohabitation, French fiscal policy continued to move towards restraint – by 0.3 per cent of GDP in both 1987 and 1988

Another Socialist Prime Minister

In the presidential elections of April–May 1988, François Mitterrand defeated Jacques Chirac by a comfortable margin. Though not required to do so, Chirac immediately submitted his resignation as Prime Minister and Mitterrand named as his successor Michel Rocard, a Socialist with a strong leaning toward free markets. The growth rate averaged 4.3 per cent in 1988–9 and unemployment declined somewhat from its peak of 10.5 per cent in 1985 to 9 per cent in 1990.

Beginning in 1991, France felt the impact of German reunification. Exports accelerated but interest rates had to be raised. Meanwhile France's adherence to the ERM strengthened. The notion of the stability of the French franc relative to the D-mark became increasingly important as a matter of national policy. The byword was 'credibility'. It was measured by the premium of French short-term interest rates over comparable German rates. Inflation and interest rates tended to converge with those in Germany in the latter part of the 1980s. By 1989 consumer price inflation in France was only 3.5 per cent compared with 2.8 per cent in Germany. The interest rate gap – both short and long-term – had narrowed to 2 per cent in 1989 as compared with about 6 per cent in 1982 and 4.7 per cent in 1985. In 1991, inflation in France, at 3.1 per cent, was below that in Germany for the first time in living memory, and French short-term interest rates were only two-thirds of 1 per cent above German rates.

By the summer of 1992, the interest-rate gap was even smaller. But in September the ERM was badly shaken. Britain and Italy had to drop out and Spain and Portugal had to devalue. France maintained its D-mark parity, but at the cost of a sharp rise in short-term interest rates and heavy intervention in foreign exchange markets.

Figure 5.1   Inflation in France and Germany

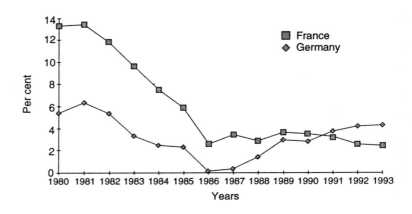

The 'franc fort' policy symbolised the transformation that had occurred in French economic policy and performance since François Mitterrand assumed the Presidency of the Republic in 1981. Inflation was historically low. While the economy had slowed, France was growing faster than many of its trade partners. Its balance-of-payments deficit was relatively small. The negatives were a high rate of unemployment (10.5 per cent) – made somewhat less painful by a generous system of unemployment compensation – and the need to maintain lofty interest rates to protect the franc in the ERM.

As for structural developments, the privatisations of the Chirac period were succeeded by a policy of 'neither privatisation nor nationalisation' as enunciated by Mitterrand in 1988. Some partial privatisations took place – for example Volvo was permitted to acquire a 20 per cent share in Renault, a state-owned company, and Mitterrand announced that he now favoured partial privatisations if they resulted in increased investment or employment. Ironically, one of the motivations for the government's more liberal policy regarding privatisation was that it brought revenue to the Treasury. President Mitterrand may have looked across the Channel at what Mrs Thatcher was doing in this respect.

Second Period of Cohabitation

In the parliamentary elections of March 1993, the Socialists suffered a crushing defeat and a second period of cohabitation began, with Edouard Balladur as Prime Minister. High unemployment was generally cited as the major reason for the election outcome.

Balladur's first budget attempted to cut the deficit by reducing expenditures and raising taxes. He soon realised that this was an error and launched a 'Balladur bond' in the amount of 110 billion francs to combat unemployment. He also launched a large privatisation programme, starting with the chemical firm Rhone Poulenc and Banque Nationale de Paris, bringing revenue to the treasury.

Unemployment continued to rise and in July speculation against the franc began in foreign exchange markets. It was based not on a belief that the franc had become overvalued relative to the D-mark but that the government and the Bank of France would have to agree to lower interest rates in order to deal with the unemployment. As is brought out in the next chapter, the upshot was a decision to increase margins in the EMS to ± 15 per cent. As it turned out, France used very little of this scope to let the franc depreciate (at least through to the spring of 1994). It stuck to the 'franc fort' policy. Meanwhile unemployment rose to 12 per cent in late 1993.

Balladur appeared to get along more harmoniously with Mitterrand than did Chirac. And his popularity in France soared – despite continued recession and rising unemployment, the July foreign exchange crisis, and farmers' opposition to the GATT agreement – to the point where he was being tipped as a candidate for the presidency. In an interview in the *Financial Times*, which named him 'Man of the Year', he said, 'It is paradoxical that the French have evidently still a good opinion of me, and yet apparently believe they are badly governed.'[3]

France, as viewed in 1993, had been transformed. It had a strong currency, a lower inflation rate than Germany and a current-account surplus. And François Mitterrand, still with two years to run in his second term, had nudged France further away from the 'exceptionalism' of its earlier history. Claude Imbert has observed that just as de Gaulle had 'applied his prestige and historic authority to the much needed liquidation of long-standing national traditions' – colonialism and the French right's resistance to change – his main opponent, François Mitterrand, later ended the exile of the French left, 'which had channelled itself away into a Marxist ideological ghetto'.[4]

One of the many ways in which the change in France may be illustrated is in the language of Mitterrand. In 1981–2, he frequently employed the word 'socialism' to justify his policies. In the late 1980s and early 1990s, that word was no longer heard from him.

Mitterrand is responsible for other changes. Paris has been somewhat transformed: the Louvre has a glass pyramid entrance designed by I.M. Pei and a new Richelieu wing (formerly occupied by the finance ministry); at La Defense a monumental arch has been constructed in alignment with the Louvre, the Place de la Concorde, and the Arc de Triomphe; and a very modern and very large new opera house exists at the Place de la Bastille.

5.2   GERMANY

Less space is devoted to Germany (and Japan) than to the United States, Britain, and France not because they are less important but because they underwent less of a transformation. In the case of Germany the big metamorphosis came only in 1990 with the reunification of East and West Germany.

An international agreement back in 1978 had a lasting effect on Germany attitudes about economic policy. Faced with sluggish economic growth and a large current-account surplus, the German government under Chancellor Helmut

Schmidt agreed to adopt a more stimulative budget policy at the annual economic summit meeting, held in Bonn in 1978. Included were a cut in taxes and an increase in expenditures with a combined effect equivalent to 1 per cent of Germany's GNP. A number of other countries took similar action while the United States agreed to pursue a more restrictive fiscal policy and to deregulate the price of oil and take other measures to reduce its oil imports.

In 1979–81, inflation in Germany worsened and the current account moved into deficit. This led a number of observers to criticise, and blame, the coordinated agreement at the summit. The fact is that the heads of government who met in 1978 could not possibly have foreseen the fall of the Shah of Iran a year later. That is what set off the second oil shock and imposed inflation and balance-of-payments deficits on all oil-importing countries. But the German view of the effects of the Bonn agreement was to influence German policymakers in the 1980s and beyond, reinforcing their distaste for 'artificial' measures aimed at stimulating the economy when it was operating well below capacity.

Germany's GDP increased only 1 per cent in 1980 and was flat in 1981, while unemployment rose slightly. In 1982, output declined and unemployment jumped to 5 per cent, compared with 3.1 per cent in 1978.

When Helmut Kohl took over the Chancellorship in October 1982, Schmidt's government had already reversed Germany's budget policy from its stance of 1978–9. The 1982 budget called for a compression of expenditures and a reduction of the budget deficit in the face of a sluggish economy. In this and other ways the change of government in Germany, in contrast with what happened in Britain and the United States, did not involve a sharp break with earlier policies.

The recovery from the 1982 recession was anaemic. GDP growth averaged only 2 per cent per year in 1983–7 and unemployment exceeded 9 per cent of the dependent labour force in 1984–5. In other European countries, economic expansion was somewhat more rapid. But Germany's inflation subsided significantly, from 5 per cent in 1982 to near zero in 1987.

With demand expanding more slowly than in its main trading partners and with a lower inflation rate, Germany's exports outpaced imports and the current account of the balance of payments moved toward a much larger surplus – from less than 1 per cent of GDP in 1983 to a peak of 4.8 per cent in 1989.

The Kohl government intensified the process of fiscal consolidation initiated under Helmut Schmidt. The structural budget deficit of all levels of government combined was reduced in 1982–5 by 3.5 per cent of GDP. While this may have had beneficial long-run effects in encouraging investment, it must have been an important factor in holding down the growth of the economy.

But there were other views on this question. The sluggishness of the German economy led to the notion among some German economists that Europe in general and Germany in particular was suffering from a hardening of the economic arteries. Herbert Giersch, former head of the Kiel Institute and well-known internationally, appears to have coined the term 'Eurosclerosis'. What he had in mind was that real wages were too high, unemployment compensation too generous, and labour laws too restrictive to encourage new hiring and to permit adequate mobility of labour. This inflexibility allegedly impeded growth, according to Giersch and others who agreed with him.

The German economy continued on a slow growth path through 1987 but growth picked up to about 3.5 per cent in 1988. The pickup followed a shift in fiscal policy from restraint to stimulus beginning in 1986. Probably more important was the increase in population owing to immigration. From 1985 to 1991, West Germany's population rose more than 5 per cent after having declined by almost 1 per cent in the previous five years. The birthrate fell by some 40 per cent from the second half of the 1960s to the first half of the 1980s.

The immigrants consisted of three groups: East Germans, ethnic Germans from the Soviet Union and Eastern Europe and people from elsewhere – mainly the former Yugoslavia, Romania, Bulgaria, and Turkey – seeking asylum. The German constitution contained both a 'law of return' for ethnic Germans and a law of asylum (the latter in the process of being amended to become more restrictive). It is estimated that more than 800 000 people immigrated in 1989, legally or otherwise. The economic effect in West Germany showed up in two ways: an acceleration of spending on housing and consumer goods but also a slow decrease in unemployment despite a faster rise in employment.

The Berlin Wall came down on 9 November 1989. It was a joyous event even though that particular date is infamous in German history: the Nazi rampage against Jews – *Kristallnacht* – occurred on 9 November 1938.

Events moved rapidly thereafter. Immigration from East Germany (the German Democratic Republic – GDR) accelerated to an estimated 2000 per day early in 1990. In the GDR output was falling and the quality of life was being affected by the departure of professionals, including medical doctors, and skilled workers. It is estimated that nearly 4 per cent of the GDR labour force left in 1989 and more than twice that many were likely to move in 1990.

In the circumstances, Chancellor Kohl felt an urgent need to stem the inflow of people. That explains the hasty announcement in February 1990 of the intention to form a currency union with the GDR. In April the governments of East and West Germany agreed on an economic and monetary union, to be established by the summer. Against the advice of the Bundesbank, the Kohl government decided on a conversion rate of east marks into D-marks at one-to-one for wages and salaries and for bank accounts up to certain levels. On the very day of the announcement, the President of the Bundesbank, Karl-Otto Poehl, was in East Berlin conferring with his GDR counterpart and agreeing with him that early monetary unification was not on the cards. The Kohl government overrode the objections of the Bundesbank because it was anxious to give East Germans a motivation to remain at home while aspiring to the living standard existing in the west. Then and ever since, political considerations have prevailed over economic good sense in the management of the unification process.

Monetary unification took place on 1 July 1990. The D-mark became the currency of the GDR and the Bundesbank became its central bank. On 3 October in an atmosphere of euphoria, the two countries were unified politically. The GDR ceased to exist.

The euphoria did not last long.

Industrial production in east Germany plunged by about two-thirds from mid-1990 to the spring of 1991 and unemployment rose from about 1 per cent of the labour force to 15 per cent in the summer of 1991.

In general, unification exposed eastern Germany to both a demand shock and a supply shock. Consumers switched their purchases from goods made in the east to previously-unavailable products from the west. The most conspicuous example was the shunning of the Trabant – a car made in eastern Germany – in favour of the wide array of German and non-German cars that could be bought in the western part of the country. East German products could not compete in the west in terms of quality and design. On top of that, there was a collapse of exports to Eastern Europe and the former Soviet Union (while west Germany's exports to those markets rose). The supply shock was based on sharply rising labour costs – as wages in eastern Germany, less than one-third those in the west – went up rapidly after unification. These wage hikes were encouraged by the trade unions in west Germany, which were concerned about a migration of industry to the east attracted by lower labour costs. While wages in the east rose steeply, productivity there was only one-third of west Germany's output per person. Thus producers in the east suffered a severe squeeze on their costs. For these reasons industrial production and GDP plunged in the east.

Meanwhile, efforts were made to deal with state enterprises in eastern Germany. A trust fund agency (*Treuhandanstalt*) took over more than 12 000 industrial firms. Its task was to privatise, restructure or close down these enterprises. Many of them were 'loss-making', had very poor environmental standards, were burdened with heavy debts or had unclear property rights. By the autumn of 1993, 90 per cent of the firms had been either closed or sold – often with subsidies to the buyers in one form or another – in what has been called 'the biggest fire sale in history', not untinged with financial scandal.[5] Some of the purchasers were foreign investors. The new owners proceeded to slim down excessive work forces and that added significantly to unemployment. Also privatised were 20 000 companies in services: retail stores, restaurants and hotels. There remained on the books of the agency some large firms that have very little economic value but which provide employment to about 300 000 workers. *Treuhandanstalt* is expected to finish its task by the end of 1994. Before it is finished it will have incurred debts of at least DM 275 billion (about $160 billion) as the result of subsidies, environmental cleanup, and restructuring of enterprises,

Initially unification brought depression to eastern Germany and prosperity to western Germany. In the latter, GDP growth, which had been 3.3 per cent in 1989, picked up to 4.9 per cent in 1990, as the result of a cut in income taxes at the beginning of the year and the shift of east German consumer and investment spending to the west after monetary unification. Much of the latter spending was financed out of transfers from the central and state government budgets in west Germany, which shifted strongly into deficit. Three years after unification the costs of unification still weighed heavily on central and state government budgets.

The acceleration in demand pushed up the rate of inflation, from just over 1 per cent in 1988 to 3.5 per cent in 1991 and around 4 per cent in 1992–3, high by German standards. The Bundesbank responded by steadily tightening its policy. Short-term interest rates in Germany rose from 4 per cent in 1988 to 8.8 per cent in 1991 and a peak of almost 10 per cent in the autumn of 1992.

The mix of fiscal and monetary policies – a large budget deficit and tight money – was similar to what prevailed in the United States in the first half of the 1980s. And some of the effects were also similar. In particular, there developed upward pressure on the D-mark and the large current-account surplus disappeared, giving way to a deficit. The D-mark appreciated further in 1992 and 1993 when crises in the EMS led to depreciations of other currencies.

In effect, the additional resources being absorbed by east Germany, and largely financed through government budgets in west Germany, came from Germany's trade partners as their exports to it increased sharply. If east Germany were still a separate country, west Germany's current account would look very different, since shipments of consumer and capital goods to the east would count as exports.

The rapid growth in west Germany gave way to a downturn in mid-1992 under the influence of high interest rates and declining orders, both domestic and foreign, to German industry. GDP fell 2.4 per cent from the second quarter of 1992 to the spring of 1993 and unemployment rose above 8 per cent in December. In eastern Germany a construction boom helped to turn the economy around. GDP rose 10 per cent in 1992 and a further 6 per cent in the first half of 1993 (as compared with the same period of 1992). But with high and rising labour costs, among other problems, industrial production was still depressed. Unemployment was 15 per cent according to the official tally. It is estimated that if 'job creation schemes and short-time working' were taken into account, the unemployment rate would be 35 per cent or more.[6] By the end of 1993 it was being said that the recession in west Germany was holding back economic activity in east Germany.

While economic conditions have improved somewhat in the east, a wide gulf remained between the two parts of the country. And it is clear that the costs – social and cultural as well as economic and financial – and time duration of the unification process were underestimated in 1990.

Within one year of unification, as one scholar has written,

it has become increasingly obvious that within the one Germany now exist two societies divided by forty-five years of separate histories, by disparate levels of economic development, and by mentalities shaped by the distinct social systems in which people have grown up, lived, and worked. The gap between the two parts of the country is therefore not simply a matter of differences in living conditions arising from economic dualism; it also reflects differences in collective experiences. The corresponding psychological distance between west Germans and east Germans has not been narrowed by the process of unification.[7]

Gunter Grass expressed similar opinions:

Many people from the East hoped to join the West with their own face, their own experiences. But the West was coming like colonial masters, treating them like children. It was a shock for many. They were astonished. There is no longer a wall or an iron curtain, but Germany is divided socially and economically. There are Germans first and second class. I'm afraid this will take longer than the wall to fix.[8]

This view is confirmed by a poll indicating that a majority of easterners consider themselves 'former citizens of east Germany' rather than part of a united Germany.

Thus, as compared with 1980, Germany is a very different country, politically and economically. It was, and may still be, the strongest economy in Europe. But it is now burdened with all the problems of transforming and supporting its eastern states, and those problems will not be solved quickly.

5.3 JAPAN

'Japan is indeed the object-lesson of national efficiency, and happy is the country that learns it.' These words were written in 1905 by a British prime minister, Lord Rosebery.[9] Their peacetime validity was demonstrated to the west only after World War II, when Japan's economic performance was phenomenal. Apart from what the economic statistics show, consumers in the United States and elsewhere became familiar with Japan's efficiency as they eagerly bought Japanese automobiles and television sets, then VCRs and compact disc players, and more recently personal computers as well. While Japan became known throughout the world as a major exporter, it is surprising to note that its economy is only slightly more open than the US economy. Japanese merchandise exports and imports in the 1980s were 10.3 per cent of its GDP. The comparable figure for the United States was 7.7 per cent. In contrast, Germany's trade was about one-fourth of its total output.

The Japanese economy had grown very rapidly in the 1950s and 1960s, roughly twice as fast as other industrial countries. It was a country of high saving and high invest-ment. The differential in growth rates narrowed consider-ably in the 1970s, when Japan was affected by the first oil shock. In addition, by then Japan had caught up with other industrial countries technologically and could no longer increase productivity rapidly simply by importing know-how. The deceleration of growth was a reflection mainly of a slower advance of productivity rather than of unutilised resources. The unemployment rate – remarkably low in Japan, partly because of life-time employment and partly because the statistics do not cover part-time workers – was 2 per cent in 1980, reached a peak of 2.8 per cent in 1986 and declined to 2.1 per cent in 1990. As the economy slowed again in 1992–3, unemployment rose to 2.8 per cent.

In the years after 1973, Japan developed a big budget deficit relative to its GNP. That deficit was second in size only to Italy's among the seven largest industrial countries. Government debt held by the public grew twelve-fold between 1973 and 1979. As a consequence, the powerful Ministry of Finance came to the judgement that Japan should, at all costs, avoid budget deficits and, if possible, achieve surpluses so as to reduce the outstanding govern-ment debt. Japan weathered the second oil shock, in 1979–80, with much less inflation and economic slowdown than most other countries. An opportunity thus presented itself to cut back the budget deficit, which was done year by year beginning in 1980. The general government deficit fell from 4.8 per cent of GDP in 1979 to 0.8 per cent in 1985. As is discussed in the next chapter, one result was the emergence of a large current-account surplus in the 1980s. Before 1980, that surplus, at its peak in 1978, was about $17 billion, or 1.7 per cent of GDP. In the 1980s, the current-account surplus grew steadily from $5 billion in 1981 to $87 billion, or 3.6 per cent of GDP, in 1987. Japan's exports increased more than 40 per cent in real terms in 1980–85 while the volume of its imports went up only 9 per cent. The increase in net exports accounted for 42 per cent of the advance in GDP in those years. And that advance was relatively slow, averaging 3.2 per cent per year.

The large external surplus subjected Japan to criticism from abroad regarding its macroeconomic policies, its trade practices, its retail distribution system and its inter-corporate relations. It was suggested that Japan should take steps to expand domestic demand and thereby use more of its saving at home. This was said to be especially desirable in view of the prospect that the yen would appreciate as the dollar came down from the high levels it moved to in the first half of the 1980s. Japan was charged with discriminating in various ways against imports. Rice imports were banned. Public works contracts were said to exclude foreign bidders. Its distribution system was hard for foreign producers to break into. And the *keiretsu* arrangements – horizontal and vertical relationships among companies in production and distribution – were also said to discriminate against imports.

Proposals for macroeconomic reform garnered additional support in Japan from the publication in April 1986 of the Mayekawa report – by an advisory group headed by former Bank of Japan Governor Haruo Mayekawa – addressed to Prime Minister Yasuhiro Nakasone. That report, and a follow-up in 1987, assembled a number of long-standing proposals aimed at reorienting Japan's use of resources towards the satisfaction of pressing domestic needs, including residential housing, public works, and increased leisure. The report gave added impetus to the idea of stimulating domestic demand in Japan.

The Mayekawa report bore some fruit in 1987, following a year of GDP growth of only 2.6 per cent. Finance Minister Kiichi Miyazawa proposed a supplementary budget to which the figure of 6 trillion yen was attached. That figure greatly exaggerated the programme's impact on the economy. In fact, fiscal policy became more restrictive year by year through 1990. Nevertheless, domestic demand, which had increased 3.8 per cent per year in 1984–6, accelerated to almost 6 per cent annually in 1987–90. GNP expanded by 5 per cent per year in those four years.

The result was that Japan outdid the United Kingdom in generating a 'bubble economy' – a speculative boom in stocks and real estate. What brought it on?

As in Britain, much of the answer lies in monetary policy. The Bank of Japan's discount rate was reduced in steps from 5 per cent in 1985 to $2\frac{1}{2}$ per cent in 1987 and market rates, both short and long-term, fell substantially. The yield on long-term government bonds came down from $6\frac{1}{3}$ per cent in 1985 to a low point of 3 per cent in the spring of 1987. The narrow money supply, which had increased $3\frac{1}{2}$ per cent per year in 1983–5, rose by 8 per cent per year in 1986–8. The easing of monetary policy, perhaps excessively, has been attributed in part to Japan's effort to support the Louvre agreement (next chapter) by preventing the yen from appreciating further relative to the dollar.

In addition to monetary policy, financial deregulation played a role in promoting the boom. Liberalisation of the financial system began in the 1970s but was speeded up in the 1980s, partly in response to prodding by the US Treasury. But the worldwide increase in capital mobility, based in part on the development of new financial instruments, made deregulation imperative if Japanese financial institutions were to compete with their counterparts abroad. Interest rates were freed from governmental ceilings, banks were permitted to attract additional types of deposits, and firms, which had earlier been largely confined to commercial banks for loans, found it possible to borrow at home in securities markets and abroad from banks and securities markets.[10]

In these circumstances, stock prices in Japan skyrocketed. From 1982 to the peak level at the end of 1989, the Nikkei average rose more than five-fold, while the Dow Jones average in New York tripled. The very high price–earnings ratio, and low dividend yield, made equity financing very inexpensive for Japanese business enterprises. The rapid advance in stock prices also created large capital gains for individual stockholders, for corporations (which hold much of each others' stocks), and for banks.

Furthermore, as discussed below, the yen appreciated sharply, rising from 260 per dollar in February 1985 to 126 per dollar at the end of 1988. This 'yen shock' (*endaka* in Japanese) stimulated investment aimed at upgrading products so that they could compete at the higher exchange rate. It also made assets abroad look inexpensive to Japanese investors.

All these factors stimulated the 'animal spirits' of Japanese corporations and led to a substantial increase in domestic investment spending, which rose, in real terms, by 48 per cent from 1986 to 1990 while real GDP went up by 23 per cent.

To the speculative rise in stock prices was added an even greater boom in the prices of real estate in the second half of the 1980s. By 1989, the total value of real estate in Japan was estimated by a Japanese government agency to have a value four times the value of all the property in the United States, which has an area 25 times that of Japan.[11]

The Japanese seemed to have discovered a perpetual motion machine for their economy. The increase in the prices of real estate and equities led to a substantial expansion of bank capital, which enabled banks to lend more to borrowers who pledged their holdings of real estate as collateral; the borrowers used part of the funds from new loans to buy more equities and real estate. Household spending increased in response to the growth in personal wealth. The household saving rate, which had averaged 16.7 per cent of disposable income in 1980–86, fell to 14.5 per cent in the next five years. This, plus the availability of cheap finance, encouraged business investment spending.

The bubble mentality made a large part of the Japanese population feel rich. They responded by spending on plant and equipment, new houses, impressionist art, expensive imported automobiles and jewellery, and on the acquisition abroad of businesses, office buildings, golf courses, hotels, and estates in Hawaii and California. In Japan more than 160 golf courses were built between 1989 and 1991. The price of memberships 'range from a few million yen up to the ¥250 million range' (about $2 million).[12]

As was inevitable, the bubble imploded. The Bank of Japan began to raise its discount rate in May 1989. The Tokyo stock market, which had quickly shrugged off the sharp drop in stocks in the United States and elsewhere in October 1987, reached a peak at the end of 1989. By early 1993 stock prices in Tokyo had fallen more than 50 per cent, and were being supported at that level through purchases by government pension funds and savings institutions. Land prices had also dropped, at least in Tokyo and Osaka, but are more difficult to measure since there are few transactions. According to one report land prices fell in each of the three years 1991–3. Prices in Tokyo dropped 14.5 per cent in the year to December 1992 and 7.5 per cent in the following twelve months.[13]

With the collapse of the speculative bubble, the real economy of Japan entered a period of slowdown and then recession. Consumers felt much less wealthy as the values of their stocks and real estate declined and they cut back on their spending. In 1992 retail sales fell for the first time in forty years. Businesses found it much more costly to raise capital and they reduced their investment outlays for this reason as well as because they had excess capacity created in the earlier investment boom. The result was a drop in industrial production by 6.1 per cent in 1992 and an additional 4.6 per cent in 1993. Business profits decreased, new commercial buildings remained empty and Japanese banks were left with a large volume of bad debts. For the first time since the 1974 oil shock Japan's GDP fell – by about 1 per cent during 1993. In these conditions, the government enacted two stimulus packages, one in 1992 and another in the spring of 1993, but their effects on overall economic activity were not visible. One can only say that the economy would have declined more without them.

Balance of Payments and Exchange Rates

While the dollar appreciated sharply relative to many currencies in the first half of the 1980s, it moved rather little against the yen. In fact the yen's effective exchange rate (its trade-weighted average value) moved up from 1980 to 1985 as other non-dollar currencies depreciated much more than the yen. Nevertheless, as noted, Japan's current-account surplus increased strongly in 1981–7. That in turn both required and facilitated Japan's role as a major supplier of capital to other countries, especially the United States. Actually, outflows of long-term capital exceeded the current-account surplus from 1981 to 1990. The difference was made up by inflows of short-term capital as Japanese banks and others borrowed abroad.

Japan might have become a major exporter of capital, acquiring assets in the United States and elsewhere, even if it had not developed a substantial current-account surplus. After all, the United States continued to undertake direct foreign investment abroad in the 1980s even though it had a deficit in its current account. It did so by borrowing abroad in other forms.

We may identify as another significant transformation in the 1980s Japan's emergence as the world's largest exporter of capital. Japanese direct investment abroad rose from little more than $2 billion in 1980 to $48 billion in 1990 and included not only manufacturing plants but also real estate and financial services in North America, Europe, and East Asia. Particularly noteworthy are 'transplants' – Japanese automobile factories established in the United States – stimulated in large part by 'voluntary export restrictions' applied by Japan on exports from the homeland. In 1993 more than half of Japanese cars sold in America came from such transplants.

Portfolio investment – purchases abroad of bonds and, to a smaller extent, stocks – rose from $3 billion in 1983 to more than $100 billion in 1986 and $91 billion in 1987.

The result was that foreign assets owned by Japanese investors increased by a multiple of twelve from 1980 to 1991, when they amounted to $2 trillion. Over the same period, their external liabilities also increased sharply, mainly in the form of borrowing from banks abroad. In effect, Japan became an international financial intermediary in the 1980s, borrowing short-term and acquiring long-term assets.

For a while, these developments aroused fears in some quarters in the United States, to which much of the capital went. There were adverse reactions to the acquisitions of properties, whether conspicuous ones like the Rockefeller Center or residential properties in Hawaii or motion picture companies. And fears were expressed that the US Treasury was too dependent on Japanese investors for the sale of its securities to finance the budget deficit. These fears turned out to be unjustified. In fact by 1991–2, long-term capital outflows from Japan had decreased and the current-account surplus was being financed by short-term outflows as Japanese banks repaid debts they had incurred in the 1980s.

The recession led to a slackening of imports and a sharp expansion of the current-account surplus, which more than tripled in dollar value from 1990 to 1992. In the first half of 1993 the yen appreciated from about 125 per dollar to just above 100 yen per dollar. This in turn made things worse for Japanese producers, already suffering from squeezed profits as the result of the recession at home.

The Political and Economic Outlook

In the midst of the recession, a political crisis came to a head in the late spring of 1993. The Liberal Democratic Party (LDP) had been wracked by a series of scandals over the years. Prime Minister Kiichi Miyazawa, who had taken office in 1991, was unable to deliver on a pledge to enact legislation on political reform. A no-confidence vote led to the fall of his government on 18 June and to elections in which the LDP lost its majority after 38 years as the ruling party. The opposition was motivated by a wish not only for electoral reform – to eliminate payoffs from business to politicians and to move to a one-representative-per-constituency system – but also to accelerate deregulation of the economy. It was aimed at what is called in Japan the 'iron triangle' – the power relationship among politicians, large corporations and bureaucrats. Bureaucrats, not a pejorative term in Japan, have over the years had enormous power in running ministries. The reformers want to deliver that power back to ministers

Morihiro Hosokawa, a former journalist and former governor of an affluent prefecture on Kyushu, was chosen by the seven-party coalition as prime minister. At age 55, he became the second youngest head of government since World War II. In September 1993 he proposed a small stimulus package, even though little of the earlier one had yet been spent, as well as 94 regulatory proposals. Some of these are designed to lower the cost of imports and utility charges to consumers and others ease restrictions on businesses and enhance competition. In November a commission appointed by Hosokawa and headed by the chairman of the *Keidanren*, Japan's main business federation, proposed the elimination or relaxation of 475 government regulations. According to a *New York Times* correspondent in Tokyo, the commission 'proposed everything from making it simpler to open large department stores and liquor shops to encouraging housing construction and easing quotas on fish imports. It called for creation of Japan's first product liability law and something that would mark a minor revolution in a country that permits dozens of cartels – strict application of the anti-monopoly laws.'[14] With support from both business and consumers, there is hope that significant deregulation will be carried out in Japan.

More generally, although Hosokawa had only a short term of office, it is possible that Japan's industrial success will now be complemented by the fulfilment of some pressing needs such as improved infrastructure and better housing, as proposed in the Mayekawa reports of 1986–7. But the first tasks are to deal with the recession and implement deregulation.

6 Economic Interactions and Economic Integration

The 1980s and early 1990s saw a continuation of the trend toward growing international economic interdependence that has been evident since the end of World War II. One manifestation of this trend is the increase in world trade relative to world output. Even more striking was the augmentation of financial interdependence – a more recent phenomenon than the growth of trade. In the 1970s and especially in the 1980s flows of funds across national borders increased by remarkably large amounts, as is illustrated later in this chapter.

The decade began, however, with interactions that were less than happy, given the high rates of inflation in 1980–81 spurred mainly by the sharp rise in the price of oil. In the seven largest industrial countries, consumer prices rose 12.7 per cent in 1980. They all tightened their monetary policies and several of them also moved toward more restrictive fiscal policies. The result was that the combined GDP of the Group of Seven slowed in 1980 and fell 0.3 per cent in 1982.

It is a reasonable supposition that in tackling the inflation problem the policymakers of each of the major countries looked inward and did not take account of the effect on their exports of the restrictive policies pursued in the other countries. This shows up in imports: the volume of imports of the Seven shrank 4.2 per cent in 1980–82. Since most of their trade is with each other, their exports slackened in 1981 and fell in 1982. This made the recession more severe than anyone expected. In other words, what happened was a failure of policy coordination among the major countries.[1]

6.1   INTERNATIONAL PAYMENTS IMBALANCES

As observed in Chapter 4, US budgetary policy shifted abruptly in 1982 under Ronald Reagan. The budget deficit, abstracting from the effects of recession in 1981–2 and recovery thereafter, quadrupled as a percentage of GDP from 1981 to 1986.

Meanwhile, Germany and Japan were trying to reduce their budget deficits and succeeding.

Although the US policy mix would by itself have tended to produce a deficit in the current account of the American balance of payments, the policies of Germany and Japan also contributed to that outcome. According to our equation on page 35 the shift in the budget deficits of Germany and Japan would have moved those countries toward current-account surpluses in any event. The combination of policies pursued by the three countries led to outsized current-account imbalances, as may be seen in Table 6.1.

A straightforward way to interpret these developments is as follows. The United States in the 1980s experienced a shortfall of saving as the government dissaved (in the form of a growing budget deficit) and private saving by households and businesses also fell off. This created the need to import saving from abroad, which took the form of a current-account deficit and was financed by net purchases of American securities and other types of lending and investing in the United States by foreign residents.

Table 6.1   Current-account balances of United States, Germany and Japan (billions of dollars)

	1980	1983	1987	1990	1992
United States	2.3	−43.7	−163.4	−90.5	−62.5
Germany	−13.8	5.4	46.3	46.6	−26.1
Japan	−10.8	20.8	87.0	35.9	117.6

Source: IMF, *International Financial Statistics Yearbook, 1993.*

In Germany and Japan, governments increased saving (by way of diminishing budget deficits) and this, in combination with private saving and investment, led them to export the excess saving in the form of current-account surpluses. These surpluses were financed by outward flows of capital undertaken by German and Japanese individuals and businesses either directly or through financial institutions.

Another interpretation can be given to these events – one that might seem too favourable to the United States. Germany and Japan were determined to reduce their budget deficits in the 1980s. They were able to achieve that aim without unduly depressing their economies in part because the United States was following the reverse policy. The growing export surpluses largely offset in the case of Japan and more than offset in the case of Germany the contractionary effect of the reduction in their budget deficits.

The appreciation of the dollar and the corresponding depreciation of the yen and D-mark in the first half of the 1980s were the instruments that helped to create the payments imbalances and the international transfer of savings. But, as noted in Chapter 4, these external imbalances would have appeared even if, somehow or other, exchange rates had been held steady. To hold the dollar down the Federal Reserve would have had to relax its monetary policy significantly, permitting lower interest rates. The result would have been higher inflation in the United States. That would have discouraged American exports and attracted imports. Similarly, if the yen and D-mark had not depreciated, Japan and Germany would have had lower rates of inflation, which would have tended to produce current-account surpluses. In other words, the validity of our equation $[(I - S) + (G - T) = M - X]$ does not depend on exchange-rate movements. It holds true under any exchange-rate regime.

Thus more by accident than design the three countries pursued complementary policies that created sizeable payments imbalances. By historical standards, these imbalances – the current-account deficit of the United States and the surpluses of Germany and Japan – were of record magnitude in the 1980s. That this was possible is related to the enormous increase in the mobility of capital that has occurred. In earlier years, it would have been assumed that a budget deficit of the magnitude of that in the United States in the mid-1980s would have the effect of crowding out domestic investment. It was taken for granted that for each country gross saving and gross investment were closely correlated. A well-known study by Professor Martin Feldstein and a colleague, published in 1980, supported that assumption.[2] But a later study shows that the correlation between saving and investment in individual countries fell substantially in the 1980s.[3]

Another significant aspect of the transformation of the world economy is that nations – at least those in the industrial world – can now tolerate, perhaps even enjoy, large divergences between gross domestic saving and domestic investment since lenders and investors in other countries are ready and willing to finance them. This may be the revival of an old rather than the appearance of a new phenomenon. The United States in the nineteenth century sustained a significant margin of investment over saving thanks to inflows of capital from Europe, especially England.[4] In more recent years it has almost been a defining characteristic of developing countries that they receive capital from abroad, enabling them to invest more than their own saving would allow.

This development – the greater ability of nations to sustain an excess of investment over saving – is one aspect of another significant alteration in the international landscape: the greatly enhanced mobility of capital across national borders among industrial countries. That change began in the 1970s but became much more evident in the 1980s. Among the factors accounting for it are financial deregulation, the dismantling of exchange controls, and the revolution in computer technology and telecommunications. New information now moves around the world instantaneously and investors and lenders are virtually as familiar with economic, financial and political conditions in other countries as with those at home. And trading can take place on a 24-hour basis.

Moreover the computer has made possible the creation of new financial instruments – such as options, interest-rate swaps, and exchange-rate swaps, known as derivatives – that facilitate the international movement of funds. An increasing proportion of this movement was in the form of purchases and sales of securities, both short and long-term. The word that appeared in the 1980s was 'securitisation' and the international activities of securities firms grew rapidly. It became possible and quite common, for example, for an American corporation to issue bonds denominated in a foreign currency, say Japanese yen, in London and to swap the proceeds back into dollars while protecting itself against the risk of an appreciation of the yen by a transaction in the forward market and an interest rate swap. Another example: trading of futures contracts on German government bonds (Bunds) is dominated by London rather than Frankfurt.[5]

A measure of the increase in capital mobility may be seen in the deposits from abroad in banks in industrial countries, which more than quadrupled from 1979 to 1991 while their total deposits increased two and one-half times. Over the same period, gross annual foreign purchases and sales of US Treasury bonds and notes each increased from about $40 billion to $2 trillion while gross foreign purchases of US stocks rose from $22 billion to $200 billion. And foreign exchange transactions in New York amounted to $192 billion daily in April 1992 compared with $18 billion in 1980.

In the early 1990s another form of capital mobility made its appearance: emerging market funds through which investors in industrial countries bought shares of stock in developing countries.

In any event, the large payments imbalances among the three industrial countries began to shrink only towards the end of the decade. During its boom, Japan's imports rose sharply and its external surplus declined. Germany's current account moved into deficit in 1991 under the impact of unification. The US deficit fell. In 1993 the Japanese and US imbalances increased again as Japan's imports fell off owing to its recession and the United States recovery led to a faster growth of imports. Once again the enlarged imbalances were easily financed by private capital.

6.2   EXCHANGE-RATE POLICIES

As the dollar rose in the first part of the 1980s, complaints were heard from abroad about the inflationary effects of rising import costs. This was especially so in France. The policy stance of the Reagan administration against exchange market intervention no doubt contributed to the widespread expectation among market participants that the dollar would continue to strengthen.

The speculative bubble of late 1984 and early 1985 shook but did not alter the policy of non-intervention. But, under the influence of a letter from Margaret Thatcher to Ronald Reagan, Secretary Regan signed on to a Group of Five communiqué in January 1985 stating that greater exchange-rate stability was desirable and that they would undertake coordinated intervention 'when to do so would be helpful'.

As it turned out, the dollar peaked in February 1985 and declined irregularly during the following six months.

In early 1985 Donald Regan and James Baker – Chief of Staff in the White House – switched jobs. Baker brought Richard Darman with him as Deputy Secretary of the Treasury. The Baker–Darman team was to reverse three of the policies pursued by the Regan–Sprinkel Treasury. One concerned intervention in foreign exchange markets.

Baker took the initiative to convene a meeting of the Group of Five finance ministers and central bank governors (soon expanded to the Group of Seven with the addition of Canada and Italy) at the Plaza Hotel in New York in September 1985. They surprised the world by announcing that exchange rates should better reflect fundamental economic conditions and that 'some further orderly appreciation of the main non-dollar currencies against the dollar is desirable. They stand ready to cooperate more closely to encourage this when to do so would be helpful'. In the words of Nigel Lawson, for the first time in many years, the Finance Ministers of the major nations had genuinely got their act together, had reached an agreement of substance, and were all speaking about it in much the same terms. This gave a new credibility to the idea of international financial cooperation in general and to the G5 (and its successor) in particular.[6]

It is no coincidence that this fundamental shift in policy came after James Baker took over as Secretary of the Treasury in the United States. Donald Regan's interest in exchange rates was minimal, judging from the book he wrote after leaving office.[7] Its index includes not one mention about the dollar, exchange rates, the balance of payments, the Group of Five, or any related subject. Baker was more pragmatic and more attuned to current policy problems. His motivation for promoting the Plaza agreement was quite clear. Shrewd politician that he is, he saw the danger of protectionism in the US Congress if exports continued to languish and imports continued to surge. He hoped to head it off with a declining dollar.

The announcement effect of the G-5 statement along with concerted intervention and a temporary increase in Japan's interest rates served to lower the dollar's value. Between February 1985 and the end of December 1986, the dollar depreciated by about 40 per cent against the yen and the D-mark. In late October 1986, the American and Japanese finance ministers announced their agreement that the dollar need not depreciate further against the yen. In return the Bank of Japan cut its discount rate. The explanation for this Baker–Miyazawa agreement appears to be that Baker was concerned that further appreciation of the yen would weaken the Japanese economy, whose exports had levelled off in real terms. What was needed was a pause in the dollar's depreciation in order to give some breathing space to Japan to implement domestic macroeconomic measures to offset the reduction in its external surplus. This reasoning was to apply to Germany and other European countries as well. Baker had been irritating his fellow ministers of finance in Europe and Japan by calling publicly for more expansionary policies in those countries and even threatening them with steeper declines in the dollar if they did not act.[8]

The Baker–Miyazawa agreement was a prelude to a broader one among the major countries, to be concluded in February, after a further sharp decline of the dollar in terms of both the yen and the D-mark.

Even before this, Baker and Darman had apparently decided that the dollar had depreciated enough for the time being. They were no doubt encouraged in this judgement by Paul Volcker, who had for some time been hinting publicly that he was not in favour of additional dollar depreciation. As the only man in US history to have participated in two devaluations of the dollar (in 1971 and 1973), Volcker was entitled to this judgement. What worried him were 'the potentially disturbing consequences of further dollar declines on confidence, on inflation, and potentially on economic growth itself'.[9]

The G-6 (Italy absented itself to protest its exclusion from a preparatory meeting) met at the French Finance Ministry – still at that time in its palatial quarters in the Louvre and now in a late twentieth-century structure at Bercy in the eastern part of Paris – and announced that

> the substantial exchange rate changes since the Plaza Agreement will increasingly contribute to reducing external imbalances and have now brought their currencies within ranges broadly consistent with underlying economic fundamentals. Further substantial exchange rate shifts among their currencies could damage growth and adjustment prospects in their countries.

While France's Finance Minister, Edouard Balladur, hoped to get an accord on a system of target zones at this meeting (French officials have never been comfortable with flexible exchange rates) the unpublished agreements were hazy on the central rates that would be aimed at and the ranges for fluctuation around them. The central rates were close to those in the markets at the time of the meeting. An inner range of ±2$\frac{1}{2}$ per cent was for discretionary intervention and an outer range of ±5 per cent was to determine mandatory intervention; yet the margins were characterised as 'soft', presumably because Bundesbank President Karl-Otto Poehl did not want to be required to undertake exchange-market intervention. According to Toyoo Gyohten, then Vice Minister in Japan's Finance Ministry, 'There was no clear and firm agreement ... The exchange rate discussion took place over dinner, while all the participants were quite busy cutting their meat and sipping their wine'.[10]

The markets did not go along with this policy declaration as cooperatively as in 1985–6. Within weeks after the Louvre meeting, the yen rose well above its Louvre rate. Market participants apparently were not impressed by the ministerial declaration of February or its strong reaffirmation at a subsequent meeting in Washington in April. In that month, the yen was 'rebased' from its Louvre central rate of 153.5 yen per dollar to 146 – an appreciation of 5 per cent.

Central banks were intervening in foreign exchange markets in an effort to keep exchange rates within the agreed margins. For 1987 as a whole, Japan's foreign exchange reserves rose by $38 billion and Germany's by $27 billion; the reported reserves of the United States fell by $4 billion. It has been estimated that total intervention purchases of dollars amounted to $117 billion in 1987 – a year in which the US current-account deficit amounted to $163 billion.[11]

The market expectation of additional dollar depreciation, and additional yen and D-mark appreciation, naturally led to rising interest rates on dollar securities, particularly rates on long-term obligations. Between March and mid-October 1987, the yield on 10-year US government bonds rose from 7$\frac{1}{4}$ to 10 per cent, reflecting the combined expectations of a worsening of inflation and dollar depreciation. As noted in Chapter 4, the increase in American interest rates helped to trigger the stock market crash in October 1987.

But even before the instability of 1987, fears had been expressed that the persistent US current-account deficits could bring on a world balance-of-payments crisis.

6.3   FEARS OF BALANCE-OF-PAYMENTS CRISIS

The growing current-account deficits of the United States led some observers to question whether the financing would continue to be forthcoming. The deficits through 1985 were covered almost entirely by private capital flows to the United States from abroad. In fact, the deficits were overfinanced by private funds since Americans were lending and investing abroad.

As it turned out, the year 1987 was a major exception to the generalisation that private capital was financing the US deficits. In that year, central banks, intervening in foreign exchange markets, acquired enough dollars to cover most of the American deficit. Precisely how large that fraction was is hard to know, since some of the dollars so acquired by central banks were placed not in banks or securities in the United States but elsewhere – in the so-called Euromarkets. Thus they did not show up in US balance-of-payments statistics as liabilities to official institutions.

What happened in 1987 generated concerns that the financing of continuing US deficits could lead to a crisis as investors became reluctant to add to their dollar portfolios. Even before that, in December 1985, the Institute for International Economics published Stephen Marris's *Deficits and the Dollar*, which predicted a 'hard landing' not only for the dollar but for the US economy, with harmful effects on other countries.[12] Marris's reasoning was that the US deficit was so large and interest obligations on its debt were growing so fast that even if the dollar were to depreciate quite a bit more, the deficit would not be cured. This would lead to a drying up of the foreign financing of the deficit. As that happened the dollar would plummet and American interest rates would shoot up, creating a recession in the United States that would drag down the economies of many other countries, both industrial and developing.

It is clear by now that Marris's fears were unfounded. The dollar did fall quite sharply in 1987; its trade-weighted average value dropped by 18 per cent. The US current-account deficit declined substantially after 1987, and the dollar rose in the second half of 1988 and in much of 1989. In 1989, the Federal Reserve and other central banks sold dollars to moderate its upswing.

A study carried out at the Bank for International Settlements showed that, despite the string of US external deficits in the 1980s, the share of dollars in the total private financial asset holdings in other industrial countries was modest – only 3.8 per cent in 1988. There was ample scope for these holdings to grow.[13]

6.4 EUROPEAN INTEGRATION

The EC moved toward greater unity, even if in fits and starts. The EMS evolved and a Europe 'without frontiers' came into being. These developments revived the idea of European Monetary and Economic Union (EMU).

European Monetary System

The EMS underwent seven exchange-rate realignments in the first four years after it was established in March 1979. These devaluations and revaluations compensated for divergences in rates of inflation among the seven countries that were members of the exchange-rate mechanism (ERM). In 1979–82 consumer prices rose 5.3 per cent per year in Germany, only slightly more in the Netherlands and Belgium, but over 12 per cent in France, and 18 per cent in Italy. Rates of inflation narrowed progressively in the next few years. By 1989, inflation ranged from 1.1 per cent in the Netherlands to 6.3 per cent in Italy. With this narrowing, interest rates also tended to converge.

After a realignment in January 1987, central exchange rates in the ERM remained unchanged until September 1992. In that interval, the belief developed that the ERM had become a fixed-rate system. As noted in Chapter 5, France's rate of inflation converged with and then fell below that of Germany, and the interest-rate differential between the two countries became very small. That was taken as an

Figure 6.1   Inflation in EMS countries

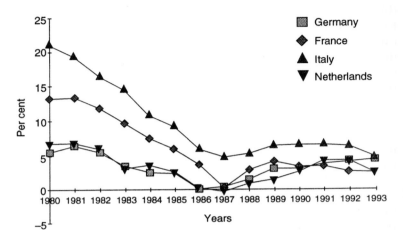

indicator of the credibility of the fixed exchange-rate relationship between the D-mark and the franc. France's determination to hold its parity with the D-mark became known as the *franc fort* policy. Belgium, Luxembourg, and the Netherlands were in a similar position relative to Germany. The fixed-rate belief evolved further towards aspiration for a common currency as proposed in the Delors Report of 1989 and embodied in the Maastricht Treaty of 1990 (see below).

The seven original members of the ERM were joined by Spain in 1989, the United Kingdom in 1990, and Portugal in 1992 – all three adopting the wide band of 6 per cent around their central exchange rates. These three countries as well as Italy had higher rates of inflation than Germany and France and, as we observed earlier, Britain probably joined the ERM at too high an exchange rate. Burdens were imposed on the system by the steep rise in German interest rates, which the other ERM members had to stay with or exceed even when economic activity began to slow down in 1990.

The result was a brusque blow to the idea that exchange rates among ERM countries could remain fixed. Speculation developed in the ERM in the summer of 1992 after a referendum in Denmark rejected the Maastricht Treaty. At the same time the dollar declined relative to the D-mark in the foreign exchange markets, following a cut in the Federal Reserve discount rate and an increase in the Bundesbank's rate. Upward pressure on the German currency made it more difficult for other ERM members to keep their exchange rates in line with the D-mark. In August, both the pound sterling and the Italian lira fell to their lower margins, requiring heavy central bank support in the markets. Meanwhile the approach of the French referendum on Maastricht, scheduled for 20 September, added additional uncertainty to the idea of a common currency and therefore to the fixity of ERM exchange rates.

In early September the Finnish markka, weakened by the economic turmoil in the former USSR, was permitted to float downward. This put pressure on the Swedish krona – though not a member of the EC, its currency was pegged to the D-mark – and the Bank of Sweden raised its marginal lending rate first to 25 per cent, then to 75 per cent, and ultimately to 500 per cent although the economy was in recession. This action struck some observers as the ultimate absurdity in the obsession with maintaining fixed exchange rates. In November Sweden was forced to let the krona float down.

On 14 September the Bundesbank lowered two of its rates by one quarter percentage point and the Italian lira was devalued in the ERM by 7 per cent. Two days later sterling, after heavy exchange-market intervention to support it, dropped out of the ERM. The next day Italy followed. Spain and Portugal later devalued. The French referendum approved the Maastricht Treaty by a small margin and the French franc held its D-mark parity but only at the cost of heavy intervention and a sharp but temporary hike in interest rates.

In the summer of 1993, another foreign exchange crisis led to the suspension of what was left of the fixed-rate ERM. That crisis was not the result of overvalued exchange rates. Rather it reflected the fact that membership in the ERM required France, in the face of rising unemployment, to maintain interest rates at the high level determined by the Bundesbank. In fact, France's real short-term rates were three times those in Germany given its lower inflation rate and its somewhat higher interest rates. Its unemployment, at 11.6 per cent, was higher than in Germany and had become an acute political issue. The overwhelming defeat of the Socialist Party in the elections of March 1993 was widely attributed to the high level of unemployment.

The crisis was triggered by the Bundesbank's decision at its pre-summer recess meeting of 29 July not to lower its discount rate along with its Lombard rate. The foreign exchange markets then moved heavily against the French franc along with most other ERM currencies, presumably on the grounds that France needed to reduce its interest rates in order to cope with unemployment. If it did so in the absence of a similar reduction by Germany, that would weaken the franc. The Bank of France and the Bundesbank intervened in the markets heavily. This led to a weekend meeting in Brussels at which it was finally decided to widen the ERM margins to 15 per cent on either side of central rates. The large amount of leeway was no doubt chosen deliberately so that markets would not expect it to be used. In fact, it was not used during the remainder of 1993.

The judgement seems clear that it had been premature to regard the ERM as a fixed-rate arrangement. Even if Germany's interest rates had not risen so steeply, the currencies of some ERM countries were bound to become overvalued, given that their rates of inflation were significantly above that of Germany. Moreover, the economies of the ERM members did not move together. Those that weakened were not able to use monetary policy to encourage economic recovery. And, as we shall see, the Maastricht Treaty put a yoke on fiscal policy.

In a speech in Washington during the crisis in September 1992, Margaret (now Baroness) Thatcher, criticising the fetish with fixed exchange rates in Europe, quipped that politicians and bankers who are pushing for a single currency in Europe treat the exchange rate 'as a virility symbol

– and I must say that, for myself, I never felt the need for a virility symbol'.[14]

Europe 1992

In any event, the convergence that was occurring in the EMS encouraged other steps towards greater integration in the EC. In February 1986 the Single European Act was signed, providing for what became known as 'Europe 1992' or the free movement of persons, goods, services, and capital among the twelve member countries of the EC. (Greece joined in 1981 and Spain and Portugal in 1986.) It also became known as 'Europe without frontiers', or 'the internal market'. Most of its provisions came into force by 1 January 1993.

A study sponsored by the European Commission – the Cecchini report – on the effects of Europe 1992 estimated that the EC will gain significantly in terms of output and employment as the result of eliminating border formalities, technical regulations applying to cross-border trade, barriers to market entry, as well as from the economies of scale in a market of 320 million people. If supported by appropriate macroeconomic policies, these effects will translate into sizeable increases in GDP, ranging from 4 to more than 6 per cent over the levels that would have otherwise prevailed.[15]

These are static or one-time effects of the formation of the single market. There could also be dynamic or continuing effects, which would show up as higher growth rates for the members of the EC. A study by Richard Baldwin produced 'back of the envelope' estimates of a permanent rise in the annual EC rate of growth amounting to between one quarter and one percentage point. Even at the lower end of this range the results would be significant over time. Apart from his numerical estimates, Baldwin's main point is that the cumulative effects of Europe 92 over time will be much larger than the one-time jump in GDP estimated in the Cecchini report.[16]

The elimination of remaining exchange and capital controls, freeing capital movements, occurred in eight of the member states in July 1990. (Spain, Portugal, Greece, and Ireland were given until 1993 to comply.) This helps to explain the large speculative capital flows in 1992 and 1993, which led to the disruption of the ERM.

European Monetary Union

The planned evolution toward a European Community that would be unified economically stimulated the idea that there should also be a common currency. Although, as noted, the notion had spread that the ERM was a system of fixed exchange rates, even permanently fixed rates in the EC were not regarded as an alternative to a common currency. That was so because the credibility of such fixed exchange rates could not be assured as long as individual nations had the possibility of realigning their currencies in the ERM.

Most ERM countries had given up the autonomy of monetary policy, instead linking their interest rates to those in Germany. That is why the ERM was also known as a 'D-mark zone'. It became clear in 1992 that the belief in the fixity of exchange rates did not assure that they could be maintained. What was needed for this and other reasons was a single currency and a single monetary policy, administered by a single central bank. That came to be regarded, by its proponents, as a natural complement to the Single European Act. It was thought that the full benefits of a unified economic area would be reaped only if the individuals and businesses in that area did not have to exchange currencies in order to undertake transactions across national borders.

Enthusiasts for economic and monetary union (EMU) also had strong political motivations, as discussed below. Another motivation – felt but rarely expressed, especially in France – was the desire to share in the formulation of monetary policy. In the ERM France's monetary policy was, in effect, decided in Frankfurt by the Bundesbank. In an EMU France would have representatives on the governing council of the European central bank and would therefore have a say in its monetary policy decisions.[17]

This was not the first time the idea of an economic and monetary union was broached in the EC. The Werner Committee report of 1970 proposed a progressive move to such a union by 1980, but the international monetary turbulence of the 1970s – the oil shock of 1974–5 and the move to floating exchange rates – made it a dead letter. The spirit of the Werner report was revived when the EMS was established. In June 1988 the European Council (the heads of government of the twelve countries)organised a committee of central bank governors and other experts, chaired by Commission President Jacques Delors, to examine the possibility of forming an economic and monetary union. The report of the Delors Committee was submitted in April 1989, calling for a three-stage move to EMU, in which there would be irrevocably fixed exchange rates or, preferably, a single currency, and a single European central bank. The report also called for coordination of fiscal policies among members of EMU and 'binding rules' limiting budget deficits and the means of financing them. The Delors report embodied the principle of 'subsidiarity' – a term originally used in papal encyclicals to indicate that social problems should be dealt with at the most immediate or local level consistent with solution. In the EMU context it is designed to limit the functions of higher levels of government (the Council of Ministers, the EC Commission, the European Parliament) to what is essential, making them subsidiary to the governments of the member states or conceivably even lower levels of government.

The European Council accepted the Delors Report and decided that its first stage would begin in mid-1990. During that stage, the internal market was to be completed, policies were to be coordinated, and the 'structural funds' – providing for financial assistance from the richer to the poorer EC members and therefore 'cohesion' in the EC – were to be enlarged.

Meeting at Maastricht in the Netherlands in December 1991, the Council adopted amendments to the Treaty of Rome (which established the European Economic Community) that were to be put to a vote in each of the member countries. In broad terms, the Maastricht Treaty provided for evolution to EMU in three stages. Union could eventuate by the end of 1996 if a majority of the member states meet the stipulated conditions but it would begin in any event by January 1999.

The agreement provided for a European central bank and for the eventual substitution of a common currency, the ECU, for the present currencies of the individual nations. It also incorporated 'convergence criteria' that would determine whether and which countries qualified for membership in EMU. These criteria involve the rate of inflation (no higher than 1.5 per cent above the average of the three countries with the lowest inflation rates), long-term interest rates (no higher than 2 per cent above the three low inflation countries), stable exchange rates (no realignments in the past two years), and 'a sustainable government financial position' (a general government deficit less than 3 per cent of GDP and a gross government debt less than 60 per cent of GDP). It is noteworthy that, in 1992, only France and Luxembourg would have qualified; Germany did not meet the budgetary criterion.

These convergence criteria have been the subject of much discussion and criticism in the economics literature.[18] One criticism is that the efforts of EC nations to fulfill the criteria are imparting a 'deflationary bias' to the European economy. The slowdown in some countries and recession in others in 1992–3 was being aggravated by efforts to curb budget deficits. However desirable that may be in the medium term – and such deficits are bloated in a number of EC countries – to do so in a recession tends to aggravate the downturn or discourage recovery.

The provisions of the treaty governing fiscal policies have also been criticised. With monetary policy and exchange-rate policy no longer available to individual member states of EMU, fiscal policy would be the only instrument left to deal with country-specific shocks – that is, events such as German unification that have non-uniform impacts on the members of the EMU. But the fiscal policy rules in the

Maastricht treaty are asymmetrical: they limit budget deficits but do not deal with fiscal policies that might be too restrictive. The need for greater flexibility of fiscal policy was pointed out in a report by the deputies of the finance ministers and central bank governors of the Group of Ten (the ten largest industrial countries) as follows:

> The political ability of countries to accept such constraints ['a pegged exchange rate regime'] in favour of a credible exchange rate commitment depends crucially on the effectiveness of their individual and collective efforts to maintain internal macroeconomic stability without monetary policy autonomy. These efforts are likely to be more successful in economies with relatively flexible wages and prices, low structural rigidities, and countercyclical fiscal stabilisers that are relatively effective and well-disciplined. Establishing effective mechanisms in these respects is necessary for countries to reap the full benefits from maintaining stable exchange rates.[19]

Comparisons have been made with the United States. Although the individual states do not conduct countercyclical fiscal policy, the Federal government's tax and transfer system partially compensates regions of the country that experience a fall of income. It has been estimated that when a state goes into recession at least 28 per cent of each dollar of income decline is offset by either lower tax payments to Washington or additional receipts (mainly unemployment compensation) from the Federal government.[20] The EC budget is and will continue to be much smaller, relatively and absolutely, than that of the Federal government in the United States. Hence that type of offsetting would be much less significant in EMU. This prediction about the size of the central budget of the future EMU rests on the principle of subsidiarity.

As it turned out, Denmark rejected the Maastricht agreement by a close vote in a referendum in June 1992 and then accepted it in a second referendum in May 1993. In France, the referendum narrowly passed. Strong opposition was being expressed in Britain but the Parliament voted for it. The attitude of German citizens was uncertain; there was a clear reluctance to give up the strong D-mark, which had provided Germany with an enviable record of price stability over the years but the government favours it.

Other objections to Maastricht involved attitudes towards 'bureaucrats' in Brussels at the European Commission. Many citizens apparently resented the powers exercised by this unelected executive body of the EC.

We need not go into additional detail on the Maastricht agreement. Some doubts exist about whether it will be approved in its present form. What seems clear is that economic integration in Europe has come a long way and is very likely to continue, whatever the rate of progress towards a common currency and all that goes with it. Apart from the economic rationale for increasing the degree of integration of the European nations, and enlarging that membership in the future to include not only other western European nations but also some countries in eastern Europe, there are strong political motivations drawing these countries closer together. As Charles Bean puts it,

> neither the costs nor the benefits of monetary union are in principle as great as critics and advocates respectively have made out. In fact, from a purely economic perspective, it seems to me something of a storm in a teacup. Why then has so much fuss been made over it? I think the answer is primarily political ... A separate currency is an important symbol of nationhood, while a common currency is an equally potent symbol of a shared political destiny.[21]

To be more explicit about it, the French government is strongly wedded to EMU because it is a way of embracing Germany, keeping it in the western Europe camp and discouraging future adventurism. The present German government shares this view.

6.5   INTEGRATION IN NORTH AMERICA

The North American Free Trade Agreement (NAFTA), signed in December 1992 among the United States, Canada, and Mexico 'is the most comprehensive free trade pact (short of a common market) ever negotiated between regional trading partners, and the first reciprocal free trade pact between a developing country and industrial countries'.[22] It incorporates much of the already-existing Canada–United States free trade agreement, extending to Mexico the obligation to liberalise trade and investment. In general, tariff barriers and most non-tariff barriers on trade among the three countries will be eliminated over a period of 10 to 15 years. The free trade area could gradually spread to other countries in the Western Hemisphere.

6.6   CONCLUSION

It is clear that economic and financial integration has intensified both on a global and a regional basis. While this chapter is confined almost entirely to industrial countries, the phenomenon of increasing interdependence extends well beyond those countries, as will become evident in subsequent chapters. The world is becoming smaller, in the sense that nations have a greater impact on each other when a change takes place in their economies. That calls for increased co-operation, if not coordination, in policymaking.

7 The Elements of Economic Reform: Eastern Europe

At the end of World War II, the Soviet Union's Red Army occupied the countries of Eastern and Central Europe (henceforth referred to as Eastern Europe). Stalinist regimes, both political and economic, were established in Albania, Bulgaria, Hungary, Poland and Romania, as well as in East Germany. In 1948 Czechoslovakia came under full Communist control but in the same year Yugoslavia, under Josip Broz Tito, broke with the Soviet Union and followed its own socialist road; in later years this included 'self-management' of enterprises and much less central planning than elsewhere in the region.

Uprisings against Stalinism in Hungary in 1956 and in Czechoslovakia in 1968 were put down by Soviet troops on the basis of what came to be known as the Brezhnev doctrine, which proclaimed that a threat to socialism in any one country was regarded as a matter of concern to all socialist countries and justified intervention. Nevertheless, Hungary, while hewing to the Moscow line in foreign policy in the years that followed, was able to undertake economic reforms, including the introduction of some market mechanisms. In the early part of the 1980s Poland moved partially away from central planning. On the other hand, Romania under the iron fist of Nicolae Ceausescu pursued an independent foreign policy but its economic regime was based on central planning and forced industrialisation of what had been a rich agricultural country. What did central planning involve?

7.1 CENTRAL PLANNING

The system of central planning, in the USSR and Eastern Europe, was based on directives from governmental ministries regarding the allocation of resources in physical terms by state-owned enterprises. These enterprises accounted for a high proportion of industrial production and, except in Poland, for most agricultural production. Both the inputs (raw materials and capital goods) and the outputs of enterprises were dictated by the plan. Prices played a very small part in this process: workers could choose among available jobs on the basis of wages paid and consumers could respond to the prices of the goods they found in the shops.

The plans emphasised heavy industry, large firms and specialised production. In most product lines, fewer firms than in the west were responsible for total output. Part of the motivation for this concentration was to simplify the task of planners in allocating resources.

Prices had little relation to world prices and energy, food and rents were subsidised for households. State-owned enterprises that were able to earn profits under the price system provided the government with tax revenue. Those that could not cover their costs were either subsidised or supplied with inexpensive credit. In the language of economists, these firms were subject to a 'soft budget constraint'; that is, in contrast to firms in a market economy, they were not required to alter or close down operations when they were unprofitable. In most countries foreign trade was primarily conducted by state trading organisations and differences between foreign and domestic prices were compensated for by taxes or subsidies.

The excess spending by enterprises combined with deficits in government budgets tended to generate inflation, which was held down – repressed – by price controls. Where that happened, households accumulated large amounts of liquid assets in the form of currency or deposits that they would have been prepared to spend if attractive goods had been available – a condition known as a monetary overhang.

Despite these shortcomings, the system of central planning produced reasonably rapid rates of growth in the first two or three decades, if the available statistics are to be believed, and they are known to be deficient. According to economist Angus Maddison, GDP growth in Bulgaria,

Czechoslovakia, East Germany, Hungary, Poland, and Romania was rather close to that in 16 OECD countries in 1950–65 and 1965–80. But in the 1980s, growth slowed much more in the centrally-planned economies than in the OECD area, as may be seen in Figure 7.1.[1]

What explains the slowdown? In part, the Eastern European nations were affected by economic and financial conditions abroad. Energy prices rose, though less than in world markets. High interest rates in the west in the early 1980s were also a factor, since the Eastern European countries had begun to borrow in western financial markets in the 1970s and some of them became heavily indebted. More generally, what applies to the Soviet Union is probably true also for Eastern Europe: a command economy finds it difficult to keep up with a rapidly changing technological frontier.[2] Even when growth rates were more satisfactory, the quality of output was inferior.

The system became increasingly inefficient, but it provided stable prices, full employment, and a relatively

Figure 7.1   Growth in Eastern Europe and OECD

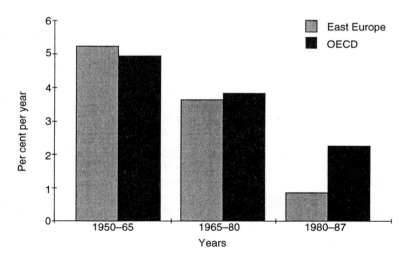

equal distribution of incomes, to which the populations of centrally-planned economies became accustomed. As reform began in recent years, it is understandable that people reacted negatively to open inflation or unemployment or seeing their neighbours become rich.

7.2   THE PROCESS OF TRANSITION TO A MARKET ECONOMY

The introduction of *glasnost* and *perestroika* in the USSR by Mikhail Gorbachev, who became general secretary of the Communist Party of the Soviet Union in March 1985, provided a more congenial atmosphere for reform in Eastern Europe. In effect, the Brezhnev doctrine was permitted to lapse.

With the breaching of the Berlin Wall in November 1989, political revolution spread through Eastern Europe (except for Albania, where the change occurred only in 1991). The era of one-party Communist rule came to an end. Until that happened, basic economic reform could not occur since it was not consistent with Communist ideology, as became evident in the Soviet Union under Gorbachev (to be covered in Chapter 8).

The political revolutions in Eastern Europe were accompanied by a desire to break away from Soviet hegemony, to move closer to western Europe, and to make the transition to market economies. Eventual membership in the European Community, with its political and economic implications, became the goal.

In some countries the process of political and economic reform was spurred by outstanding leaders. In Czechoslovakia's 'velvet revolution' Vaclav Havel was a symbol of freedom and Vaclav Klaus, a strong believer in free markets, did much to shape the economic reform. Lech Walesa became Poland's democratically-elected president. Leszek Balcerowicz, Deputy Prime Minister for Economy from September 1989 to October 1991, bravely applied stringent macroeconomic policies and put Poland ahead of most of its neighbours on the road to economic reform. Elsewhere – in

Hungary, Romania, Bulgaria – reform went forward but its leaders were hardly charismatic. In Hungary, for example, the style of the late Prime Minister Jozsef Antall has been described as 'serious and reserved rather than charismatic, and his political objective has been to oversee fundamental changes with minimum upheaval.'[3]

Economic reform – making the transition to a market economy – is a difficult process for which, as noted earlier, there is no precedent and no blueprint. It has been compared by many, including Lech Walesa, to converting a fish soup back into a fish.

In the words of David Lipton and Jeffrey Sachs, who were advisers to Solidarity in Poland:

> Even with a consensus on the ultimate aims of reform, the tactical difficulties of creating a market economy are profound. Fundamental social, political, and economic changes must be carried out in the context of a deep and worsening economic crisis, inexperience in managing a market economy, fragile political institutions, the residual pressures of the communist power structure throughout society, the reemergence of historical enmities, and often very deep ethnic fissures.[4]

Moreover, as has become evident, the process imposes painful costs on numerous groups in society as the result of unemployment, open inflation, and the high cost of consumer goods. The initial euphoria at liberation has given way to a realisation that the transition is bound to take a long time, as we have already noted in the case of east Germany.

Underlying the various changes required by the transition to a market economy is the withdrawal of governments from detailed decision-making, introduction of a system of incentives on the part of managers and workers – incentives to produce more efficiently, to respond to market signals, to innovate and to undertake reconversion aimed at changing the composition of output so as to supply products for which a demand exists at home or abroad.

The transition to a market economy involves three categories of reform:

(1) Macroeconomic stabilisation via fiscal and monetary policies designed to reduce inflation and inflation expectations once prices are liberalised;
(2) Institution building to put in place the necessary features of a market economy: property rights, a system of commercial and bankruptcy law and an efficient accounting system; a banking and payments system, non-bank lenders and financial markets that can provide the financial lubrication needed in a market economy; a properly functioning central bank in place of 'monobanks' that mainly finance government deficits and state-owned enterprises on the basis of central plans; anti-monopoly regulation; introduction of a tax system that does not rely solely on the earnings of state enterprises; the creation of a social safety net, especially unemployment insurance and possibly a labour-intensive public works programme;
(3) Structural reforms starting with the elimination of price controls and subsidies so that prices can perform their function of influencing the distribution of demand and supply and so that, given the exchange rate, prices are in line with those in world markets; the downsizing, restructuring, or closing of 'loss-making' enterprises, including the so-called industrial dinosaurs; the establishment of markets and market-type relationships among firms; privatisation and a system of corporate governance that provides incentives for efficiency on the part of managers; the liberalisation of foreign trade and, at some point, the establishment of currency convertibility.

The various reforms are interrelated. They are all necessary. A major question has to do with the order in which they are carried out – what has been called the sequencing of reforms. Some aspects of sequencing are clear, but it is not possible to map out the entire process in advance. Moreover, it will differ from country to country depending on its history, traditions and political situation.

In the words of Vaclav Klaus, who became Prime Minister of the Czech Republic:

> I like to compare the transformation process with chess playing. When we want to play chess, we must know how to play. We must know how to move various pieces on the chessboard. We must know the basic opening strategies. But it's not possible to know the situation on the chessboard after the fifteenth or twenty-fifth move.[5]

Still, some priorities can be set forth. Macroeconomic stabilisation has to come early, along with price liberalisation and the elimination of most subsidies on consumer goods. Inflation, open or repressed, existed in most of the eastern countries. In Poland, consumer prices rose on average by more than 30 per cent per year in 1980–88. In Hungary the inflation rate was 8 per cent per year over the same period. In the other countries inflation was repressed, showing up in shortages of goods, queues at shops and a large monetary overhang.

The other aspects of reform – establishing the institutions of a market economy and restructuring inefficient enterprises – clearly take time, maybe a decade or more.

A question around which controversy prevails is whether to employ a rapid approach – otherwise known as 'big bang' or 'shock therapy' (the latter being an 'emotionally-loaded' and biased term[6]) – or a gradual approach to the introduction of reforms. The big bang approach was adopted for price liberalisation and macroeconomic stabilisation in Poland, Czechoslovakia, Bulgaria, and Romania, while Hungary pursued a policy of gradualism. The result in the former countries was a burst of inflation and then a subsidence. This steep rise of prices was regarded as an effective means of absorbing the monetary overhang. Consumer prices in Poland rose 250 per cent in 1989 and almost sixfold in 1990 before inflation tapered off to 40 per cent in 1993. Bulgaria had a somewhat similar experience, but Romania's inflation rate continued to accelerate through 1993, partly because a rapid depreciation of its exchange rate raises the cost of imports. Czechoslovakia managed the transition to a relatively free price system with a much smaller rise of prices. In 1993 the Czech Republic's inflation rate was 21 per cent.

As Michael Bruno, Chief Economist at the World Bank and former Governor of the Bank of Israel, sums up the price liberalisation experience:

> the overriding fact remains that in most of the cases far-reaching liberalization has been achieved, together with a reasonable measure of macroeconomic stability, in spite of a highly distorted starting point and immense economic and political risks. Finally, from the consumer's perspective, the qualitative change that has taken place in the market environment probably outweighs the statistical measure of price increase.[7]

In other words, sellers now have to compete in quality and price for the consumer's attention and the consumer has a wider choice than under central planning.

Perhaps inevitably, the beginning of reform was accompanied by sharp drops in output, as is shown in Table 7.1.

As the IMF has pointed out, 'official statistics almost certainly overstate the contraction – and, in some countries, understate the recent expansion – because they do not fully reflect the growth of new private enterprises or the informal

Table 7.1   Output changes in Eastern Europe (per cent per year)

	1990	1991	1992	1993
Bulgaria	−9.1	−12	−7.7	−4
Czechoslovakia*	−1.6	−14.7	−7.2	0
Hungary	−3	−10	−5.0	−1
Poland	−11.6	−9	1	3
Romania	−5.6	−15	−15.4	−4

* Czech Republic after 1991.

Source: OECD, *Economic Outlook*, December 1993, p. 117.

sector'. Data tend to be collected only from large state-owned enterprises. New enterprises and the informal sector do not always get counted.[8] An example of 'informal activity' is the large number of sidewalk retail establishments that have sprung up on the main avenues of Bucharest and other cities in Eastern Europe.

Accompanying the output declines have been substantial increases in unemployment. From near zero in 1989 unemployment rose by 1993 to 17 per cent in Poland and Bulgaria, 13 per cent in Hungary, 9 per cent in Romania, and 4 per cent in the Czech Republic. In addition, there exists a sizeable amount of hidden unemployment as non-viable state-owned enterprises continue to provide jobs, financing themselves with credit. There may also be some hidden employment reflecting moonlighting and jobs in private establishments that are not picked up in the statistics.

A significant part of the decline in GDP in these countries was the result not of their economic reform measures but of the disruption of CMEA trade. Exports and imports among the former Soviet Union and the Eastern European nations, including east Germany, is estimated to have fallen by 50 per cent in 1991, when this trade reverted to world market prices and payment in convertible currencies. The sharp rise in the prices of energy imports from the former Soviet Union had a depressing effect on enterprises in Eastern Europe. Moreover, chaos in the former Soviet Union led to a sharp contraction of its imports – which many state enterprises in Eastern Europe were accustomed to supplying. The pattern of trade under CMEA had involved exports of manufactured goods, including armaments and some agricultural products, from Eastern Europe to the Soviet Union in exchange for raw materials, natural gas and oil at subsidised prices.

Although the collapse of CMEA trade accounted for much of the decline in output in Eastern Europe, Hungary and Poland were able to increase their exports to industrial countries from 1989 to 1992 by more than enough to offset the drop in exports to the former Soviet Union and Eastern Europe.

Another part of the output decline resulted from shortages of raw materials and energy previously imported from the Soviet Union. In other words, disruption of CMEA trade had both a demand and a supply effect on Eastern Europe.

That the fall-off in production was not solely the result of reform measures is demonstrated by the fact that output dropped in the successor states of the Soviet Union before reform programmes and stabilisation policies were adopted.

7.3   PROGRESS AND PROBLEMS OF REFORM

In general, macroeconomic stabilisation, price liberalisation and the opening of economies to foreign trade came quickly. Structural reform measures have been adopted at a slower pace. Part of the explanation for the sustained recessions is that central planning has been abolished but the institutions of a market economy are not yet fully in place.

The problem of responding to market incentives is especially acute in the case of the large state-owned enterprises. Movement away from socialist planning involves two types of ownership change: the springing up of new private firms and dealing with state-owned enterprises by privatising them either intact or broken into parts or closing them down.

The huge state-owned industrial dinosaurs in heavy industry, including armaments, are a major problem. They will have to shrink in size and some will have to disappear since they are unable to compete in quality or price in a competitive system where new firms are created using up-to-date technology and imports are free to enter. But mass unemployment poses clear political dangers and this has slowed the process of liquidating or privatising state-owned enterprises. Meanwhile the dinosaurs are kept going with bank credits.

Privatisation

According to Scott Thomas, economist in the US aid mission to Poland, privatisation:

originally meant sale or liquidation of productive assets. The concept has broadened considerably in usage, especially in the context of post-Communist economies. It can mean selling the business and leasing the land and fixed assets. It can mean leasing the business, too. It can mean selling, leasing or giving away some or all of the assets in the enterprise concerned to management and workers. It can mean retaining government ownership of a large minority interest. It can mean stripping away viable assets for sale or giveaway, and leaving behind for the state nonviable assets, along with non-performing loans and other liabilities. It can mean giving to all adult citizens, for free or for a nominal fee, vouchers that can be used to bid for shares in public factories. It can mean hiring foreigners to run holding companies charged with administering public factories in blind trusts for those citizen-owners. It can mean providing public loans and grants to state-owned enterprises for investments that will 'prepare' them for sale, or to write business plans for the same purpose. It can mean all of these things, and still include the sale of some factories to the highest bidders. In practice, with respect to the larger enterprises, it almost never has meant liquidation.[9]

What is left out of this recitation is the sale to foreign investors, which has been important especially in Hungary and also, to a smaller degree, in Poland and the former Czechoslovakia. Given the limited amount of capital in the hands of residents of Eastern European countries, a major alternative is to allow foreign investors to buy into state-owned enterprises. But there are obvious political limits to this option. In Hungary numerous enterprises that make consumer goods are now largely owned by foreign multinational companies. This has aroused some resentment and lessened public enthusiasm for privatisation. In Poland workers have demonstrated against a proposed sale of a majority of shares in a state-owned cement company to a Belgian firm. A poll among state-sector industrial workers revealed that half oppose privatisation and only 3 per cent approve of foreign ownership.[10]

Another technique is the distribution to the public of vouchers that carry the right to bid for shares – 'ingenious and unconventional mass privatisation programmes designed to help create capitalism without capital' as described by Anthony Robinson in the *Financial Times*.[11] This method was utilised in what are now the Czech and Slovak Republics in 1992 as a means of accomplishing a rapid transfer of some state-owned enterprises into private hands. In the process, hundreds of private investment funds, akin to pension funds or mutual funds in the west, were established through which a majority of citizens surrendered their vouchers and obtained shares (which became tradable on the Prague stock exchange in 1993). The assumption is that the investment funds will act to oversee the activities of the enterprise managers in a way that enhances efficiency and productivity, including restructuring or downsizing of the privatised firms. But there is no assurance that the investment funds will improve corporate governance and management. This is demonstrated by the effects of a new bankruptcy law that came into effect in the Czech Republic in April 1993. It is estimated that up to one-third of the 1500 enterprises sold in 1992 through the voucher scheme will be found to be technically bankrupt. Much of the reason is that they have incurred heavy debts as their sales fell off with the collapse of CMEA trade and with recession in western Europe. The bankruptcy process need not mean dissolution; it may facilitate a settlement between debtors and creditors.

It is clear that even if privatisation is a necessary condition, it is not a sufficient condition for producing efficient, market-oriented firms. The mere transfer of ownership from the state to private shareholders does not accomplish a restructuring and conversion of enterprises to a condition where they are viable in a market economy, nor does it establish a competitive environment.[12]

In Poland, 'internal privatisation' has occurred: the existing management and workers have been allowed to buy, to lease, to take over, or to sell the assets of the enterprises. The last of these practices, known as asset stripping, can lead to the demise of the enterprise but it does accomplish some privatisation. In the spring of 1993 a voucher programme was finally approved by the Polish legislature and implemented.

Privatisation in Hungary has not involved vouchers and the distribution of shares. Rather, firms are sold directly by the government to foreign or domestic investors, sometimes to existing management – known as self-privatisation or spontaneous privatisation.

The process of dealing with state-owned enterprises has begun but it is slow and will take a long time. And many of the dinosaurs will eventually have to go out of existence. Meanwhile two other forms of ownership change – the creation of new private firms, referred to as greenfield investment, and the privatisation of small businesses, mostly in trade and services – go on apace. The greenfield investments are taking place largely in consumer goods and services including hotels – that is, sectors neglected by central plans that focused on heavy industry. As of June 1992 the number of such 'small privatisations' ranged from 100 000 in Poland to 70 000 in Hungary and 20 000 in the former Czechoslovakia to less than 100 in Bulgaria.[13]

More generally, the share of GDP produced in the private sector has increased but the estimates vary. According to a compilation by the European Bank for Reconstruction and Development, that share was between 8 and 20 per cent in the Czech Republic in 1992, between 27 and 35 per cent in Hungary and between 42 and 50 per cent (including co-operatives) in Poland.[14]

7.4   TRADE AND INVESTMENT WITH THE WEST

While trade among CMEA countries fell sharply after 1990, some of the Eastern European countries were able to increase their exports elsewhere, especially to western Europe. Poland's exports to all industrial countries rose, in dollar value, by about 80 per cent from 1989 to mid-1992 while its total exports increased only 20 per cent. Czechoslovakia's exports to industrial countries went up by 50 per cent in 1992 but its total exports were no higher than in 1989. Hungary also raised its exports to industrial countries – by 80 per cent from 1989 to 1992. The European Community's share of Eastern European exports rose from about one-fourth in 1989 to one-half in the summer of 1992. Thereafter the recession in western Europe began to depress those exports.

The European Community signed trade agreements with the eastern nations. But recently the EC imposed a quota on steel imports from the Czech and Slovak Republics at one-half the levels of 1992 and limited imports of textiles and meat. The eastern countries have been complaining bitterly about inadequate access to western European markets in general. The EC countries defend themselves by pointing to recessions and high unemployment.

Direct investment from abroad has gone primarily to Hungary ($2.9 billion in 1991–2) and the former Czechoslovakia ($2.2 billion in 1989–92).

There is a connection between trade policy and new direct investment in Eastern Europe. If investors fear that western markets will not be open to exports from the east, they will hesitate to open new or acquire existing plants there.

7.5 THE OUTLOOK

A survey of Eastern Europe in The *Economist* in March 1993 offered the opinion that: 'In three years, the countries of Eastern Europe have transformed themselves from command economies to something that is more than half way to capitalism. It seems unlikely that this achievement will now be overthrown.'[15] That appears to be a reasonable conclusion.

Although progress has been made, a considerable number of east Europeans are disenchanted with economic reform – owing to inflation and unemployment. The upturn in output and decline in inflation in Poland are encouraging signs. And the OECD has predicted that output would rise in 1994 in all the Eastern European countries except Bulgaria and Romania.[16] Still, the structural reform aspects of the transformation will take a long time to complete. And political unrest cannot be ruled out if unemployment – now partly suppressed as state-owned enterprises of doubtful viability continue to meet payrolls – increases significantly further. The transformation is not being helped by weak economic activity in western Europe or by the barriers there to exports from the east. Popular dissatisfaction shows up in the election victories of former Communists in Poland and Hungary.

One should not mistake the trees for the forest. The main point is that what were basically undemocratic countries with command economies in 1980 now have mostly popularly-elected regimes that have started down the road – long though it may be – toward market economies.

8 Chaos and Reform in the Soviet Union and Russia

When Mikhail Gorbachev came to power in March 1985, he was presiding over a large economy, rich in resources but also inefficient and isolated from the world economy. In the 1960s the USSR produced *Sputnik* and Khrushchev boasted that the Soviet economy would 'bury' the west. In the 1970s the Soviet Union had to import large amounts of grain. In the 1980s its growth rate slowed and dissatisfaction with its economic performance began to be openly expressed. The inadequacies of central planning described in the previous chapter applied, of course, to the Soviet Union, from which central planning was exported to Eastern Europe.

Soviet statistics are of doubtful validity. But even when refined by western scholars they show rates of growth of more than 5 per cent per year in the quarter century ending in the mid-1950s despite the severe destruction of World War II. The country was industrialised and millions of peasants were drawn away from agriculture into factories, where they enjoyed rising standards of living.[1]

That spurt of centrally-planned industrialisation and growth was achieved under Stalin by brutal methods in which human rights were ignored and the environment was despoiled. Nevertheless it permitted the Soviet Union to become a military superpower and to have influence throughout the world.

In later years, particularly in the 1970s and 1980s, the growth rate slowed markedly. In Gorbachev's words:

At some stage – this became particularly clear in the latter half of the seventies – something happened that was at first sight inexplicable. The country began to lose momentum. Economic failures became more frequent. Difficulties began to accumulate and deteriorate, and unresolved problems to multiply. Elements of what we call stagnation and other phenomena alien to socialism began to appear in the life of society. A kind of 'braking mechanism' affecting social and economic development formed. And all this happened at a time when scientific and technological revolution opened up new prospects for economic and social progress.

He went on to state: 'In the last fifteen years the national income growth rates had declined by more than a half and by the beginning of the 1980s had fallen to a level close to economic stagnation.'[2]

There were several reasons for the slowdown. Growth had depended much more on increasing inputs – labour and capital equipment – than on rising productivity. Additions to the labour force were made possible in part by steady advances in the participation of women. By the early 1970s, 85 per cent of adult women were in the work force, compared with 60 per cent in the United States. Moreover growth of the labour force tapered off in the 1970s. For these reasons, employment growth slowed. Similarly plant and equipment investment could not keep expanding rapidly without impinging unduly on the availability of consumer goods. The growth of both gross and net investment declined sharply between 1970 and 1985.[3] And, of course, military expenditures were a burden, accounting for a higher proportion of GDP in the USSR than in the United States.

Meanwhile productivity gains did not compensate for these changes that began to limit economic growth. Total factor productivity – output per unit of labour and capital – increased only one-half per cent per year in 1950–73 compared with 3.35 per cent in OECD countries and 1.73 per cent in developing countries. In 1973–84, total factor productivity declined 1.4 per cent annually in the Soviet Union while it rose by 1.28 per cent per year in the OECD nations.[4] One explanation is that as technology became more complex (though it lagged far behind that in the industrial countries), the system of central planning was less and less capable of efficiently allocating physical inputs and outputs of individual enterprises. Another is that neither managers nor workers had the incentive to increase efficiency.

Furthermore the concentration of production in one or a few plants was counterproductive since it meant that a shortfall of output in one enterprise had a big effect on the enterprises it supplied.

Apparently the command economy was capable of industrialising but was ill-suited to the management of an industrialised economy.

The poor economic performance can also be attributed to a passive and dependent workforce. In both industry and agriculture the incentive system discouraged individual effort and pride of workmanship. Kyril Tidmarsh, former Moscow correspondent of *The Times* of London, writes that working-class professionalism was discouraged by 'the leveling of wages and the narrowing of differentials, regardless of skills or output'. Moreover 'undesirable "dirty" jobs eventually had to be remunerated with inappropriately high pay. ...'. The result was that low-skilled workers 'thus became higher paid while the high skilled saw their pay decline'. This was of course a perverse incentive.

> Every operation in industry had a quantitative labor 'norm' that workers had to fulfill for basic pay. Productivity above the norm was sometimes rewarded. It was well known, however, that dramatic or continuing norm-beating would lead to an upward revision of the work goal. For decades, therefore, the system encouraged workers to produce below potential.[5]

As a result of all this the Soviet economy was a shortage economy. Consumers were accustomed to standing in lines and even to paying bribes to secure favourable treatment from salespeople in shops.

The quality of the goods produced was also unsatisfactory in the eyes of Soviet consumers. Despite shortages, consumers were refusing to buy some goods in the 1980s. General Secretary Andropov, in a speech in 1983, 'lamented that the quality of many consumer goods – including TVs, radios, cameras, and watches – was so low that they simply could not be sold and instead sat in warehouses.'[6] In addition, many products, including computers and communications equipment, were technologically obsolete.

On the other hand, the Soviet system provided its citizens with full employment, stable prices and what they regarded as an equitable distribution of income. Economic reform was bound to clash with these cherished features of the system.

The unsatisfactory performance of the economy was openly discussed by Yuri Andropov during his brief tenure as General Secretary of the Communist Party beginning in November 1982 and ending with his death in February 1984. He and his successor, Konstantin Chernenko – who died 13 months after taking office – set the stage for Gorbachev's reforms.

8.1   GLASNOST AND PERESTROIKA

Mikhail Gorbachev, trained in the law at Moscow State University, spent twenty years as a local politician in Stavropol in southern Russia where he was born. His southern accent was at times the butt of jokes in Moscow, to which he was called in 1978 to be in charge of agriculture for the Communist Party. He was made a full member of the Politburo in 1980. In March 1985, he became the youngest general secretary of the Party in the history of the Soviet Union. He immediately projected a new style of leadership, in sharp contrast to his predecessors. He displayed vigour, a smiling countenance, an attractive and stylish wife, and a willingness to mingle with the populace. It is reported that in nominating Gorbachev to be general secretary, Andrei Gromyko said that 'this man has a nice smile, but he has got iron teeth'.[7]

Shortly before he became general secretary, Gorbachev used the term 'radical reform' – startling in the Soviet context – to signal his intentions.

In addition to economic reform (on which more below), Gorbachev's early moves included *glasnost* – greater openness and self-criticism in society, accountability of public officials, and an end to censorship. *Glasnost* also carried the de-mythologising of Stalin much further than Khrushchev had ever done. At the Moscow airport in the autumn of 1988, I was startled to see a donation box for the victims of Stalin, into which departing travellers were invited to deposit their left-over rubles.

Glasnost also included a shift in attitudes towards the outside world. A 'world view' was adopted with respect to ecology and international economic relations. Soviet officials began to admit their interdependence with other countries and to think about joining international economic institutions such as the GATT and the International Monetary Fund and World Bank. The change in viewpoint can be illustrated by a personal recollection. In the late 1970s the Soviet Ambassador to the United States, Anatolii Dobrynin, was invited to The Brookings Institution for lunch. During the discussion I started to put a question to him with the words 'In this interdependent world....' He interrupted and, wagging a finger at me, said 'Soviet Union not interdependent.'

In Gorbachev's philosophy *glasnost* was closely linked to *perestroika* – economic restructuring – since the latter required public participation and backing in the face of entrenched opposition by the bureaucracy.

Gorbachev also pursued the anti-alcohol campaign started by Andropov. Involving a reduction in the production of alcohol, shorter hours for liquor stores, and a rise in the legal drinking age, it was aimed at increasing productivity as well as at improving the quality of life. It became the subject of both jokes and bitter complaints and did not last long, in part perhaps because it resulted in a loss of revenues to the government and an enlarged budget deficit.

Economic reform was Gorbachev's first priority. That is what *perestroika* was all about. He stressed the need for an 'acceleration' of economic development: a more rapid rate of growth of the economy and a distinct improvement in the quality of output, though it was probably naive to expect this combination of outcomes to be realised. Among the means he pressed for were modernisation of machinery and equipment and a wage policy that raised the incomes of those with higher skills. As it turned out, the increase in investment combined with the budget deficit resulted in a pickup in inflation.

Reform moved ahead in 1987 with a decision that appeared to eliminate centrally-determined annual plans and to give state enterprises operational autonomy, including self-financing, but subject to rewards or penalties depending on their performance. Yet state orders still covered 90 per cent of industrial output in 1988, and Gorbachev and his colleagues in the Kremlin continued to hold ministries responsible for the quality of output in their sectors. Firms were given more freedom to set their prices and wages and both rose more rapidly in 1988–9. Another reform was the authorisation of private and cooperative enterprises in the supply of consumer goods and services, but employees of state enterprises could not be hired full-time in these activities. By end-1990 245 000 cooperatives were in existence employing more than 5 per cent of the labour force and accounting for almost 7 per cent of GNP.[8]

A major political reform was proposed by Gorbachev in 1988 and was implemented in 1989: the separation of the functions of the Communist Party and the government. The Party would give up its economic responsibilities. A real parliament – the Congress of People's Deputies – would be created and it in turn would elect a smaller full-time Supreme Soviet. In 1990 Gorbachev was elected president by the Congress. A constitutional amendment provided for the popular election of the president beginning in 1995.

The late Ed Hewett noted in the penultimate paragraph of his book *Reforming the Soviet Economy*, published in 1988, that every Soviet leader since Stalin had tried in his own way to reform the system. Gorbachev

> seems to be a different kind of leader ... But he is also the product of the old system. He has been educated by it and is a politician who has succeeded by working the system. His approach reflects the continuity of his background: in part it is a refutation of the past and in part it is a recasting of past policies. Those links to the past bring with them the weaknesses of past approaches.[9]

8.2 CRISIS AND BREAK-UP

As is evident from the quotations from Gorbachev and Hewett above, the Gorbachev economic reforms did not go very far. The central planning bureaucracy in Moscow was reduced in size and authority. State enterprises were given more autonomy but there was no system of market prices to provide signals and guide their decisions. A striking example: the output of a heavy machine-building factory in the Urals, which employed 50 000 workers in the 1980s, measured its output in terms of tons of machinery, whether the products were machines, oil drilling equipment, bull-dozers, or washing machines.[10]

Furthermore competition was virtually non-existent either domestically or from imports. In fact, many of the state enterprises were monopolies. Also there was no macroeconomic policy. The budget deficit increased in the second half of the 1980s as revenues from alcohol and oil exports declined while expenditures for investment and defence increased. And too much money was being created by the central bank.

The result was stagflation: the USSR experienced a decline in GNP in 1990 by just over 2 per cent as manufacturing production, agricultural output and oil extraction dropped. Prices, though still legally controlled, rose faster as enterprises exploited their monopoly powers and followed a long-standing practice of shifting production to ostensibly new products for which they were entitled to raise prices. Shortages and hoarding of goods became more acute and that in turn led enterprise managers to hoard stocks of raw materials. Also the monetary overhang grew as consumers found themselves with even larger amounts of unwanted rubles.

In these conditions, public dissatisfaction increased, encouraged no doubt by knowledge of what was happening in Eastern Europe in 1989. Strikes occurred – a virtually unprecedented event in Soviet history.

Numerous comprehensive reform plans were put forward with much publicity but were not accepted by the leadership. Some partial reform decrees were promulgated but were not always implemented. Boris Yeltsin, an ex-member of the Politburo who was to become president of the Russian Republic in 1991 in a historic free election, emerged as a strong advocate of economic reform and gathered around him the most able economists anxious for reform. At a Communist Party Congress in July 1990 he dramatically turned in his party membership card. Meanwhile Gorbachev tried to take a middle road between reformers and conservatives. At the same time various republics, especially but not only those in the Baltics, were clamouring for and in some cases seizing greater autonomy from Moscow. They issued declarations of sovereignty and began to sign economic co-operation agreements with each other.

The economic and political fragmentation was highlighted by the resignation in December 1990 of Foreign Minister Eduard Shevardnadze, who warned of the possible approach of a 'dictatorship'.

Total output in the Soviet Union declined more steeply in 1991, by 11.8 per cent according to the IMF. Among the reasons were a shortage of imported supplies owing to the scarcity of foreign exchange and the collapse of trade with Eastern Europe.

The wholesale price system was liberalised at the beginning of 1991 with a view to improving incentives. Some retail prices were also raised. In April there was a major reform of retail prices, which raised them on average by 60 per cent. For the year 1991 as a whole retail prices almost doubled.

In the spring of 1991, Gorbachev and the leaders of nine of the fifteen republics agreed on a new union treaty that gave additional powers to the republics. The treaty, which was strongly opposed by conservatives in Moscow, was scheduled to be signed on 20 August 1991.

As history records, a coup was attempted on 19 August by Gorbachev's vice president, Gennady Yanayev, and seven other officials who had been appointed by Gorbachev. They announced that Gorbachev, who was on vacation in the Crimea, could not carry on his duties owing to ill health

and they were assuming power and declaring a state of
emergency. Tanks rumbled into Moscow. The coup leaders
held a press conference that was covered by CNN and
people all over the world were able to observe their grim
nervousness and insecurity.

Large numbers of Muscovites gathered in the streets to
oppose the coup and Boris Yeltsin, in a memorable act,
stood atop a tank in front of the Russian Republic parliament building – the so-called White House – to denounce
the coup as 'reactionary' and 'anticonstitutional'. On the
next day 50 000 people assembled at the same place, where
they were addressed by Shevardnadze. Similar demonstrations took place in other cities.

On the international front the coup was supported by
Saddam Hussein, Muammar Qaddafi, and Fidel Castro.[11]

The coup – or *putsch* as it is often called in Russia – was
opposed by Russia's defence minister, a retired general, who
advised the troops not to follow the commands of the coup
leaders. Gorbachev, whose communications with Moscow
and elsewhere had been cut off, returned to Moscow with a
Russian delegation sent by Yeltsin. Soon the coup leaders
were arrested.

On his return to Moscow Gorbachev, at a press conference, proclaimed his loyalty to the Communist Party
while calling himself a true believer in the socialist idea.
This and the coup itself were among the catalysts that
sealed his fate and led to the dissolution of the Soviet
Union and the independence of the republics. Public
opinion swung to Yeltsin and other republican leaders.
On 23 August the activities of the Russian Communist
Party were suspended by decree. The next day Gorbachev
resigned as its general secretary and dissolved its Central
Committee. That put an end to the era of Bolshevism that
began in 1917. Later that autumn the Constitutional
Court of Russia ruled, after a lengthy trial, that the Communist Party was illegal as a national entity but that communists could meet at a local level. Among the thirteen
judges on the court, twelve were former members of the
Communist Party.

In the words of Georgi Arbatov, 'the *coup d'état* became the Party's *coup de grâce*.'[12]

As David Remnick, former *Washington Post* correspondent in Moscow, puts it, 'Russia faced a great historical moment, an elected president occupying the Kremlin for the first time in the thousand-year history of Russia, the hammer and sickle gone from the flagpole, the regime and empire dissolved.'[13]

In December 1991 the republics, other than those in the Baltics, agreed to form the Commonwealth of Independent States (CIS). This ended the Soviet Union. Gorbachev resigned as president on Christmas Day.

His resignation speech, addressed to 'Dear Compatriots, fellow citizens' noted that the country has

> plenty of everything: land, oil and gas, other natural riches, and God gave us lots of intelligence and talent, yet we lived much worse than developed countries and keep falling behind them more and more.
>
> ...
>
> The reason could already be seen [when he found himself at the head of state]. The society was suffocating in the vise of the command-bureaucratic system, doomed to serve ideology and bear the terrible burden of the arms race.

Mikhail Gorbachev will go down in history for having transformed what was the Soviet Union in many ways: moving it away from the totalitarian ideology and practices that dominated all of his predecessors; abandoning the notion of a class struggle at home and an arms race abroad; opening the society to free speech and a free press, tolerating dissent, encouraging freedom of religion, emigration and political freedom generally, including contested elections; withdrawing Soviet troops from Afghanistan; changing foreign policy, especially relations with the other superpower, the United States; liberating Eastern Europe and allowing it to go its own way; and starting the process of economic reform even if he failed to pursue it adequately.[14]

8.3 RUSSIA

It is not possible to cover developments in all fifteen of the republics of the former Soviet Union. We shall focus mainly on Russia.

The Russian Federation is the largest country in the world in area and the sixth largest in population (about 150 million). It consists of sixteen autonomous republics, five autonomous regions, and ten autonomous 'national regions'. There are also Russians in the other republics. For example, more than half the population of Alma-Ata in Kazakhstan and Bishkek in Kyrgyzstan are ethnic Russians, as are one third of the people in the capitals of Tajikistan and Turkmenistan.

Boris Yeltsin, the president of the Russian Federation, was born in 1931 in Sverdlovsk (now Yekaterinburg) in the Ural mountains. He attended the Urals Polytechnic Institute and then worked as a construction engineer in his home area until 1968, when he became a Party functionary, serving on the Sverdlovsk District Central Committee. Shortly after Gorbachev took office as general secretary, he brought Yeltsin to Moscow to head the Central Committee's construction department. He was named a candidate member of the Politburo in 1986 and also first secretary of the Moscow City Party Committee, a position in which he became very popular with Muscovites. In October 1987 at a plenum of the Central Committee Yeltsin criticised the leadership for the slow pace of reform and was expelled from the Politburo. In 1989 he was elected to the Congress of People's Deputies from Moscow with 89 per cent of the votes. As noted earlier, he was elected president of the Russian Republic in 1991.

It has been written that under

Stalin's regime a maverick such as Boris Yeltsin would have been shot; under Khrushchev he would have been jailed; and under Brezhnev he would have been sent to an insane asylum. Because of the transformation that Gorbachev engineered in Soviet politics, Yeltsin was able to arise again and challenge his one-time patron.[15]

Yeltsin has been characterised as 'a deeply ambiguous figure: by turns courageous and backsliding, clear and muddled, uncompromising and hesitant. Yet his gut instinct for a more liberally inclined Russia has not deserted him and his shaky popularity remains higher than that of any contender ...'[16]

Chaos and Reform

Yeltsin inherited an economy whose output had fallen about 14 per cent, with a large budget deficit, heavy external debts and meagre foreign exchange reserves. Oil production, its largest earner of hard currency, had dropped drastically. And little structural reform had been accomplished.

Some aspects of economic reform proceeded more rapidly in Russia in 1992. It began with the deregulation of most prices before a macroeconomic stabilisation policy had been put in place. Thus prices soared in early 1992 except for those that remained under control, including energy and rents. Oil prices were raised but remained well under the level of world prices. From December 1991 to December 1992 prices paid by urban consumers are estimated to have risen almost 2600 per cent – or more than 90 per cent per month.[17] Inflation declined somewhat, though temporarily, in the spring of 1993. Whatever its other effects, the hyperinflation put an end to rationing and soaked up the monetary overhang.

The steep rate of inflation was attributable to the outsized budget deficit – more than 20 per cent of GDP in 1992 according to the IMF – and the credit-creating activities of the central bank. In both cases the funds were used to subsidise state-owned enterprises. This was in effect a form of unemployment insurance on a large scale. The subsidies and credits to loss-making state-owned enterprises enabled them to meet their payrolls. The alternative would have been massive unemployment, with possible serious political repercussions. Another reason for the inflation was that Russia was lending large amounts of rubles to other republics, enabling them to buy Russian goods.

Inflation along with the general political and economic uncertainty led to capital flight. Everyone who could do so exchanged rubles for foreign currencies, mainly dollars. Thus the ruble's exchange rates depreciated rapidly, raising the domestic cost of imports. Consequently some imports were subsidised, adding to the budget deficit.

Most of the other republics of the CIS were still using the ruble and the inflation in Russia necessarily spread to them to the extent that they were not creating their own inflations. They too had to liberalise their prices and let them go up. Otherwise their output would have been siphoned off to Russia, attracted by its higher prices.

Privatisation and Industry Reform

The institutional and structural categories of economic reform, identified in Chapter 7, have been implemented only slowly except for price liberalisation. A privatisation programme is being pursued vigorously by Deputy Prime Minister Anatoli Chubais. Numerous new firms have been created, especially in the service industries. Many new banks have been established – 1500 or more by mid-1992 – but they are not full-scale commercial banks. Most of them have been set up by state enterprises, to which they lend partly on the basis of credits from the central bank. That Russia is far from having an effective banking system is indicated by the fact that it takes weeks, if not months, for a payment to be made from one enterprise to another.

A major economic problem is the existence of many large industrial enterprises of uncertain value and viability. They are being propped up with subsidies from the state budget and credits from the central bank and from other enterprises.

As MIT Professor Stanley Fischer, former Chief Economist of the World Bank, has written:

> While economic growth in the formerly socialist economies will come more from new firms than from the transformation of existing firms, the state sector in most of the formerly socialist economies is so large that restructuring is essential. Because the capacity of the state is limited, most of the restructuring will have to come through privatization.[18]

Fischer goes on to point out that some of the very large firms that are dominant in medium-sized towns need to be restructured by the state before privatisation is possible. This is so because a decision by private owners to close such plants in whole or in part would cause severe hardships for the local employees and the state would have to intervene in any event.

Along similar lines, Brandeis University Professor Joseph Berliner argues against rapid privatisation of large state-owned enterprises. He points out that 'marketization' has to come first: the structural and institutional reforms identified in the previous chapter; without them privatisation will not produce the efficiency gains expected from it. Moreover, many of the large enterprises would have to be subsidised even if they became private.[19]

In late 1992 vouchers were issued to every man, woman and child in Russia – a programme similar to that introduced in the former Czechoslovakia. Predictably workers and managers as well as 'conservative' politicians, including former President Gorbachev, were critical of this action. The vouchers were eligible for exchange at auctions for shares in enterprises put up for privatisation. The vouchers can also be bought and sold by the citizenry and by investors from abroad. A substantial portion of the shares – either 40 per cent or 51 per cent – could be acquired by the employees and managers; if they chose a majority of the shares, they paid more heavily.

The motivation behind this scheme is not only the obvious economic one – improving the efficiency of the enterprises by introducing the incentives associated with the profit motive – but also political: to give the public a stake in private enterprise and make the reform process irreversible.

While thousands of enterprises have been privatised, the outcome remains uncertain. A mere change of the ultimate owners from the state to citizens does not by itself assure significant improvement in the quality of management, productivity and hence the quantity and quality of output of large enterprises. It is noteworthy, and worrisome, that most of the enterprises that were privatised up to April 1993 are majority owned by their managers and workers, who have an understandable resistance to new investment and restructuring if the result is a laying off of workers.

President Yeltsin's reform measures met strong opposition from his vice president and in the Congress of People's Deputies from both former communists and members of what is called, ironically enough, the military–industrial complex (for those too young to remember or with short memories, a term coined by President Eisenhower shortly before he left office). In October 1993 Yeltsin ordered the parliament disbanded, calling for new elections. This led to another crisis when the parliament resisted and attempted a coup by first trying to take over a television station. Yeltsin secured the support of the military leaders who proceeded to shell the very same White House where Yeltsin defied the revolutionists of 1991. Yeltsin prevailed and elections in December approved a new constitution but also sent a large number of nationalists, former communists and anti-reformers to the new Duma, the lower house of parliament.

Toward the end of January 1994 economic reform appeared to be in retreat as Prime Minister Chernomyrdin formed a new government saying that 'the period of market romanticism is now over'.[20] He proposed dealing with inflation, which worsened during the period of political turmoil, by non-monetary means, which sound like price controls. Two of the principal reformers in the previous government, Yegor Gaidar and Boris Fyodorov, refused to participate in the new one. And two chief foreign advisers to the government, Anders Åslund of Sweden and Jeffrey Sachs of the United States, were asked to step aside.

The prospects for continued reform appeared dim. Yet in the first few months of 1994 Chernomyrdin pursued an anti-inflationary budget policy and encouraged continued privatisation.

8.4 THE OUTLOOK

Russia abounds in problems – political, economic, and social.

Privatisation – in both senses: new firms being organised and old ones moving into private ownership – is under way. Some enterprises that made armaments are turning out consumer goods such as washing machines. Structural and institutional reform are creeping forward. A start has been made on allowing citizens to buy and sell farm land. Macroeconomic stabilisation has progressed. Inflation is down but output is depressed, though not as much as the official statistics indicate.

As reform moved ahead haltingly, it was accompanied by some of the excrescences of a free, non-totalitarian society. Crime is rampant and a 'mafia' exists. Corruption and bribery were present under the old system but they are apparently more blatant now. Those individuals who have become rich, legally or illegally, ride around in Mercedes or BMWs while pensioners have difficulty making ends meet. The difference between the rich and the poor is greater than at any time since before the Communist revolution. Ironically many of the *nouveau riche* are former Communist Party *apparachiks*. How important these conditions were in the way people voted in December 1993 is unclear.

Winston Churchill's characterisation of Russia as 'a riddle wrapped in a mystery inside an enigma' may still be apt. It represented the most serious uncertainty facing the world, politically and economically, in early 1994.

8.5   OTHER REPUBLICS

Most of the successor states of the Soviet Union are in serious economic difficulties and some are experiencing civil wars. They are all feeling the effects of the break-up of what had been an integrated economy in which most of them were dependent on Russia for oil and gas at subsidised prices.

The Baltic states (Estonia, Latvia and Lithuania) and Ukraine have separated their monetary systems from the ruble area, issuing their own currencies. They are therefore suffering even more severely from the rise in the prices of energy.

And all of them face the same economic reform problems as Russia.

9 From Mao to Deng: Economic Reform in China

China's experience with economic reform has been very different from that of the other countries in transition. Politically China has not moved towards democracy. It remains a Communist one-party state. Its elderly 'paramount leader', Deng Xiaoping, speaks of his death as going to an appointment with Karl Marx.

Nevertheless, China with the largest population and the third largest area of the countries of the world, is more decentralised – politically and economically – than Russia and the nations of Eastern Europe. That has allowed for local initiatives and experiments that, if successful, can spread elsewhere. Substantial economic reforms have been adopted but on a gradual basis. There has been no shock therapy. Nor has there been a significant amount of privatisation of state-owned enterprises. But new private firms have come into existence. A substantial part of China's output is now produced by entities that operate according to market principles. As *The Economist* has written:

> Plunges do not appeal to the Chinese, who call their method of reform 'crossing the river by feeling the stones underfoot.' As early as the mid-1980s, Chinese economists were arguing that quick wholesale reform has the same defect as central planning: it requires the government to take too many big decisions on questions, such as the right sequence of reform or the right way to privatise, that it knows too little about. Far better to experiment cautiously, letting different regions and different companies try different things. If they work, extend them, If not, bury them.[1]

China's reform has been based on marketisation rather than privatisation. And it has differed from region to region. The coastal provinces – notably Guangdong – have developed rapidly on the basis of Deng Xiaoping's 'open door' policy. This has authorised joint ventures with foreign capital, mostly from Hong Kong. Much of the output has been exported. The interior provinces have moved ahead on the basis of saving in the local agricultural sector, which made possible the formation and growth of town and village enterprises (TVEs).

China has avoided the drastic declines in output that have afflicted all the other countries in transition. In fact, its growth performance in the past fifteen years has been astonishing. In 1993 the government was trying to cope with an overheated economy that grew by about 13 per cent in both 1992 and 1993.

The country that Napoleon called a 'sleeping giant' has awakened.

9.1   PRE-REFORM DEVELOPMENTS

Mao Zedong led the Chinese Communist revolution, which came to fruition in 1949. Under his direction China carried

Figure 9.1   Growth of China's GNP

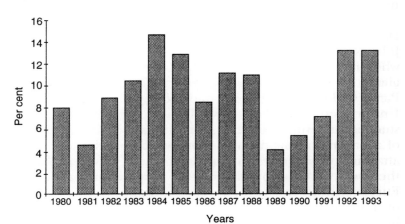

out a major and bloody land reform in which landlords were killed and peasants took over ownership of properties that they had formerly leased. Later, agriculture was collectivised, industry was nationalised and heavy industry was encouraged as China adopted the Soviet system of central planning, advised by thousands of Soviet technicians. Central planning was relaxed somewhat but continued in force even after the split with the Soviet Union in the late 1950s.

In 1957 Mao initiated the Great Leap Forward, which involved establishing peoples communes in the countryside and abolishing private plots. The average commune consisted of 5000 households. The peasants were mobilised to build roads, dams and irrigation networks. The next year a programme of local steelmaking was launched in the communes and elsewhere: many hundreds of thousands of small furnaces were built throughout the country but inadequate provision was made for supplying the raw materials needed and the steel proved to be mostly useless. The programme was a total failure and was soon abandoned but only after agricultural production plummeted because of the diversion of peasant labour from its usual activities. The result was a famine in which 20 to 30 million people died from starvation or malnutrition. China's GDP, which had doubled from 1950 to 1958, fell by almost one-fourth in the next three years.

Mao believed in permanent revolution and continuous class struggle. According to the late eminent China scholar, John K. Fairbank, he took on the self-image of an emperor when he instigated the Cultural Revolution in 1966.[2] It was aimed at intellectuals and 'revisionists' in the Communist Party (CCP) who were accused of taking the 'capitalist road'. Universities and secondary schools were closed and students, carrying little red books containing the 'thoughts' of Chairman Mao, were mobilised as Red Guards, first attacking their university presidents and professors. Then they went on a rampage destroying libraries, recordings of European classical music, works of art, and other trappings of 'bourgeois life'. Intellectuals, artists and musicians were humiliated, persecuted, and sometimes killed or led to commit suicide to avoid beatings. Others were sent to rural areas where they were required to do degrading work. Many officials of the CCP were ousted from office. Among the absurdities perpetrated during that period, vehicles in Shanghai were told to advance at red lights and stop at green lights, as the Red Guards reasoned that the revolutionary colour should not be associated with coming to a halt. When the country was close to civil war the Red Guards were disbanded.

It is estimated that a million people were killed during the Cultural Revolution and many times more were victimised. 'Central to it all was the assumption of conspiracy – "hidden enemies and traitors" among the intellectuals within the CCP ...'.[3]

Despite all the turmoil, China made economic progress under Mao, who died in 1976. The growth rate from 1952 to 1978 was respectable – around 6 per cent per year. But, as in the Soviet Union, Chinese economic growth in the 1960s and 1970s was the result almost entirely of increased investment and employment. Productivity was stagnant as the Great Leap Forward and Cultural Revolution created economic chaos. But more than that was involved. According to Fairbank, the 'dead end of involution – growth of product without development of greater productivity per person – that had held the Chinese farmer back for centuries still held him back in 1950–1978.'[4]

Nevertheless, as Brookings Institution scholar Harry Harding has noted, China created an industrial base, 'exploded its own nuclear bomb, launched earth satellites, built primitive computers, and synthesised insulin'.[5]

9.2 THE BEGINNINGS OF REFORM

The foregoing events provided fertile ground for Deng Xiaoping's initiation of economic reform. The people were ready for a change, both in the countryside and in the cities. Moreover, although China's economic performance had been favourable as compared with other centrally-planned economies, it lagged far behind its East Asian neighbours, the 'four little dragons' – that is, Hong Kong, South Korea, Singapore and Taiwan. China's per capita GNP increased by 3.6 per cent per year during 1960–76. In Japan, Korea and Singapore these increases were twice that large and Taiwan's per capita growth was 6.2 per cent annually.[6] This widening gap also motivated China's reformers.

Not long after Mao's death, Deng Xiaoping was restored to his position as vice-chairman of the CCP and vice-premier. He became the leader of a group in China's power structure that was critical of the Cultural Revolution and favoured a more pragmatic approach to policymaking, particularly economic reform. Under Deng, China also turned outward in foreign policy, normalising relations with the United States and sending 10 000 academics and technicians to study there.

Deng Xiaoping was born in 1904 in Sichuan province in central China. Like Mao, he grew up in rural China in a well-to-do family and received a better education than the average farm boy. In 1920 Deng sailed for France with an uncle, where he worked in factories and became a communist. In 1926 he studied for several months in Moscow on his way back to China. After working in the Shanghai Communist underground for a few years, he was sent to Guangxi province to organise the peasants into a military force in order to try to capture Canton and other large cities from Chiang Kai-shek's Kuomintang. Thus his military career began. He later became a military commander, organising his troops from scratch and learning tactics and strategy along the way. Eventually he came to direct field armies of hundreds of thousands of soldiers.

After the revolution, Mao made Deng the proconsul, in effect, of southwestern China. His task was to build the area into an independent economic entity as a defence against the possibility of an American nuclear attack on eastern and northern China. By 1954 he was a member of the Politburo and number four in the party.

In 1967, during the Cultural Revolution, he was condemned for, among other infractions, being too pragmatic and insufficiently ideological: he used the slogan 'What matter black cat, white cat? So long as it catches mice it's a good cat' in relation to agricultural policy. He was banished to Jiangxi province where he did manual work. In 1973 he returned to Beijing to his earlier position as vice-premier. But in 1976 he was dismissed again, when Mao said that Deng 'knows nothing of Marxism-Leninism'. Finally in July 1977 he was reappointed and eventually took over Mao's reins.

Under Deng's leadership, economic reform proceeded in spurts and its pace varied from region to region. One reason for this was that differences of view existed between moderate and radical reformers. (In China those more in favour of reform are said to be on the right side of the political spectrum in contrast to ideological Marxists on the left; in the former Soviet Union these designations are reversed.) Another reason for the uneven pace of reform was that the economy experienced occasional bursts of inflation as central planning was relaxed.

9.3 REFORM IN THE COUNTRYSIDE

The first spurt of reform focused on rural China. The communes were abolished and under the 'household responsibility system' farmers took over the management, though not the ownership, of land. Prices paid for agricultural products were raised and peasants were permitted to sell above-quota output at still higher prices and to retain the extra earnings. In 1985 the state's mandatory procurement quotas were replaced by a system of contracts with farm households for a limited number of products, giving even more freedom to farmers. Later, as output increased, the state introduced a system of support prices.

Under these improved incentives, agricultural productivity accelerated. Farm output, which had grown only 1.6 per cent per year in 1971–7, increased by 6.7 per cent per year in 1978–83.[7] This was, in Fairbank's words, 'a triumph for Deng's reforms'. But he goes on to write,

Anyone who concludes that Chinese agriculture, having seen the light and wanting to be more like us, has gone 'capitalist' is making a grievous error. The contract system must be seen as the latest phase of statecraft in how to organize farmers in order to improve their welfare and also strengthen the state.[8]

Fairbank's observation is supported by the fact that local governments often blockade the grain market, prohibiting sales to traders, until the compulsory procurement quota is filled at the contract price, which is below the market price.

Rising income in the countryside created the savings that financed increased investment in the economy as a whole. The productivity increase also provided the basis, in terms of available labour, for towns and villages, and to a lesser extent private parties, to establish non-agricultural enterprises that operated outside the central plan, selling their products at market prices and reinvesting profits. Their output increased on average by 29 per cent per year in 1979–86. By 1992 TVEs numbered about 19 million employing more than 100 million people and were responsible for about one-third of China's total output. The effect on living standards is striking. From the early 1980s to the early 1990s, average living space per person doubled in rural China and luxuries like refrigerators, washing machines and colour television sets are in evidence. 'China has turned its back on Stalinist collectivism of agriculture, although it may be some time before it completely repudiates it.'[9]

Nevertheless one should not exaggerate the degree of prosperity in rural China. The benefits from the faster growth of productivity in agriculture are rather unequally distributed. In a number of provinces rural poverty is still acute. And peasants have demonstrated against higher taxes in some regions as they became aware that their incomes lag far behind those in urban areas. This led in June 1993 to cuts in a number of taxes and fees imposed on farmers.

The piecemeal raising of prices paid to farmers over the years was not passed on to consumers of rationed agricultural products such as grain and edible oils. As a result, subsidies grew large. In 1991 and 1992 the prices of these rationed products were raised sharply, contributing to the inflation that took hold, as discussed below.

9.4   INDUSTRIAL REFORM

Reform came later and less comprehensively in industry (apart from TVEs). In 1978 state-owned enterprises accounted for more than 80 per cent of industrial output. As in other centrally-planned economies, these enterprises were not subject to a hard budget constraint. Despite some reforms, a large proportion of them (the estimates vary from one-third to two-thirds) operate at a loss and are kept going by subsidies and bank loans at low interest rates.

Initially, after 1978, state-owned enterprises were permitted to undertake some production outside the plan but state control remained pervasive. One reason is the so-called 'iron rice bowl': the enterprises provide housing, medical care and education to workers and their families along with lifetime employment. Social peace depends on the continuation of these arrangements.

Other reforms followed. In the mid-1980s the 'contract responsibility system' – similar to the household system applied successfully in rural areas – was introduced for state enterprises. It sought to separate management from ownership and appeared to shift authority from state planners to plant managers. The latter were permitted to sell above-plan output at negotiated, rather than at governmentally fixed, prices and to reinvest the profits where they exist. And some prices were liberalised. Later, wholesale markets developed for the sale of output not subject to the central plan and for the purchase of inputs. Nevertheless the lack of incentives in centrally-planned systems that we have observed in Eastern Europe and Russia is also evident in China's state-owned enterprises. While the proportion of inputs and outputs of state enterprises that is subject to central planning is shrinking, these enterprises are not the dynamic factor in China's economy. It is the TVEs and other 'collectives' – enterprises affiliated with tiers of government below the central or provincial level – along with private companies, including joint ventures and foreign firms, that are the mainspring of China's rapid growth. The share of non-state enterprises in industrial output increased from just under one-fifth in 1978 to more than half in 1992. Correspondingly, a growing proportion of total output is sold at market prices: about two-thirds of agricultural and industrial output and four-fifths of retail sales in 1992.[10]

Deng Xiaoping gave a boost to the non-state sector in early 1992 by visiting southern China, where such activity flourishes, and simply saying 'Do it faster'. In March of that year references to a planned economy were deleted from the country's constitution. And in October 1992, the CCP 'formally embraced paramount leader Deng Xiaoping's view that the market system was not incompatible with the ideas of socialism and called for the establishment of a socialist market economy'.[11]

In the summer of 1993 the government 'announced plans to transform one-third of state-owned companies into limited-liability corporations responsible for their own profits and losses. That would mean that if the companies suffered persistent losses, the Government would not bail them out and they could go bankrupt'.[12]

9.5 MACROECONOMIC DEVELOPMENTS

Neither fiscal nor monetary policy is especially effective in China partly because the country is decentralised. The central government budget is burdened with subsidies to loss-making state enterprises, and revenues from profitable enterprises decreased after they were permitted to retain earnings. The People's Bank, which has been converted to a central bank and deprived of its commercial banking functions, appears to have limited influence on the lending activities of the state-owned commercial banks. And the formulation of monetary policy was complicated by the fact that the agricultural sector was being monetised – that is, the farming community was increasingly using and holding cash.

As a result China has experienced episodes of inflation – 18 per cent in 1988–9, according to official statistics that are of questionable accuracy. The central government reacted by cutting state investments, postponing a price liberalisation, urging local authorities to restrain enterprise wage policies and tightening monetary policy. Measured retail prices rose only 2.1 per cent in 1990.

The official GNP statistics apparently exaggerate China's growth rate. But even if the data displayed in Figure 9.1 are discounted somewhat, they represent an impressive performance. It resulted, as elsewhere in Asia, from high rates of saving and investment – ranging between 30 and 40 per cent of GDP in the 1980s and early 1990s.

The growth rate of GDP speeded up to 13 per cent in 1992 and was about the same in 1993. The result was a revival of inflation to an annual rate of 15 per cent in the spring of 1993, the highest since 1988–9. The boom was fed in part by a large jump in foreign investment and investment outlays by state enterprises. Inflation brought with it hectic speculation in real estate and a depreciation of the yuan.

In early July 1993 the governor of the People's Bank was forced to resign and was replaced, at least temporarily, by Vice Premier Zhu Rongji, a member of the Politburo and a possible successor to the premier, Li Peng. One reason for concern at the highest level was the unrest – even violence – among peasants suffering from inflation and aware that they were not keeping up in terms of income with their urban countrymen. But the leadership appears also to be concerned that too stringent a crackdown on credit in order to reduce inflation could lead to higher unemployment and social unrest.

9.6   INTERNATIONAL TRADE AND INVESTMENT

Since 1980 China's exports have grown more than twice as fast as world trade. Shoppers in many countries are well aware of the great variety of Chinese goods available, particularly labour-intensive manufactured consumer goods. In this respect China is competing heavily with the traditional Asian NICs.

The process started with the establishment of four 'special economic zones' (SEZs) in two coastal provinces in 1979–80. Firms in these zones, both state-owned and others, were permitted to operate outside the central plan and to attract foreign investment. In 1984 14 coastal cities were allowed to operate in a similar manner. Later, still other areas were declared to be 'open economic zones'.

Economic reform of the trade regime has made it possible for 'thousands of individual manufacturing firms and local foreign trade companies ... to conduct international trade transactions'.[13]

The striking export performance is related to foreign investment in China, which rose from less than $400 million in 1982 to $27 billion in 1993.[14] Much of this investment is coming from Hong Kong and Taiwan and is located mainly in the coastal provinces. Hong Kong entrepreneurs began shifting manufacturing facilities to China in the mid-1980s, attracted by lower labour costs as wages rose rapidly at home. But some of the investment from Hong Kong has involved the purchase of state-owned firms. Taiwanese businesses followed suit more recently, especially in the case of labour-intensive products. Half of the increase in China's exports in 1990–2 was generated by these foreign firms.

In addition Hong Kong has become an important intermediary for China's trade. In 1990 36 per cent of China's exports were re-exported through Hong Kong and 25 per cent of its imports came through Hong Kong.[15]

In general, China has become much more open to the world economy. Between 1980 and 1992, exports and imports tripled as a proportion of GNP.

9.7 POLITICAL AND SOCIAL CONDITIONS

China today is a far different country from what it was under the ideological zealotry of Mao Zedong.

It is true that Deng Xiaoping, while encouraging economic reform, has attempted to maintain the Communist Party's political control. In 1979 he enunciated the 'Four Cardinal Principles' that China was expected to abide by: the socialist path, the dictatorship of the proletariat, the leadership of the Party and Marxism-Leninism-Mao Zedong thought.

Much has changed since then. Living standards have soared. Not only are Chinese citizens eating better, they are enjoying modern conveniences. In 1981 there was one colour television for each 100 urban households; ten years later there were 70. The number of washing machines per 100 urban households rose from six to 80 and the number of refrigerators from 0.2 to 50.[16] Recently, in its effort to cool the overheated economy the government banned the building of new golf courses!

It has to be stressed that this well-being is not equally distributed. It is most evident in the coastal provinces. In about one-third of the provinces, income per capita has been growing at about 3 per cent annually, compared with 6 per cent or more in Guangdong, Xingjiang, Yunnan and other coastal provinces.

Along with this economic improvement has come the spread of education and greater political freedom. The CCP is still firmly entrenched in power but it no longer attempts to control as much of the details of peoples' private lives as in the past. 'The world should be relieved that, for the Chinese, going into business has replaced joining the Communist Party as the way to success.'[17] The populace is now much more aware of ways of life outside China, thanks to television and a proliferation of satellite dishes. Here again we encounter the political and economic effects of the telecommunications revolution. The CCP no longer has a monopoly on news.

Short-wave radios, direct dial international telephones, fax machines and personal computers are also becoming available, facilitating international communication. It is questionable, given these facts and the reforms of the economy, whether the CCP can maintain its control. According to Nicolas Kristof, former *New York Times* bureau chief in Beijing:

> the Government sometimes resembles not so much a Communist monolith as a disorganized conglomerate. The Politburo, acting as a fractious board of directors, often ignores tacit disobedience.
>
> Even if the central Government ordered a major crackdown [on TV] it is unclear that it would be enforced outside the capital. Local governments, always lethargic about implementing edicts they dislike, are making money by running cable television systems that depend on satellite television.[18]

It also should be noted that greater economic freedom has brought back corruption, crime, and prostitution.

9.8 THE OUTLOOK

China's economic performance is likely to continue on an impressive scale for some time. And the state-enterprise sector of the economy will probably continue to shrink. While much economic reform has occurred, China has not become a full-fledged market economy.

Politically, China is nominally a Communist nation but as Kristof writes, 'No Communist country, at least, has ever so fully embraced stock markets, satellite television, private colleges, Avon ladies, music video and radio talk shows.'[19]

Questions remain. What regime will succeed Deng Xiaoping? What model of politics will succeed communism which is disappearing as an economic ideology? Will new pro-democracy movements arise in a more educated society, as happened before the Tiananmen Square massacre of June 1989? And, given the communications revolution, which made the entire world aware of what happened at Tiananmen Square, would the Communist authorities dare to crack down again?

For the longer run we may hope that economist Lawrence Summers was correct when he wrote in 1992:

> It may well be that when the history of the late 20th century is written, in a hundred years, the most significant event will be the revolutionary changes in China, which will soon be communist only in a theoretical sense. The rise of China may well be the transcendent event.[20]

10 Other Asia: Dragons, Tigers and an Elephant

The economic dynamism now so evident in China has been a feature of Hong Kong, South Korea, Singapore and Taiwan for many years. These four countries have been called 'the four little dragons' in Asia – China being the large dragon – and 'the four tigers' in the west. The dragon is a symbol of serene and prestigious power in Asia. The tiger, while also powerful, is regarded as less majestic and self-confident. Thus because Korea, after decades of highly successful economic performance, encountered some problems in 1993 (discussed below), Koreans tended to characterise their nation as a tiger rather than a dragon.

In any event, the four countries became industrialised and grew rapidly in the 1960s and 1970s as 'newly-industrialised countries' (NICs) and 'newly-industrialised economies' (NIEs). That process persisted in the 1980s and early 1990s as the composition of their output continued to shift away from labour-intensive products towards those embodying more capital and higher technology. Also in the 1980s Malaysia, Thailand and Indonesia emerged as fast-growing industrial powers. A distinguishing feature of most of these countries is that they combined rapid growth with increasing income equality. The entire area, including China and Japan, became more integrated economically as intra-regional trade and investment flows swelled. More recently India, symbolised by the large but slow-moving elephant, joined the parade by undertaking fundamental structural reforms and beginning to open its economy to the rest of the world.

10.1 THE FOUR TIGERS

In the 1970s the economic performance of the four tigers was remarkable. Their growth rates ranged from 8 to 10 per cent per year. Their economies were characterised by high saving and domestic investment, a well-educated labour force, orientation towards exports, a relatively equal distribution of income, low taxes and a considerable degree of government intervention in the economy – sometimes referred to as industrial policy. While they continued to prosper in the 1980s their manufacturers had to adapt to competition from both labour-intensive goods from lower-wage countries nearby and high-technology products from industrial countries.[1] This pattern of regional development, as comparative advantage shifts from the technological leaders to their neighbours, has often been likened to a formation of flying geese.

Korea is somewhat typical and it has had a greater demonstration effect on other developing countries than Taiwan or the city states, Hong Kong and Singapore. In the 1950s South Korea was a very poor country, much of its economy having been destroyed in the war with North Korea. In 1961 its exports were mainly raw materials and agricultural products and its annual per capita income was less than $1000. Land reform and government assistance led to rapid advances in agricultural productivity so that in the 1970s Korea had the highest rice yields per acre in the world.[2]

Industrialisation in the 1960s, encouraged by General Park with tax incentives and low-interest loans from the government, involved high rates of investment – 25 per cent of GDP in 1965–70. In the 1970s, emphasis shifted to heavy industry, including chemicals. By 1979 manufacturing in Korea accounted for about one-third of its total output compared with 12 per cent in 1967. Concurrently its exports had increased more than 22 per cent per year in real terms, more than three times as fast as world trade. Exports were encouraged in a variety of ways: duty-free imports of raw materials for export industries, cheap credit and tax preferences. Korean construction companies took advantage of the economic boom in Middle East oil-exporting countries after 1973; in 1980 more than 130 000 Korean construction workers were in the Middle East, contributing to Korea's earnings of foreign exchange.

The entrepreneurial system was organised and industrialisation was encouraged on the basis of groupings somewhat similar to the *zaibatsu* in Japan. Governmental incentives were provided to successful firms that were permitted to diversify to become holding companies or conglomerates, known in Korea as *chaebols*.[3] The larger of these conglomerates have names that are now familiar worldwide: Hyundai, Samsung, Daewoo and Lucky-Goldstar. In the 1970s they were especially prevalent in heavy industry and in 1978 they accounted for 43 per cent of value added in manufacturing.[4] More recently they have produced automobiles, semiconductors and personal computers.

The rapid development in the 1970s had its costs. Inflation accelerated, largely because monetary policy was unable to perform its function. Instead the banks were used by the government to implement its industrialisation policy – encouraging heavy industry such as machinery, construction equipment and petrochemicals – by making 'policy loans' to favoured sectors at negative real interest rates and depriving other sectors of credit (a condition known as financial repression). Such policy loans accounted for almost three-fifths of total bank loans in 1980 and then declined somewhat. In these conditions the economy became unbalanced. Excess capacity appeared in the machinery, shipbuilding and nonferrous metals industries while the lighter industries experienced excess demand, which showed up partly in rapid wage advances.

Korea's heavy investment in the 1970s was based in part on external borrowing. Its current-account deficit averaged $1.2 billion per year in the 1970s and then increased sharply with the second oil shock. But rapid export growth held down the relative burden of debt service payments. In 1982 the IMF listed Korea among the twenty most heavily-indebted countries but by 1985 it was not among the fifteen debtor nations singled out for the Baker plan.

At the start of the 1980s Korea experienced its first decline in real GDP since the 1950s. A very poor harvest combined with the oil shock, recession abroad and high interest rates in industrial countries provide part of the explanation, along with the structural imbalance noted above. Consumer prices rose more than 28 per cent in 1980 under the impact of the steep rise in oil prices and a depreciation of the Korean won. The current account registered a deficit of $5.3 billion, equal to 8.5 per cent of GDP. All this happened as the government changed with the assassination of President Park in October 1979. It led to a shift in macroeconomic policies and to alteration of Korea's development strategy. Both fiscal and monetary policy were reformed and an incomes policy restrained price and wage advances. Zero-based budgeting was introduced and the budget deficit was cut in half as a proportion of GDP. The Bank of Korea, which had been imposing credit ceilings on individual banks, adopted more conventional instruments of monetary policy: reserve requirements, open market operations, and the rediscount mechanism.[5] In the decade ending 1992, annual inflation averaged 5.1 per cent, whereas it had been well above 10 per cent in the previous two decades. GDP grew on average by more than 9 per cent per year, among the highest growth rates in the world.

Structural reforms included a move away from the policy of import substitution, at least for non-agricultural goods. Import quotas were liberalised and tariffs were lowered. They are expected to average no more than 8 per cent in 1994. The freeing of imports still left a ban on a list of some thirty products from Japan – a result of Korea's 35 years as a Japanese colony and its desire to avoid undue reliance on Japan. A start was also made on removing government controls over the financial system, especially regulation of interest rates on bank loans. More generally, the government tried to shift away from picking 'winners and losers' in its industrial policy towards a more 'generic' approach. According to the World Bank, government intervention 'since 1979 has focused on the restructuring of distressed industries, support for the development of technology, and the promotion of competition'.[6]

In 1987 Korea's first democratic election in many years put a former general in the presidency. In 1992 a civilian,

Kim Young Sam, was elected president on a platform that promised gradual withdrawal of the government's controls over the economy as well as a drive against corruption.

Korea's growth rate fell to 4.8 per cent in 1992 as exports were affected not only by the slowdown in the world economy but also by Korea's relatively high wage costs. Plants that made and exported labour-intensive products such as shoes and apparel were losing sales as China and other lower-wage countries undersold them. While Korea's exports of higher technology goods to China increased rapidly, its industrial production levelled off in 1993.

Remarkably, Korea's real GDP almost tripled from 1980 to 1992 and it emerged as an industrial power whose output is shifting towards capital-intensive products. The deregulation process in industry and finance has begun and the nature of industrial policy has changed. But Korea's economy is still subject to a considerable amount of government intervention. Its philosophy of the relationship of government to industry is more like that of Japan than in the Anglo-Saxon tradition.

10.2   MALAYSIA AND THAILAND

Malaysia, with a population of about 18 million, is rich in natural resources, including tin, rubber and petroleum. In the 1970s it developed exports of light manufactured products – textiles, shoes, and apparel – in free-trade and export-processing zones on the basis of direct investment from abroad. The stock of direct investment in 1980 was six times as large as that in Korea. Malaysia has recently had the highest ratio of foreign direct investment to total investment – above one-half – among Asian countries (with the single exception of Singapore).[7]

Partly on this basis Malaysia industrialised rapidly in the 1980s. Manufactured goods as a share of total exports increased from 18.8 per cent in 1980 to 70 per cent in 1992. Among its manufactures are semiconductors, disk drives, other electronic products and automobiles. A domestically-produced car – the Proton – supplies two-thirds of the home market and is exported to 17 countries.[8]

The economy grew 8.4 per cent per year in 1986–92 and the inflation rate, though it moved up in the booming economy, remained below 5 per cent annually. Malaysia's prosperity has led its government to undertake the construction of the world's tallest structure, an office building in the capital city, Kuala Lumpur.

Thailand, with a population of 58 million, has seen its economy grow at about the same rate as Malaysia's and its inflation has been a little higher. It too has experienced a shift in output and exports from rice and other commodities to manufactures. An explicit export promotion policy was adopted in 1981 and import barriers began to be lowered. In other respects the Thai government has intervened less actively in the economy than Malaysia and Korea. In the latter part of the 1980s incoming direct investment increased sharply, to more than $2 billion per year, much of it from Japan. By 1990 more than three-fifths of Thailand's exports were manufactured products compared with one-fourth in 1980. Although Thailand too was beginning to feel the competition of lower-wage firms in China and Vietnam, its export volume more than doubled from 1987 to 1992.

10.3   INDONESIA

Much larger in area and population than the other countries covered above, Indonesia consists of more than 10 000 islands, many of which are uninhabited, stretching over about 3000 miles. With over 190 million people, Indonesia is the fourth most populous country on the planet. The densely populated island of Java accounts for two-thirds of Indonesia's industrial output.

President Suharto, in his sixth five-year term, runs a strong, if not authoritarian, central government. Its economic policy is dominated by so-called 'technocrats' or the 'Berkeley mafia' many of whom earned economics degrees in the United States. They have imposed budgetary discipline and monetary stability.

As an oil and gas producer (and a member of OPEC) Indonesia enjoyed windfalls in the two oil shocks. Its export earnings rose from about $1 billion in 1970 to more than $22 billion in 1981, when oil and gas accounted for four-fifths of exports. The increased foreign exchange earnings were used to improve health services, public infrastructure and especially education. Primary school education is nearly universal. But the government also invested in state-owned enterprises in heavy industry that required tariff protection.

The falloff in oil prices in 1983 and 1986 required economic adjustments. In addition to stabilising macroeconomic policies the government opted for export promotion and outward orientation of the economy. Tariffs were cut substantially in 1985, the currency was devalued in 1986 and export incentives were introduced. Economic growth picked up in the latter part of the 1980s. The main manufactured exports were plywood and textiles. In recent years, with oil revenues lower, Indonesia has been the recipient of foreign direct investment which has financed the creation of labour-intensive industries producing shoes, apparel and electronics no longer made in Korea and other higher-wage countries in Asia.

From 1986 to 1992 annual economic growth exceeded 9 per cent, 'the highest sustained growth rate since independence'.[9]

10.4 THE EAST ASIAN MIRACLE

A study published by the World Bank in 1993 – *The East Asian Miracle* – recounts and analyses the remarkable economic performance of the countries of East Asia. Among the characteristics of that performance are high growth rates based on heavy investment, rather low inflation, 'shared growth' in the sense that income is distributed relatively equally, rapid export expansion and industrialisation towards higher value-added and technologically more advanced products. What are the explanations for this record and what can other developing countries learn from it?

As the study and a number of commentaries on it pointed out,[10] the East Asian nations got the fundamentals right. Their fiscal and monetary policies were effective. Beyond that necessary condition, they invested in education. They oriented their economies towards exports, which promoted competitiveness and efficiency. In addition they were open to investment from abroad.

More controversial is the fact that in various degrees their governments intervened in the economies to promote industrialisation and exports. As the report states:

> Policy interventions took many forms: targeting and subsidizing credit to selected industries, keeping deposit rates low and maintaining ceilings on borrowing rates to increase profits and retained earnings, protecting domestic import substitutes, subsidizing declining industries, establishing and financially supporting government banks, making public investments in applied research, establishing firm- and industry-specific export targets, developing export marketing institutions, and sharing information widely between public and private sectors. Some industries were promoted while others were not.[11]

In evaluating these policies and their relevance for other developing countries, the report concludes that

> promotion of specific industries did not work and therefore holds little promise for other developing economies. Directed credit has worked in certain situations but carries high risk [in a world of very mobile capital where firms not favoured by directed credit can borrow abroad]. The export-push strategy has been by far the most successful of the three sets of policy intervention and holds the most promise for other developing countries.[12]

In any event, as we have observed, the trend in the past decade has been away from specific industrial policies.

10.5 INDIA

From the time of its independence in 1947 India has been one of the most democratic countries in the third world. It has, however, been subject to social unrest based on religious friction between Hindus and Muslims. The economy was, until recently, highly regulated and its performance was disappointing. Poverty and illiteracy are still widespread.

Jawarharlal Nehru, prime minister from 1947 to 1964, was influenced by Fabian socialist thinking in Britain and impressed by the Soviet Union's economic performance under central planning. Moreover the colonial heritage created a fear of foreign domination and hence a desire for self-sufficiency. A planning commission, presaged by a planning committee under Nehru in the 1930s, was established after independence, chaired by the prime minister. It prepared a series of five-year plans, beginning in 1951, that set out production goals and investment guidelines. An overriding purpose was to reduce poverty. Among the other objectives were the prevention of monopoly power, protection of small producers and the maintenance of a balance in economic development among India's diverse regions. These objectives were implemented by a system of licences regulating the activity of firms including the types of products they turned out and their ability to expand or contract their scale of production. It has been reported that, before recent reforms, 'a single application to set up an industrial plant had to satisfy as many as eighty-six different enactments and control agencies before receiving approval'.[13] In addition, many industries were nationalised. Of the 25 largest businesses in terms of sales in 1992, fourteen were owned by the government.

Imports were limited by both quantitative controls and very high tariffs (averaging over 100 per cent). Imports increased only 1.2 per cent per year in 1965–80. Direct investment from abroad was discouraged. As Finance Minister Manmohan Singh has wryly observed, India's experience of having one foreign trading company arrive (the East India Company early in the seventeenth century) and end up ruling the country had an influence on India's attitude towards direct investment from abroad.

India's system of controls over industry has been characterised as follows by Columbia University Professor Jagdish Bhagwati:

> The Indian planners and bureaucrats sought to regulate both domestic entry and import competition, to eliminate product diversification beyond what was licensed, to penalize unauthorized expansion of capacity, to allocate and prevent the reallocation of imported inputs, and indeed to define and delineate virtually all aspects of investment and production through a maze of Kafkaesque controls. This all-encompassing bureaucratic intrusiveness and omnipotence has no rationale in economic or social logic; it is therefore hard for anyone who is not a victim of it even to begin to understand what it means.[14]

This set of policies did not yield impressive results in terms of economic growth, successful industrialisation or the alleviation of poverty. From 1950 to 1980 real GDP increased by 3.7 per cent annually and per capita GDP went up by 1.7 per cent per year. Manufacturing output as a share of GDP was 19 per cent in 1990, having risen from 16 per cent in 1965. In comparison manufacturing comprised 34 per cent of GDP in east Asia and 25 per cent in Latin America in 1990. Yet investment in India was not low. In the 1960s it averaged 16.5 per cent of GDP and in the 1970s, 19.7 per cent. The problem was that resources were not being used efficiently and productivity rose only slowly.

The most positive development was not in industry but in agriculture. In the mid-1960s higher-yielding types of wheat and rice along with fertiliser, pesticides and improved irrigation were introduced. The result – the 'green revolution' – was a significant increase in the output of grains and the elimination of famines and the need to import grains. Nevertheless farm output increased only 2.8 per cent per year from 1965 to 1980. Two-thirds of the Indian work-force is in agriculture but it produces only one-third of the nation's total output.

India's experience of sluggish growth appears to be similar to what was observed in the Soviet Union: although saving and investment increased as a percentage of GDP, productivity growth was very slow. In the case of India, Bhagwati placed the blame for this poor record on (1) extensive bureaucratic controls over production, investment, and trade; (2) inward-looking trade and foreign investment policies; (3) a substantial public sector, going well beyond the conventional confines of public utilities and infrastructure. He adds another factor: 'India's failure to spread primary education and to raise literacy to anywhere near the levels that other countries have managed.'[15] In 1990 just over half of adult men and two-thirds of adult women were estimated to be illiterate.

One result of the policies outlined above was a shortage of electric power, rail transportation and communications facilities. Under Rajiv Ghandi, who succeeded his mother, Indira Ghandi, as prime minister after her assassination in October 1984, expenditures aimed at enlarging the capacity of and modernising such infrastructure were increased. Given the magnitude of the needs for investment, efforts were made to attract private capital into these areas of economic activity.

More important, Rajiv Ghandi began a process of structural economic reforms. Bhagwati suggests that Ghandi, a former pilot with Indian Airlines (the domestic carrier) and therefore the first prime minister who had worked outside politics, understood the disadvantages of the comprehensive system of controls on industry.[16] Ghandi proceeded to dismantle licensing in 25 industries. This included, for some industries, what in India is called 'broad-banding' – that is, permitting a variety of products in the general field in which the firm was licensed.

These and other reforms put through by the Ghandi government were, according to Bhagwati, 'a small step in the right direction; they generated enthusiasm simply because India seemed finally to be going down the right road.'[17] The reforms apparently encouraged a speed-up of economic activity. Industrial production rose 49 per cent in 1985–90 compared with 39 per cent in the previous five years.

Rajiv Ghandi had to leave office in 1989 in a corruption scandal and was assassinated during an election campaign in 1991. That brought P.V. Narasimha Rao to the prime minister's office and Manmohan Singh to the ministry of finance. Their first task was to deal with a macroeconomic crisis. The budget deficit had increased markedly in the 1980s and the inflation rate rose to almost 14 per cent in 1991. The current-account deficit and the foreign debt increased for several reasons: the Gulf war temporarily raised the cost of oil imports and cut off workers' remittances from the Middle East; exports to the former Soviet Union decreased; and the political uncertainties engendered by the assassination of Rajiv Ghandi led to capital flight. Foreign exchange reserves fell from $5.4 billion at the end of 1986 to $1.2 billion at the end of 1990 and even less during 1991. Questions were beginning to arise about India's ability to service its foreign debt.

The crisis forced the new government to act on these macroeconomic problems but also led it to reconsider the structural policies that had been pursued for many years. The successful performance of Korea and other East Asian countries probably had an influence in this respect.

An agreement with the IMF, under which India borrowed about $2.5 billion in 1991–2, involved policy conditions calling for reforms that a number of Indian economists had been advocating, especially after Rajiv Ghandi started the process. Thus in 1991 the question became not whether to reform but 'in what sequence, with what speed, with what chance of success?'[18] It began in July 1991.

The macroeconomic programme was standard. The budget deficit was reduced by an amount equal to 2 per cent of GDP within one fiscal year by cutting subsidies to agriculture and to state enterprises. In the next fiscal year the deficit was lowered by an additional 1 per cent of GDP. Monetary policy was tightened and the Indian rupee was devalued by 19 per cent.

Among the structural reforms, the extent of industrial licensing was severely curtailed: licensing, which had been in effect for decades, was abolished for all but 18 industries. But the 'no exit' policy remains in effect: firms with more than 100 employees are not permitted to discharge workers or to close down. Also eliminated were barriers to entry of new firms in areas previously reserved for public enterprises. At the same time an anti-trust system was set up.

While privatisation has not occurred, shares in profitable public enterprises were sold – first to financial institutions and later to private individuals as well. But, as Jagdish Bhagwati and Yale Professor T. N. Srinivasan have observed, 'the programme offered only a marginal stake in public sector enterprises to the private sector without any efficiency implications'.[19] Another reform measure reduced the potential size of the public sector by lowering the number of industries reserved to it from eighteen to eight. But the state enterprises are still not fully exposed to market competition or to a hard budget constraint.

With regard to foreign trade, export subsidies were abolished when the rupee was devalued and exporters were permitted to retain 30 per cent of their foreign exchange earnings. In March 1992 fairly complete convertibility on current account was introduced, though with a dual exchange rate – one of which was more favourable to essential imports. A year later the exchange-rate system was unified. Tariffs were lowered in both 1992 and 1993 but they still supplied a substantial portion of government revenue. Approval of foreign investment in India was made much more automatic in a wide range of industries and potential investors have responded though not on a massive scale. In the financial system a number of liberalising and deregulating measures were taken.

India has clearly started down the road to a significantly less state-controlled economy. Much remains to be done. Many restrictions on economic activity still exist. Public enterprises, even when they are not loss-makers, are inefficient and a drain on the budget; in 1990 they absorbed 44 per cent of investment funds but produced only 27 per cent of GDP.[20] A good case can be made for major privatisation, even of loss-making enterprises.[21] Subsidies to farmers, consumers and public enterprises, among other recipients, amount to more than 10 per cent of total government expenditures. Foreign trade needs much more liberalisation especially in the case of consumer goods, which are subject to both quantitative restrictions and high tariffs. Finally the financial system needs to be freed up so that it can perform its function of allocating credit where it does the most good in promoting efficiency and growth.

The likelihood that the Rao government will be able to continue reforming the Indian economy increased when state elections in November 1993 handed a defeat not only to the Hindu nationalist Bharatiya Janata party, which happens to favour reform, but also to leftist parties which do not. Finance Minister Singh made it known that he intended to introduce additional reforms in his budget to be presented in early 1994.

Meanwhile inflation declined to about 6 per cent and the economy was growing at a rate of 5 per cent in 1993. The inflow of capital, including a return of flight capital, led to a rebuilding of foreign exchange reserves to about $13 billion at the end of 1993.

It remains to be seen whether the elephant can be induced to move more rapidly.

11 Middle East and Africa: Oil, Wealth and Poverty

This chapter is concerned with a vast area running from the oil-rich Arabian peninsula with its sparse population through Egypt and its North African neighbours and on to the diverse but relatively under-developed countries of Sub-Saharan Africa. The term 'Middle East' does not denote a clearly defined geographical area. It sometimes refers to the entire region from Afghanistan to Mauritania, including Turkey. Other designations separate the so-called Maghreb countries: Algeria, Morocco, Tunisia and Libya; with Mauritania they are also referred to as North Africa as distinct from the Middle East. Whatever the grouping, these countries are mostly Islamic and, except for Iran and Turkey, make up a large part of the Arab world.

A precise designation is not necessary for our purposes. As in the case of other parts of the globe, we shall examine a few countries in which significant transformation has occurred. First it is necessary to take account of the impact of OPEC.

11.1 THE RISE AND FALL OF OPEC

The Organization of Petroleum Exporting Countries (OPEC) was founded in 1960 at a meeting in Baghdad among four Middle East oil-exporting countries – Iran, Iraq, Kuwait and Saudi Arabia – and Venezuela, the largest oil exporter in the Western Hemisphere. Although its membership grew to thirteen nations – including, among larger ones, Algeria, Indonesia, Libya and Nigeria – OPEC attracted little attention until 1973 when it became a household word by inflicting the severest shock to the world economy since World War II. After a partial oil embargo was declared by its Arab members during the Arab-Israeli War in

October 1973, OPEC announced two price increases. The oil price tripled from 1974 to 1975 (and crept up an additional 25 per cent by 1978). OPEC had become, at least for the time being, an effective cartel. Since in the short run the demand for oil is inelastic – that is, a change in price induces a relatively small change in the amount demanded – the cartel can increase its revenue by restricting the amount supplied as it raises the price. But, as became clear later, the OPEC members were not able to apply this simple principle. They could not agree on the division of the cartel's total output and it tended to exceed desired levels. Later, as the share of non-OPEC countries in world oil output increased, the cartel weakened further.

The sharply higher oil price in 1974–5, on top of already fast-rising commodity prices, aggravated inflation in oil-importing countries. The average price of all imports of industrial countries and non-oil developing countries rose about 75 per cent between 1972 and 1974. The oil-price increase also depressed the economies of the importing countries. The effect was like that of a large new sales tax.

The current-account surplus of the OPEC nations as a group rose spectacularly in one year, 1974, from $9 billion to $65 billion and, as noted in Chapter 2, they acquired large amounts of assets abroad. As a result of the newly-found power of the oil cartel, a number of fears arose among people in oil-importing countries: would OPEC raise the price again? Would it withhold oil, causing hardships of many kinds in importing countries? Would OPEC nations disrupt financial markets by withdrawing their substantial holdings of newly-acquired foreign assets or use them to buy up large parts of the economies of other countries? Given these worldwide concerns, journalists flocked to meetings of OPEC ministers. And they reported on every word and change in facial expression of Saudi Arabia's long-time oil minister, Sheik Ahmed Zaki Yamani.

As it happened, the oil-exporting countries quickly expanded their domestic spending and therefore their imports. By 1978 the OPEC current-account surplus had disappeared. Then the second oil shock occurred in 1979–80, as the result not of an OPEC decision but of the drop in Iran's oil output and a worldwide scramble to acquire oil in anticipation of still higher prices. The price advanced sharply once more, by about 160 per cent. Again the OPEC current-account surplus shot up, to reach $104 billion in 1980. As in 1975, the industrial world went into recession while inflation skyrocketed. The average import prices of industrial countries rose 46 per cent from 1978 to 1980. The non-oil developing countries were hit hard again by this combination of events.

The higher oil prices beginning in the early 1970s had predictable long-run effects on demand and supply. The price system worked, in the sense that new sources of supply of oil were developed in non-OPEC countries and the demand for oil decreased in response to the higher prices. New oil supplies came from the United Kingdom, Norway, the North Slope of Alaska, Mexico and other developing countries. Consequently OPEC's share in world oil exports fell from 88 to 67 per cent between 1979–81 and 1986. At the same time energy consumption in general and oil use in particular were economised. Automobiles became smaller and more fuel efficient, especially in the United States. Supplies of other forms of energy increased. After rising rapidly for many years, oil consumption in the industrial countries fell by more than 18 per cent between 1979 and 1985 while GDP increased 14 per cent. The members of OPEC were unable to agree on a concerted reduction in the total amount they supplied. This led Saudi Arabia, which had been acting as the 'balance wheel' – cutting its exports almost 75 per cent from 1980 to 1985 – to 'flood the market' and force the price down.[1] The average price of crude oil, which had decreased a little in 1981–83, dropped from $28.25 per barrel in 1984 to $13.80 per barrel in 1986. In this 'third oil shock', the effects in oil-importing countries were just the reverse of those when the price rose. And the OPEC current account, which had already moved into small deficit, registered a $33 billion deficit in 1986.

Except for a temporary spurt during the Gulf war the price of oil tended to decline during the recession of the early 1990s. In late 1993 the real price of oil – the price adjusted for the rise in the average price of exports of oil-importing countries – was not far from what it had been before the first oil shock. Sheik Yamani is quoted as saying that 'oil is not an ordinary commodity like tea or coffee. Oil is a strategic commodity. Oil is too important a commodity to be left to the vagaries of the spot and futures markets, or any other type of speculative endeavor'.[2] But that is precisely what has happened. OPEC appears to have lost its influence and prominence. That may, however, not be the end of the story. Just as high oil prices in the 1970s and early 1980s discouraged demand and stimulated new supplies, the current relatively low price may do the opposite and, in time, lead to upward pressure on oil prices again.

11.2 TURKEY

A member not of OPEC but of the industrial countries' Organisation for Economic Cooperation and Development (OECD), Turkey is one of the larger nations in the Middle East in terms of both area and population (59 million). Mostly in Asia, partly in Europe, Turkey has been a cross-roads for many centuries. On a visit to Antalya on the southern coast, I walked on the remains of a street on which Alexander the Great trod. Turkey has a common border with no less than seven countries: Syria, Iraq, Iran, Armenia, Georgia, Bulgaria and Greece.

In 1923 it became the first republic in the region. Mustapha Kemal Ataturk succeeded in converting his country into a modern, democratic, industrial, secular state, in which education and industrialisation were encouraged. In 1932, in advance of a number of European countries, he established women's suffrage. Turkey now has the first woman prime minister among Muslim Middle Eastern countries and women account for two-fifths of the physicists and chemists and one-sixth of the lawyers and doctors.

In economic, but not in social, policy Turkey under Ataturk became a model for other Middle Eastern countries after World War II. In the 1930s Ataturk had nurtured Turkey's industrialisation and development with pervasive state intervention, including 'five-year plans' and import substitution. Many public enterprises were established, protected by high tariffs and import restrictions. Here as in Latin America (see Chapter 12) the doctrine of *dependencia* flourished.

Turkey since 1980

The interventionist policies introduced by Ataturk did not prevent the development of a private sector in the economy.

> The public sector, concentrated in capital-intensive industries with large economies of scale, was to provide the inputs necessary for private industry and agriculture. Indeed, by 1980, the private sector, typically operating smaller plants producing consumer goods, accounted for about 70% of manufacturing value added.[3]

The economy had grown at respectable rates – about 6 per cent per year – in the post-war period up to the late 1970s. Then an economic crisis emerged. Unemployment was close to 10 per cent and concentrated in the cities. The state-owned enterprises required support from the budget – in amounts above 3 per cent of GDP – and inflation exceeded 10 per cent in 1980 while the current-account deficit soared. These were among the reasons, along with political unrest, for the military coup in that year. Trade unions were 'weakened or destroyed with the usual violence [of a military government]'.[4]

Somewhat as in Chile, as we shall see, the military government initiated a process of economic reform and macroeconomic stabilisation, relying on able technicians including Turgut Ozal, who continued to pursue these policies as prime minister after a return to civilian rule and elections in 1983. Export-led growth was adopted in place of import substitution. Over the years tariffs have been reduced and import controls have been eased; Turkey is aiming to form a customs union with the European Community in 1995 and eventual membership. Many prices were raised in an effort to make state-owned enterprises profitable and reduce the budgetary support they were receiving. A process of privatisation was begun and is proceeding, partly motivated by the government's desire for increased revenue. From 1981 to 1990 Turkey's GDP growth averaged 5.4 per cent per year and the current-account deficit shrank to manageable size. In 1992 Turkey had the highest rate of growth, and also the highest inflation rate, among OECD countries.

Ozal, who was elected president in 1989, died suddenly in April 1993. His long-time political rival, Suleyman Demirel, succeeded him. Mrs Tansu Ciller – like Ozal, a professional economist – became prime minister, pledging to pursue economic reform as well as women's rights.

While reform has much further to go, Turkey is a less regulated, more outward-oriented country than it was in 1980. But it has not solved the problem of maintaining macroeconomic stability. And politically it still faces the problem of Kurdish separatism in the southeastern part of the country.

11.3   SAUDI ARABIA

The desert kingdom of Saudi Arabia is the largest oil producer in the area and will be the focus of our attention among countries in the Gulf region. Its population in 1973 was 6.6 million in a land area one-third the size of the United States. Even before the first large oil-price advance, Saudi Arabia had been developing. It has been called 'a unique model of nation building in which a country has been able to transform its polity from the conditions of the eighteenth century to those of the twentieth century within three decades'.[5] In 1973 its exports, consisting almost entirely of oil, exceeded its imports of goods and services and it was accumulating reserves. The dollar value of its exports more than quadrupled in 1974. Foreign exchange reserves reached a peak of $28 billion in 1981, but that was only a fraction of the government's foreign holdings.

According to *The Economist,* government assets abroad in 1981 amounted to $110 billion and private Saudis had about $50 billion abroad.[6]

The enormous increase in export earnings, virtually all of which went to the government, provided the basis for a variety of infrastructure and other investment expenditures, including ports, airports, roads, schools, hospitals, housing, desalinisation plants, electric power facilities, new cities and heavy industries, especially petrochemicals and oil refineries. Even wheat is being grown, at a reported cost of $300 per ton[7] – three times the world price – supported by heavy subsidies and irrigated with water from underground aquifers that were discovered in the process of drilling for oil. Wheat production increased from about 3000 tons in 1975 to 1.7 million tons in 1985 and the country became an exporter of small amounts of wheat. Substantial expenditures on a military build-up were also undertaken. Defence spending amounted to nearly one-fifth of GDP in the years 1973–85. In addition, many social services, including education, were enlarged and supplied free to the Saudi population, who pay no taxes. The labour force to carry out many of these activities was supplemented by a sizable influx of foreign workers – not only from other Arab countries. According to official Saudi statistics – about which some doubts exist, given the difficulty of carrying out censuses – 43 per cent of all employees in 1979–80 were non-Saudis (and only 0.4 per cent were Saudi women).[8] Workers' remittances from Saudi Arabia amounted to $11.6 billion in 1990 and $13.7 billion in 1991.

As a result of the step-up in economic activity, Saudi Arabia's real GDP tripled between 1970 and 1980, while its population increased by one-half. Inflation averaged nearly 16 per cent per year in 1973–9. The face and economic structure of the country changed enormously in the 1970s. And so did the lives of Saudi Arabians. The proportion of the population living in the desert declined from about 60 to 46 per cent and in small towns it fell from 20 to 12 per cent. By 1980 more than two-fifths lived in cities of 100 000 or more people.

In international relations the country played a major role in OPEC. Its aim was to keep the price from going too high in opposition to OPEC members with much smaller oil reserves – and therefore shorter time horizons – or with political motivations in relation to oil-importing countries. In the management of its foreign exchange reserves the finance ministry and the Saudi Arabian Monetary Authority were well aware that they had a stake in the stability of the western markets in which their assets were invested. Belying a number of predictions, they did not try to use the assets abroad as leverage to gain political or economic advantage. It was clear to them that a threat to pull their funds out of a market would lead to a sharp fall in prices in that market long before their assets had been fully withdrawn.

Developments in the 1980s

In 1980 manufacturing other than that based on oil accounted for less than 3 per cent of Saudi Arabia's GDP. The government was encouraging the development of diversified manufacturing firms including those involving joint ventures with investors abroad. Two new cities, Jubail and Yanbu, were constructed by the government, complete with all the infrastructure needed to support manufacturing activity. By 1991 7 per cent of GDP came from manufacturing.

The oil boom faded in the early 1980s. The volume of Saudi Arabia's oil exports in 1985 was only 27 per cent of its level in 1980. The current account has been in deficit since 1983. With both the price and volume of oil exports down, the trade surplus declined from a peak of $81.9 billion in 1981 to a trough of $3.1 billion in 1986. In the early 1990s, when Iraq's production was off the market, Saudi Arabia's trade surplus rose a bit. But large payments abroad for services and official transfers in connection with the Gulf war kept the current account in deficit – by $27.7 billion in 1991 and $19.4 billion in 1992. The deficit must have increased considerably in 1993, when the price of oil dropped sharply. Saudi Arabia's foreign assets are estimated to have decreased from $138 billion to $51 billion or less from 1983 to 1993.[9]

Saudi Arabia's development programme in the 1970s and 1980s was undertaken largely by the government, whether directly or through the Saudi Basic Industries Corporation (SABIC). In the second half of the 1980s some privatisation was carried out and the development plan aimed at promoting the private sector. Part of the motivation was the declining income of the government as oil prices sagged. At the beginning of 1994 King Fahd announced that budgeted expenditures would be cut by 20 per cent, as revenues had fallen off with the decline in oil prices. Until this announcement, Saudi Arabia represented an exception to the general tendency we have observed towards less government involvement in the economy. The reasons were more pragmatic than ideological, given the enormous revenues accruing to the government during the oil boom.

On balance, Saudi Arabia's GDP stagnated after 1982. It declined through 1985 and then advanced at about 5 per cent annually through 1991. Population grew by 4.6 per cent per year in 1980–91. As a result, per capita GDP decreased, on average, by more than 3 per cent per year over the decade to 1991. That left it 50 per cent higher than in 1970 for an annual growth rate in per capita GDP of only 1.9 per cent over the two decades.

Nevertheless the quality of life improved. During the 1980s life expectancy increased from 54 to 69 years and adult literacy rose from 25 to 62 per cent. Between 1975 and 1990 primary school enrolment increased from 42 to 62 per cent and secondary school enrolment went up from 12 to 48 per cent. While in 1970 the proportion of girls in primary school was less than half the number of boys, by 1990 that proportion had risen to 84 per cent. In secondary schools it rose from 16 to 79 per cent.[10]

Saudi Arabia continues as an absolute monarchy in which the large royal family functions in leadership roles throughout the economic and political systems. An appointed consultative assembly (the Shura Council) has been established and held its first meeting in December 1993.

11.4   EGYPT

Egypt came into the 1980s with a highly-regulated economy in which public enterprises were responsible for 27 per cent of GDP and 60 per cent of value added in manufacturing. These enterprises often required subsidies and were protected by high tariffs and import substitution policies. Like many Middle East countries Egypt had been influenced by developments in Turkey under Ataturk. In the 1970s and early 1980s Egypt benefited, as an oil producer, from the high oil prices and also received remittances ($2.7 billion in 1980) from its migrant workers who were employed in Saudi Arabia and elsewhere. The end of the oil boom led the government to undertake sizeable public expenditures, which enlarged both the budget deficit and the current-account deficit and created a heavy foreign debt burden.

A reform programme – pursuit of *infitah* (economic opening or liberalisation), which started in the 1970s under Anwar Sadat – was revived in 1990, under the aegis of the IMF. It involves improving the efficiency of loss-making public enterprises, some privatisation and some reduction of tariffs, as well as macroeconomic policies aimed at budget-deficit reduction and a lowering of inflation. The reform programme has been pursued cautiously, partly because President Mubarak is concerned about worsening unemployment and thereby encouraging the militant Islamic fundamentalist movement, which has made itself felt, among other acts, by attacking tourists (thereby harming an important source of foreign exchange), attempting to assassinate officials and setting off a bomb in one of the pyramids.

Nevertheless the budget deficit was brought down drastically and inflation dropped from near 20 to about 12 per cent in 1993. Privatisation of 300 state-owned enterprises is going ahead at a slow pace. Meanwhile unemployment remains high and Egypt faces the problem, both economic and political, of absorbing a half million or more new workers each year into employment.

11.5 OTHER MIDDLE EASTERN COUNTRIES

The story is quite similar in other countries of the region. While some have benefited more than others from oil resources, they share the experience of coping with high unemployment despite overmanning in state-owned enterprises. In some nations, such as Algeria, high unemployment, especially among those more educated, nourishes Islamic fundamentalism. There has been movement away from the Ataturk model towards less state intervention in economies, encouragement of private activity and greater openness to the outside world. But it is far from complete. According to Said El-Naggar, former professor at Cairo University:

> It is difficult to justify that, in many Arab countries, the government continues to be involved in such activities as grocery and department stores, bakeries, flour mills, printing, bookshops, advertising, hotels, travel agencies, contracting, cattle and poultry farming, fisheries, and scores of other activities. These are normally the kinds of activities that are better and more effectively undertaken by the private sector.[11]

11.6 SUB-SAHARAN AFRICA

The nations of Sub-Saharan Africa other than South Africa do not require a great amount of space here. That is so not because there is little to say about that region but because hardly any economic transformation has taken place there.

In the period since 1980 'the continent of woe', as IMF Managing Director Michel Camdessus describes it, has experienced declining income per capita, rapid population growth, the worst drought of this century in 1992, the spread of Aids, rising foreign debt (mainly to official lenders) and environmental degradation. In some countries civil strife, if not civil war, exists and governments barely function. In the twelve years ending 1992, per capita GDP fell by more than 15 per cent. Life expectancy at birth is 51 years and half the population is illiterate.

Part of the explanation for the economic woe is that most of these countries are highly dependent on basic commodities – including oil, copper, cocoa, coffee, cotton, tea and tobacco – for export earnings and the prices of these products have tended to decline in the past decade, especially during the recession of the early 1990s. Sub-Saharan Africa's terms of trade have deteriorated steadily since 1984. Moreover, there has been loss of market share in some of these commodities to other developing countries.

More broadly, with a few exceptions the Sub-Saharan countries have failed to diversify beyond the production of primary commodities. Domestic investment is relatively low, foreign investment has gone mainly to oil-exporting countries and foreign aid is insufficient even where it is used effectively.

There are a few exceptions to this sad economic story. Botswana, with its diamonds, grew about 9 per cent per year in 1980–92. Burkina Faso, Burundi, Chad, Congo, and Mauritius had GDP growth rates above 5 per cent per year. They have been joined since 1985 by Djibouti, Gambia and Mali. These nine countries account for only 7.6 per cent of the population of Sub-Saharan Africa.[12]

This is not the place for prescription. For that one may turn to the World Bank and the International Monetary Fund with their structural adjustment programmes, some of which have produced successful results.

11.7 SOUTH AFRICA

South Africa is in the midst of a remarkably peaceful, and historic, political transformation. In time there will undoubtedly be economic transformation as well.

The country has been described as one in which a first world and a third world live side by side. How the relationships between these two worlds will evolve is impossible to predict but they will certainly change fundamentally, with significant economic consequences.

12 Democratisation and Reform in Latin America

The 1980s became known as 'the lost decade' in Latin America. For the region as a whole, GDP grew little more than 1 per cent per year compared with almost 6 per cent in the previous decade. As a result, per capita GDP fell by more than 10 per cent in the 1980s. There were few exceptions – Chile and Colombia among them – to this declining trend in real income. The recession of 1981–2 in the industrial countries and the debt crisis that erupted in the summer of 1982 had much to do with the sharp turnaround in the economic well-being of Latin America in the 1980s. But the early 1990s saw substantial improvement as economic reforms were adopted and some debt relief was obtained.

Meanwhile, and perhaps remarkably, Latin America moved towards more democratic political regimes despite the economic tribulations. In 1979 military dictatorships or juntas ruled in much of South and Central America. Elected presidents governed only in Colombia, Venezuela and Costa Rica. By 1993, although political uncertainties existed in Peru and Venezuela, every country in Latin America had a popularly-elected president.

This chapter first considers Latin America as a whole and then examines Mexico's transformation in some detail, followed by briefer observations on Argentina, Chile and Brazil.

12.1 BACKGROUND

Most nations of Latin America grew at a rapid pace in the 1960s and 1970s – an average of 5.7 per cent per year in the entire region. After 1973, a number of these countries became heavy borrowers from banks in the industrial world. As noted in Chapter 2, the banks were accumulating deposits on a massive scale from oil-exporting countries and were looking for profitable outlets for these funds. They used the technique of syndicated loans – shared by many banks – denominated mainly in dollars and bearing variable interest rates tied to the 6-month Eurodollar rate in London (London interbank offer rate, or Libor). The banks actively peddled these loans to South American borrowers, both governmental and private. The term 'loan pushing' came into use as the surpluses of OPEC nations were 'recycled' to promising-looking developing countries. The borrowers in turn welcomed the loans as a means of financing both the increased cost of imported oil and higher domestic investment.

During most of the 1970s the interest rates on these loans were very low when measured in real terms. It became conventional to judge real interest rates by comparing nominal rates with the annual increase in the export prices of the borrowers. For the heavy debtors, most of which were in South America, the average interest rate on loans from private creditors – mainly commercial banks – ranged from 7.5 to 9 per cent while export prices were rising on average by more than 14 per cent per year. To debtors it looked like a bargain. And the debt piled up. In Latin America as a whole, total long-term debt – that with a maturity of more than one year – increased from $27.8 billion in 1970 to $238.5 billion in 1982. The ratio of long-term debt to GNP rose from 18.3 to 33.5 per cent.[1]

How were these sizeable capital inflows used by the borrowing countries? They were able to finance enlarged current-account deficits. The deficit of the region rose from $7.6 billion in 1974 to $41.6 billion in 1982. While interest payments also increased, as noted, the debtors were in receipt of 'net transfers' – the excess of new borrowing over interest payments. That in turn financed higher domestic investment. In some countries it also financed capital flight, motivated by tax evasion or fear of political instability or expected inflation and currency depreciation.

Nevertheless, the process looked sustainable to many observers as the debtors appeared to thrive. Therefore the maturing loans were easily rolled over or refinanced with new loans. Among the more memorable statements of the period was that of Walter Wriston, Chairman of Citicorp in New York, to the effect that governments do not go bankrupt. It is only fair to report that I wrote in 1981: 'Given the high rate of investment, the strong rate of growth, and the availability of oil, it is hard to believe that Mexico will not continue to look like a good credit risk.' But I also noted that 'if real interest rates [in industrial countries] do not come down soon, the outlook for debt-financed economic development is bleak.'[2]

12.2 ONSET OF THE DEBT CRISIS

Whether or not the recycling could have continued smoothly under normal conditions is a moot question. The disruption of the process began with the Iranian revolution and the fall-off of Iran's oil exports, which had accounted for nearly 10 per cent of world oil output. The international price of oil rose in a series of jumps in 1979–80, cumulating to a price increase of almost 150 per cent.

As in 1973–4, inflation speeded up and economic activity slowed in many countries. To combat the inflation, central banks in industrial countries tightened monetary policy and interest rates rose steeply. Libor, which had averaged 9.2 per cent in 1978, was 16.7 per cent in 1981. That in turn caused the interest payments of the debtors to balloon. Latin American interest payments increased from 12.2 per cent of exports earnings in 1978 to 30.3 per cent in 1982.

The combination of sharply higher interest rates, slackening exports to industrial countries in recession and higher costs of imported oil enlarged the balance-of-payments deficits of the debtor countries. Ironically the debt crisis started not in what looked like the most vulnerable country, Brazil, but in an oil-exporting nation, Mexico, that had appeared as highly creditworthy. In August 1982 Mexico temporarily suspended its debt service.[3]

When Mexico suspended, the banks quickly cut back their lending to all debtors and that threw all of them into crisis. In order to continue to meet the interest obligations on their debts to banks and other creditors abroad, the debtors had to conserve foreign exchange by reducing their imports. That required them to slash their domestic investment. In Latin America the volume of imports fell by 37.7 per cent in 1982–3 and investment as a proportion of GDP declined from 23.4 per cent to 17.0 per cent from 1980 to 1983. The result was a drastic slowdown in economic growth and in per capita output.

Why did the debtor governments not default – that is, stop paying interest so that they could use their scarce foreign exchange to buy imports? Various answers can be given. It has been said that the heads of state of the largest debtors did not want to disconnect their economies from the world financial system nor to risk a foreign policy rupture with the United States. More specifically, they depended on foreign commercial banks for short-term credit to finance their trade and did not want to see it withdrawn. And the debtor governments must have been motivated by the wish to maintain creditworthiness in the hope of future inflows of capital. Also, if they were to stop all debt service, capital flight probably would have intensified.[4]

12.3   DEALING WITH THE DEBT CRISIS

Initially the debt crisis had two aspects: the squeeze on debtor countries as noted above and the danger that many banks in industrial countries would be in serious trouble if the debtors defaulted. Motivated by these two concerns the IMF, then under the leadership of Managing Director Jacques de Larosière, induced the banks to undertake 'concerted lending' to many of the debtor countries as a condition for loans to the debtors by the IMF along with its 'seal of approval' on their policies. But such lending soon petered out. The banks were reluctant to put additional loans on their books when repayment was uncertain and the market prices for such loans – which were traded among banks and other investors – were at a fraction of their face value.

In the autumn of 1985 US Treasury Secretary James Baker announced a plan aimed at restoring growth in the debtor countries. He may have been motivated by a fear that Mexico would suspend its interest payments again in the face of the decline in oil prices.[5] The Baker plan called on the commercial banks in industrial countries and on the multilateral development banks (the World Bank and its regional counterparts in Latin America, Asia, and Africa) to increase their lending to the debtor countries by a total of $40 billion over three years. As it turned out, new lending fell well short of that goal.

Then in March 1989 Baker's successor, Nicholas Brady, proposed a plan involving debt and debt service reduction as well as new lending by the commercial banks – all of which was to be assisted by new credits to the debtors from the IMF and World Bank. Debt reduction programmes were worked out for Argentina, Costa Rica, Mexico, Nigeria, the Philippines, Uruguay and Venezuela.

Although the result was a relatively small decrease in the annual interest payments of the debtors, the Brady plan appears to have had a catalytic effect, especially in Mexico. In combination with Mexico's economic reforms, it led to a large inflow of private capital – both a return flow of Mexican capital that had fled the peso and foreign direct and portfolio investment. A similar inflow of funds occurred in other debtor countries.

Since 1989, when the Brady plan was announced, the debt burden has decreased significantly. For the fifteen most heavily-indebted developing countries (most of which are in Latin America) the ratio of interest payments abroad to exports of goods and services fell from 23.3 per cent to 17.3 per cent between 1988 and 1992. In Mexico, according to Finance Minister Pedro Aspe, that ratio declined from 43.6 per cent to 18.5 per cent between 1982 and 1991.[6] In addition, substantial inflows of capital have enabled the debtor countries once again to incur and finance current-account deficits. The aggregate current-account deficit of Latin American countries increased from $6.0 billion to $34.4 billion from 1990 to 1992. That in turn made possible higher rates of domestic investment and a resumption of economic growth. In Latin America as a whole, GDP growth in 1991–2 picked up to 2.9 per cent – almost three times the rate in the 1980s. There was a large amount of variation behind that average figure; Argentina, Chile and Venezuela grew by 8 per cent or more. The average was held down by slow growth or stagnation in Brazil and Peru.

What made all this possible was a return of confidence on the part of foreign investors and domestic residents who had engaged in capital flight. Much of the inflow took the form of purchases of stock (some through the many emerging market mutual funds that have sprung up) and direct investment. Companies in Latin America issued $4.1 billion of stock on international markets in both 1991 and 1992 and more than that in the first half of 1993.[7] Almost half of the capital inflow consisted of what the IMF calls 'non-debt-creating flows'. The inflows were so substantial that foreign exchange reserves in Latin America more than tripled between 1989 and 1993, reaching more than $103 billion. While welcome, the large inflow created some problems for the monetary authorities. Prices of real estate and equities have risen. In some countries the exchange rate has appreciated, and restrictive monetary policy has been undermined, leading central banks to seek ways to sterilize the inflows.

The resumption of capital flow to Latin America in the early 1990s sparked some concern about a new debt crisis *à la* 1982. That cannot be ruled out, given Latin America's history of debt problems going back to the nineteenth century. And a part of the inflow, the debt-creating part, must have been a reflection of the relatively low interest rates in the United States, which were bound to rise at some point. Yet there were important differences between the situation in 1993 and what happened in the 1970s and early

1980s. For one thing domestic economic policies in most countries of Latin America are more effective now: budget deficits are smaller and inflation is lower. The debtor countries are less vulnerable to an increase in interest rates in the United States and elsewhere, given the form of the capital inflows. Moreover the recipient countries have been accumulating reserves, as noted, and that provides a cushion against a cessation or reversal of the inflow of capital.[8]

Meanwhile structural economic reforms of various types have been pursued, including deregulation, privatisation, and the lowering of trade barriers. The latter includes Mercosur, a trade agreement among Argentina, Brazil, Paraguay and Uruguay.

Perhaps the most striking example of economic transformation in Latin America since 1980 is that of Mexico.

12.4 MEXICO

Mexico is the second most populous country in Latin America, and its history, both political and economic, has been very much influenced by its contiguity with the United States. 'Poor Mexico, so far from God and so near to the United States', said Porfirio Diaz, long-time dictatorial president in the late nineteenth and early twentieth centuries.

Structural economic reform in Mexico has been spectacular in recent years. Although it started under the presidency of Miguel de la Madrid Hurtado (1982–8), it has moved rapidly and comprehensively since Carlos Salinas de Gortari succeeded him in December 1988.

The reforms, it has been written,

are part of a fundamental shift in the government's development strategy, which aims at a substantial increase in the role of market forces and private incentives in the economy, while limiting that of the state to establishing the appropriate legislative and administrative framework for the private sector to create productive employment and wealth.[9]

The Mexican government appears to have discarded three elements that influenced its economic philosophy for many years: fear of domination by the United States, a large ownership and regulatory role for the public sector and import substitution rather than open trade. Salinas's enthusiastic embrace of NAFTA is evidence of these changes.

In other words, Mexico has abandoned dependency theory (*dependencia*), which earlier had widespread popularity in Latin America and elsewhere. According to that thesis, developing countries were dependent on industrial countries and were exploited by them. This was thought to hinder development in the Third World while industrial nations profited from their economic relationships with those developing countries.[10]

Mexico's economic reforms show up, according to Finance Minister Aspe, in land tenure and use, deregulation of industry, privatisation of state-owned enterprises, import liberalisation, tariff reductions and promotion of direct investment from abroad, freeing up of the financial system and an improved budget policy.[11] As it undertook these reforms, Mexico also succeeded in lowering its inflation rate to well under 10 per cent compared with an average of more than 90 per cent per year in 1983–8. It also achieved a budget surplus, thanks in part to receipts from privatisation, after many years of large deficits. In these circumstances, it has, as noted, attracted enormous amounts of both Mexican flight capital and foreign capital.

While economic reform has proceeded in a breathtaking manner, Mexico's political system continues to be dominated by the Institutional Revolutionary Party (PRI) and each outgoing president in effect chooses his successor in what has been called 'democracy by designation'. (A Mexican friend has pointed out to me that the two post-war American presidents who served two full terms and were therefore ineligible for re-election – Eisenhower and Reagan – chose their successors.)

Background

Under the presidency of José Lopez Portillo (1976–82) large new oil discoveries were made, raising Mexico's proven reserves from 6 billion to more than 70 billion barrels between 1975 and 1982. Oil revenues increased from less than one-fifth to more than half of export proceeds. On the basis of this bonanza – at the higher oil price engineered by OPEC in 1973 – Lopez Portillo was able to 'administer the abundance' by undertaking massive public sector expenditures. The budget deficit rose from 4.7 per cent to 15.4 per cent of GDP in the Portillo years. Mexico's larger oil reserves also enhanced its creditworthiness in the eyes of bankers abroad. As a result, its external debt rose $50 billion to reach $85.8 billion in 1992.

Although Mexico looked like a good credit risk, its prospects began to deteriorate in 1981. The price of oil, which had risen sharply again in the second oil shock, turned down. The United States, Mexico's chief trade partner, went into recession. As noted earlier, interest rates on dollar obligations rose steeply. Thus Mexico's annual interest payments went up 250 per cent, from $2.2 billion in 1978 to $7.7 billion in 1982. When policymakers failed to react quickly to these unfavourable developments, private Mexican capital poured out of the country in anticipation of a depreciation of the peso. Capital flight is estimated to have exceeded $11 billion in 1981 – about 40 per cent of export earnings. In early 1982, with foreign exchange reserves dropping, the peso was devalued and a moderate budget-deficit reduction was announced.

According to Brookings Institution scholar Nora Lustig, Lopez Portillo, in his last year in office,

> felt betrayed by the private sector, which he believed took advantage of the many subsidies provided during the oil boom and yet did not respond to his call for cooperation, but rather engaged in continuous and massive capital flight. As an alternative he turned to the labor sector and

to the members of his cabinet who were more on the left and pro-state, a move that also explains his subsequent decision to nationalize the banking sector.[12]

In these conditions banks abroad cut back on their lending and Mexico's reserves ran low in 1982. The Federal Reserve propped them up for a while with overnight loans to the Bank of Mexico at the end of each month, thereby 'window dressing' the size of Mexico's published reserves.[13] The rationale was that Mexico needed to buy time until the new president – already known to be Miguel de la Madrid – took office and would agree to a stabilisation pact with the IMF.

But the banks had stopped lending and capital flight had increased as Mexico's inflation soared. Foreign exchange reserves were exhausted and in August the Mexican authorities declared a temporary standstill on debt service payments to creditor banks.

The Mexican government, in Lopez Portillo's last months in office, imposed exchange controls in an effort to stem the flight of capital, devalued the peso again, and, as noted, nationalised the banks.

Many reasons can be cited for this débâcle in Mexico.[14] One faulty assumption, held by both the lending banks abroad and the Mexican authorities, was that the oil boom would go on indefinitely.

Coping with the Debt Crisis

De la Madrid's government, with Jesus Silva Herzog remaining as finance minister and Angel Gurria as chief debt negotiator, achieved greater consensus than that of his predecessor. It set about reducing the outsized fiscal deficit and devaluing the peso – a combination of policies aimed at improving the trade balance but which also worsened inflation. At the same time principal payments on the external debt were rescheduled and interest payments were resumed, helped by a credit agreement with the IMF. A medium-term goal of the government was to reduce inflation, which had risen from 17.5 per cent in 1978 to more than 100 per cent in 1983. One result was a sharp decline in real wages, by more than 30 per cent in 1983–5.

Meanwhile net transfers, which had been a positive $6.4 billion in 1981, turned negative, amounting to $8.8 billion in 1984. Mexico's GDP declined by more than 5 per cent in 1983 and, partly for this reason, the target for the current account of the balance of payments was over-achieved: there was a surplus in 1983–5. Considering that net transfers were negative and foreign exchange reserves were low, Mexico did not have the means to finance a current-account deficit.

Despite the drastic stabilisation programme, another run on the peso occurred in mid-1985. This led to an additional round of restrictive fiscal and monetary policies and another peso depreciation. Successive efforts at fiscal policy reform were frustrated in part by the large deficits of state enterprises, which were financed by the central government.

Of greater long-run significance, a structural reform measure was adopted: trade liberalisation was begun. The proportion of imports not subject to licensing, which had been zero in December 1982, rose from 16.4 per cent in December 1984 to 64.1 per cent in July 1985.[15]

Mexico City suffered a severe earthquake in October 1985, which brought small amounts of financial relief from the IMF and World Bank. And then in 1986 the world price of oil fell. Mexico's export price dropped from over $25 to $12 per barrel. Although non-oil exports had been growing, oil still accounted for more than two-thirds of export proceeds in 1985. This loss of export earnings amounted to 6.7 per cent of GDP. As a result of this and the 1985 stabilisation programme, Mexico's GDP fell by 3.9 per cent in 1986 as domestic investment declined by more than one-fifth.

To deal with the loss of export earnings and continue to pay interest on its debt, the government had to devalue the peso again. This led to another acceleration of inflation as import prices shot up but the trade balance remained in surplus and foreign exchange reserves rose somewhat. This devaluation was successful in part because real wages were flexible downwards: nominal wages did not rise in line with prices. In this as well as other respects, Mexico differed from some other Latin American countries.

With the advent of the Baker plan, Mexico received in late 1986 $6 billion in new loans and much of its public and private debt was rescheduled with longer maturities and a seven-year grace period. The easing of Mexico's external financial position provided the basis for the government to initiate several reforms in 1987–8: an 'economic solidarity pact' aimed at lowering inflation by reduction in the budget deficit, moderate wage indexation, agreements with industry on inflation targets, additional trade liberalisation and privatisation of public enterprises.[16]

The pact brought the inflation rate down in 1988 but economic growth was only 1.3 per cent. That led the new government that took office in December 1988 under Carlos Salinas de Gortari to announce a 'pact for economic stability and growth'. It was aimed at holding inflation down and attracting capital inflow by Mexicans and foreign investors. Such an inflow of funds would reduce or reverse net outward transfers, which had averaged $7.2 billion per year in 1983–8 (not counting capital flight).

Then in March 1989 the Brady plan was proposed and Mexico became the second country to take advantage of it. Although the final agreement with the commercial banks was not signed until February 1990, it was retroactive to July 1989. The agreement provided debt relief in three forms: a reduction of principal by 35 per cent on a portion of the debt, a lower and fixed interest rate of 6.25 per cent on another portion, and new 15-year loans.[17] The banks were free to choose among these three options. The net result was a decrease in Mexico's annual interest payments by $1.4 billion and additional loans of about $670 per year for four years.

While the annual interest saving was not large, the agreement was greeted by the Mexican authorities with a degree of enthusiasm that was puzzling at the time. I later concluded that 'they accepted the best bargain they could get and, having done so, tried to strengthen the confidence of investors at home and abroad in the economic prospects of their economy'.[18] The agreement was followed, at least for a while, by a drop in domestic interest rates. It also provided the backdrop for a number of structural reforms. In May 1990 the Salinas government announced its intention to re-privatise the banks, which Lopez Portillo had nationalised in 1982. This announcement had a highly favourable effect on market sentiment and apparently induced a return of some flight capital. As a result, short-term interest rates fell from 46 per cent to 32 per cent in the second quarter of 1990 when inflation was running at an annual rate of about 20 per cent.

The tax system was reformed in 1987 and 1989 in order to encourage private investment. Among the measures adopted were reductions in the highest personal income taxes, elimination of taxes on dividends, a decrease in the value-added tax, and a cut in income taxes for lower income groups. The loss of revenue was made up by a special tax on the assets of all firms and elimination of some tax exemptions.[19]

For many years government ownership of enterprises was widespread, in fields of economic activity that included oil production, sugar refining, automobile manufacturing and insurance. Privatisation of state enterprises began under de la Madrid: from 1982 to 1988 the number of state-owned firms was reduced from 1100 to 420 through mergers, liquidations and sales.[20] The process was accelerated after 1988 by the Salinas government. 'More than 80 per cent of the 1115 state-run companies that existed in 1982 were no longer in the hands of the government by the end of 1991.'[21] The largest privatisation was of Telefonos de Mexico, with a value of $1.8 billion.

As Aspe has observed, the private sector was privatised first, by removing subsidies on inputs and interest rates and by dismantling trade barriers so as to 'wean private industry away from an unhealthy dependence on the public sector'.[22]

Another basic reform under President Salinas was in rural Mexico, where the *ejidos* – akin to communes – can now be transformed into privately-owned farms. Mexican agriculture had been inefficient and output was stagnant.

Deregulation has been carried out in industry. One example: free entry was permitted into the trucking industry, which is vital in Mexico where the railway system is underdeveloped. The result was improved service and lower charges.[23]

Benedicte Larre has written that the reform of trade policy in Mexico since 1985

> is one of the most drastic breaks with the country's interventionist traditions; it is designed to expose the economy to international competition and to reverse the legacy of several decades of import substitution policy, which has led to a steady decline in the ratio of exports to GDP.[24]

Mexico joined the General Agreement on Tariffs and Trade (GATT) in 1986. Its trade liberalisation measures consisted of the elimination of import licences for many products, tariff reductions and the encouragement of direct investment from abroad. Import licences covered 83 per cent of imports in 1984 and 9 per cent in 1991. The average tariff dropped from 27 per cent in 1982 to 13 per cent in 1991. The flow of foreign direct investment to Mexico increased from less than $500 million in 1985 to $5.4 billion in 1992.

The financial system has also been reformed. Not only were the banks privatised but interest rates were deregulated and banks were given greater freedom of action to move in the direction of universal banks, as in Germany.

While Mexico's industry had grown rapidly under the earlier policy of protectionism and import substitution, its growth, like that in Eastern Europe and Russia, was extensive in nature; that is, it relied on increasing inputs of labour and capital rather than on rising productivity. The available evidence, though it is subject to some qualifications, shows a pick-up in the advance of productivity after the mid-1980s.[25]

In the summer of 1990 President Salinas suggested talks with the United States on a free trade agreement, which led to the Nafta proposal, later joined by Canada. This was the final step in Mexico's discarding of its fear of American dominance as well as the culmination of Mexico's actions to liberalise its trade. The major benefit to Mexico from

NAFTA would come from an increased inflow of investment capital from the United States.

The Outlook

Illustrative of the change in official thinking in Mexico about the role of the central government in economic affairs is the recent proposal by Salinas to make the central bank – the Bank of Mexico – independent. This type of measure appears to have become a litmus test of governments' adherence to free market principles. In this and other ways, as *The Wall Street Journal* put it in mid-1993, 'Mr. Salinas is using the sweeping powers of the Mexican chief executive to diminish the power of his successors.'[26]

Illustrative of the changed attitude abroad towards Mexico is the invitation it has received to join the Organization for Economic Cooperation and Development (OECD) in Paris, which is generally regarded as an association of industrial countries. Although the growth rate slowed in 1992–3 as Mexico's exports were affected by recession in the industrial countries, the OECD, in its first published survey of a developing country, forecast that Mexico's growth would accelerate to 6 per cent annually in the mid-1990s.

While industrial nations were once distinguished from developing countries by their current-account surpluses, that is no longer so. As we have seen in earlier chapters, a number of industrial countries have had current-account deficits for some time. Mexico's current-account deficit was $22.8 billion in 1992, financed largely by direct investment and portfolio capital inflows.

In general Mexico has undergone a striking economic transformation. Of course the country still has many serious economic problems. Environmental pollution is severe, especially in Mexico City. Income distribution is highly unequal. Poverty is widespread and it worsened during the period of declining per capita GDP in the 1980s. From 1977 to 1989 real earnings per worker fell by 37 per cent; in the next two years they rose by 11.7 per cent.[27] But dissatisfaction exists, as shown by the uprising in southern Mexico in early January 1994.

Another question concerns Mexico's political system. The dominance of the PRI has lessened somewhat; the opposition party PAN is now in control of three of the Mexican states. Movement away from the one-party system and truly 'democratic elections would be a big step.

Still, the latest Mexican 'revolution', if it continues to bring prosperity to the Mexican people, is bound to have a 'demonstration effect' elsewhere in Latin America, encouraging further pursuit of economic reforms throughout the region.

12.5   ARGENTINA

In the first three decades of this century Argentina was by far the wealthiest 'developing' country. Anyone who visits Buenos Aires is reminded more of Paris and Rome than of the capitals of third world countries. In 1900 and 1929 Argentina's per capita GDP was about three times that of Brazil, almost twice that of Japan and roughly equal to GDP per person in Austria, Italy and Norway. That early prosperity was based on Argentina's agricultural land. The pampas have been called 'the most fertile tract of land in the world'[28] and they provided ample export revenues in the decades before 1930. By 1987 Argentina's per capita GDP was slightly lower than Brazil's and only a little more than one-third that of Italy.[29]

A military junta ruled Argentina from 1976 to 1982 when, after the Falklands/Malvinas fiasco, it resigned. In 1983 Raul Alfonsin was elected to the presidency. The country had been plagued by economic instability and triple-digit inflation from the mid-1970s. In Alfonsin's first year the budget deficit was more than 14 per cent of GDP and consumer prices rose 344 per cent. Inflation was even worse in 1984–5. Various attempts by the Alfonsin government to stabilise the economy – mainly the Austral Plan of 1985 and the Primavera Plan of 1988 – were undermined by continued fiscal deficits. Inflation fell to 90 per cent in 1986 but only temporarily. In 1989 it exceeded 3000 per cent or more than 2 per cent per day. It is not surprising that Argentinians moved their funds out of pesos into dollars in large amounts.

In those conditions of hyperinflation and rampant capital flight, Carlos Menem, a member of the Peronist party and governor of the state of La Rioja, was elected president in 1989. He did not give the impression of being an economic reformer who would tackle both the macroeconomic and structural problems of Argentina. In the first peaceful transfer of power since 1928, the economic crisis led Alfonsin to resign and cede the office to Menem five months early – in July 1989.

The chaos created by hyperinflation made for a public mood that welcomed economic reform. Menem immediately announced a series of measures that included a sharp cut in the budget deficit through both expenditure restraints and tax increases, a tight rein on monetary policy, a devaluation of the currency, liberalisation of imports and tariff reductions and a privatisation programme. 'Mr. Menem has adroitly used his Peronist credentials to reverse almost everything Gen. Peron did.'[30]

While hyperinflation continued in 1990, the price advance slowed sharply in 1991. By mid-1993 annual inflation was about 10 per cent. This was the result not only of fiscal reform but of an unusually stringent monetary policy: by law the central bank may add to bank reserves and therefore to the money supply only to the extent that Argentina's foreign exchange reserves rise. The exchange rate has also been stabilised and is pegged to the dollar. Meanwhile the economy's growth rate picked up to 8.8 per cent per year in 1991–2 from 2.5 per cent in 1970–79 and a net decline in the 1980s. Thus the macroeconomic situation in Argentina is at its most favourable in a long while.

At the same time a highly regulated economy was liberalised. By presidential decree numerous restrictions on economic activity were eliminated. Tariffs were also slashed, confronting Argentine businesses with more intense competition from abroad. Privatisation has proceeded at a rapid pace and employment by the state (including state-owned enterprises) is expected to have declined from 290 000 in 1989 to 41 000 at the end of 1993.[31] Among the firms sold off are the national oil company YPF (*Yacimientos Petroliferos Fiscales*), the railways, and the telephone system and other utilities. Privatisation brought revenues to the treasury and has led to more efficient management but it has also elicited demands for regulation of the prices charged by the utilities. Privatisation has also strengthened confidence in the reform intentions of the government, thereby encouraging a repatriation of flight capital. It is estimated that Argentinians held as much as $50 billion abroad.[32] Argentina's foreign exchange reserves rose from $1.5 billion at the end of 1989 to more than $14 billion at the end of 1993. This return of capital was also based on the fixed exchange-rate policy. But that policy, important as it is in instilling confidence, is creating a problem for Argentine exports. The real exchange rate has appreciated as the peso remains pegged to the dollar while other currencies have depreciated. Although creating a problem for exporters, this policy has the advantage of putting pressure on domestic firms to increase efficiency so as to be able to compete with imports. At some point, though, greater flexibility in the exchange rate will no doubt have to be introduced. For the time being, in 1993, the pegged peso is a symbol of the economic stability that the Menem government has brought to 'the new Argentina'.

In the summer and autumn of 1993, Argentina's inflation was at the lowest level in 24 years, the economy was growing briskly and unemployment was below 9 per cent.

12.6   CHILE

Chile is the paradoxical case of a country that, under a repressive political regime, was the first in Latin America to undertake structural economic reforms. In a violent coup in 1973 General Augusto Pinochet took over from the so-called Marxist government of Salvador Allende. During Pinochet's 17 years as dictator, a 'dirty war' was waged against opponents of the regime and human rights were violated. But economic reform was also carried out. It included privatisation, deregulation, substitution of a flat 10 per cent tariff for most import restrictions, elimination of price – but not wage – controls and pursuit of effective fiscal and monetary policies. Also, the composition of tax revenues was altered by the adoption of a value-added tax and a reduction of income tax rates, while the taxes on wealth and capital gains were abolished. By 1977 the economy was growing rapidly and consumer prices were rising at double rather than triple digit rates. 'Almost all of the economic reforms recommended to highly indebted countries after the onset of the debt crisis in 1982 were implemented in Chile in the 1970s.'[33] As John Williamson has observed:

> For a long time the adoption of those policies by the Chilean government threatened to give them the kiss of death, partly because of the political odium the Chilean regime had earned by its ruthless seizure of power and by the authoritarian way in which it subsequently governed.[34]

Chile was affected by the debt crisis and experienced a 14 per cent drop in output in 1982. But in contrast to most of its Latin American neighbours, it recovered quickly and its economy grew vigorously – an average of 6.3 per cent per year – in 1983–9.

Privatisation recurred in the 1980s. In 1986–8 the divestment of state-owned enterprises – various public utilities and the national airline – was of greater magnitude, relative to the size of the country, than the British privatisations of 1980–87. A number of criticisms have been levelled at these privatisations, including a charge of favouritism toward high-income groups, subsidies to foreign investors and lack of regulation of privatised natural monopolies.[35] And the copper mines, nationalised by Allende, remain state-owned enterprises.

In 1990, after a democratic election, Patricio Aylwin took over the presidency on a platform that endorsed the ongoing economic policy. Some changes have been introduced, including a rise in the minimum wage. In 1992 the Chilean economy grew by more than 10 per cent, consumer prices rose about 15 per cent and the current account was in deficit by less than $600 million.

According to Governor Andres Bianchi of the Central Bank of Chile, the improved economic performance

> is not the most important recent development in Chile's economy. That place is taken by a revolutionary ideological change. Whereas in the past several deep ideological rifts on matters of economic management divided the Chilean establishment and the Chilean people at large, a broad consensus has now emerged about the essential elements of policy needed to grow and modernize the economy. This has far-reaching implications not only for economic growth but also for the country's social and political development.[36]

12.7   BRAZIL

One cannot examine Latin America without taking account of Brazil, the largest country in the region in terms of both area and population and a major industrial, as well as agricultural, producer. Brazil does not appear earlier in this chapter because it has experienced less of a transformation than many of its neighbours. On the other hand, Brazil has had a relatively favourable growth record. In the 1970s its GDP increased on average by 8.9 per cent annually, while its population rose 2.4 per cent per year. In the 1980s, when many Latin American economies stagnated or declined, it grew by 1.4 per cent per year.

But Brazil has not achieved its full potential. It has suffered from bouts of hyperinflation: in only one year of the 1980s did its consumer prices rise at less than a three-digit rate and in two years, 1989 and 1990, inflation was between 1000 and 3000 per cent. As both cause and effect of inflation, wages and many other prices were indexed to the cost of living.

At the beginning of the 1980s, Brazil was a highly regulated economy in which 60 per cent of industry consisted of state-owned enterprises. Numerous imports were banned and others were subject to extremely high tariffs – the highest in Latin America. And Brazil had, and still has, a very unequal distribution of income. Any visitor to Rio is conscious of the shanty-filled *favelas* that ring the surrounding hillsides. In contrast to hilly American cities, it is the poor who have the better views.

A new civilian government under President José Sarney (1985–90) attempted to stabilise the economy with the Cruzado plan involving a price freeze, de-indexation, and a new currency, the cruzado, in which three zeros were removed from prices. The Cruzado plan and its successor failed, owing in large part to lax fiscal and monetary policies. In 1987 Sarney announced that Brazil was suspending interest payments on its foreign debt, piling up arrears.

The government of Fernando Collor de Mello, beginning in March 1990, initiated more thorough economic reforms. Especially after Marcilio Marques Moreira assumed the post of minister of economy in May 1991, the government's credibility regarding macroeconomic policy and structural reform was strengthened both at home and abroad. The budget deficit was reduced somewhat and monetary policy was tightened. Inflation was brought down in 1992 despite a freeing of prices. On the structural side, deregulation and privatisation were begun. Import barriers were lowered and restrictions on direct investment from abroad were relaxed.

But President Collor was forced out of office as the result of a corruption scandal and in October 1992 was succeeded by his less decisive vice-president Itamar Franco, who brought in a new economic team. In his first six months in office there were four different ministers of economy.

In the early months of 1994, prices were rising more than 40 per cent a month and the economy was growing again after stagnating in the two previous years. It is not clear how long Brazil can live without a coherent economic policy. A prerequisite may be political reform to make possible more effective governance. That requires that the political parties, of which there are seventeen in the Congress, become less 'volatile'.[37]

It is appropriate to conclude with the familiar Brazilian quip that Brazil is the country of the future and always will be.

13 Problems and Promises of an Uncertain Future

To assert that the world looked very different at the end of 1993 from what it was in 1980 is an understatement. Who would have predicted in 1980 that the Soviet Union would cease to exist, that Russia would be attempting to privatise its state-owned enterprises or that Eastern Europe would be liberated to pursue democracy and free markets? Or that regions of China would become thriving market economies growing at a breathtaking pace? Or that the two Germanys would be unified and the process would create serious economic problems for western Germany? Or that François Mitterrand, after winning the presidency on a socialist platform would later in the 1980s be presiding over an economy hardly more socialist than its neighbours and having a strong currency and lower inflation rate than Germany? Or that Mexico would abandon its import substitution policies, open its economy to the rest of the world and have shares in some of its privatised companies traded on the New York Stock Exchange along with those of many other 'emerging markets'? Or that India would rid itself of many of its tight controls over its industries and, despite memories of the East India Company, open itself to foreign investors? Or that Korea, already a 'newly industrialised country' in 1980, would achieve such a high level of real wages that some of its firms would migrate to China and Vietnam attracted by lower wages? Or that Saudi Arabia would have a large balance-of-payments deficit?

The world has changed drastically. Because dynamic societies are much more unpredictable than those that are static, this book must end on a note of uncertainty. My crystal ball is as cloudy as that of most economists. Someone has said that while weather forecasters can at least tell if it is currently raining, all the best economists can do is to figure out if it rained in the past. In any event the state of the world today is such that prediction would be hazardous. That is particularly

203

so in regard to Russia and some of the other former Soviet republics. Lincoln Steffens, returning from a visit to Russia in 1919, said,'I have been over into the future and it works.' It took a while but that turned out to be a terribly mistaken forecast. It didn't 'work' in Russia or Eastern Europe or China.

We can be fairly confident that the movement away from the command economy and all that went with it will not be reversed. But it is hard to go further in trying to foresee the future of Russia. The results of the election of December 1993, which, among its other repercussions, brought the word 'fascism' back into the headlines, starkly underlined the fact that the transition is creating severe hardships and unhappiness for many Russian citizens. Just what type of political and economic system and foreign policy Russia will end up with is a matter of conjecture and, it may be added, considerable apprehension in the rest of the world.

That is probably the most problematic aspect of the future as one tries to discern it at the end of 1993. While uncertainties exist elsewhere – for example, in South Africa – what happens in Russia can have a much larger impact on the rest of the world.

Much of the transformation reviewed in this book is the story of reduced involvement of governments in economies. The point has been made again and again that governments have not done well at operating industrial enterprises and that they have over-regulated economic processes, including international transactions. Much of the world is cutting back those functions of government. Yet there are important roles for governments in seeing to it that economies operate so as to maximise the well-being of citizens. This chapter turns to that topic first. Then it presents some of the problems, challenges and hopes for the future that are thrown up by the transformations of 1980–93.

13.1   THE ROLE OF GOVERNMENTS IN ECONOMIES

Precisely because so much of what has been recounted in earlier pages stresses the benefits of getting governments

'off the backs' of the public, to revert to the Thatcher–
Reagan rhetoric, I want to stress here how vital some governmental activities are to the proper functioning of economies
and societies. The lessening of government involvement
that has been applauded has to do either with functions that
the private sector is better able to carry out – such as the
production and distribution of goods and services – or with
excessive regulation of such functions both domestically and
across national borders. What needs to be emphasised now
is that there are other roles that only governments can
perform and they need not be minimal.

The most obvious and least controversial governmental
activities are macroeconomic policies. Monetary policy is
necessarily a state function. The fact that there is a widespread trend towards making central banks independent –
the latest such moves having occurred in France, Mexico and
Spain – does not contradict this point. Central banks that are
not required to take instructions from finance ministries are
still governmental institutions. In the early years of decoloni-
sation after World War II, newly-independent states made an
effort to establish their identity by setting up both central
banks and national airlines. The former are intrinsically in
the public sector; the latter need not be, and there has been a
recent tendency to privatise them.

Fiscal policy, although it is somewhat in abeyance these
days, as discussed below, is the other arm of macroeconomic
policy that is essentially a government activity. Through
their budgets governments spend and tax and borrow,
thereby affecting the income and output of their economies. These functions can sometimes be fashioned so as to
combat recession or inflation and to encourage economic
growth and price stability. At the same time the tax receipts
and spending of governments vary automatically with
changes in aggregate demand and in total economic activity,
thereby mitigating the severity of inflations and recessions.

The next section returns to a discussion of the present-day
constraints on the utilisation of fiscal policy in the industrial
countries. Here, the point is simply that monetary and fiscal
policy are legitimate, and necessary, functions of government.

Those legitimate functions go well beyond macroeconomic policies. They include the provision of so-called 'public goods', and of goods and services for which there are benefits to society over and above those to the individuals consuming them – in the language of economists, 'externalities'. Governments also provide a social safety net, including unemployment compensation and other welfare payments. Regulation of the private economy in a broad range of activities from anti-trust enforcement to environmental protection is another function that only governments can perform.

Public goods are goods and services that the private economy cannot be expected to produce and sell to individual households or businesses either because they are indivisible (like national defence) or because a price cannot be charged for them (again like national defence as well as lighthouses and sidewalks) or because those who do not pay cannot be excluded from using them (like flood control). Other examples of public goods are fire and police protection and crime prevention, roads and bridges (although tolls are possible in some cases), traffic lights in cities, many forms of welfare payment, and basic research and development outlays (because the results become public knowledge and therefore private R & D activity cannot yield full financial benefits to its originators).

In other cases the goods or services could be supplied by the private sector but they are natural monopolies such as railways, ports, and public utilities. The alternatives are to let such goods or services be provided by private business with governmental regulation of their prices and terms of service or to have the government supply them. In continental Europe postal, telephone and telegraph services (PTT) are usually provided by governments while in the United States most of them are supplied privately but are regulated by government agencies.

Another category of government functions could technically be (and some are) left to the private sector but it is socially undesirable to ration them by price. Primary and secondary schools are the outstanding example here. In principle, governments could stay out of education, leaving it completely to the private economy. The result would be that those with lower incomes would be excluded at some point in the education process. Public education assures a minimum level of learning for the entire population, which is of benefit to society as a whole – not only to those who would otherwise be excluded. In other words each member of society is better off if his or her fellow-countrymen are educated. That justifies government participation either by supplying the service directly or subsidising private education.

Finally, governments have a legitimate regulatory function such as anti-trust activity, safety regulations for airlines, environmental standards for industry, and child labour laws, among others.

Enough has been said to make the point. The transformations of the period since 1980 have reduced the functions of governments. In some countries – particularly in Britain under Margaret Thatcher and in the United States under Ronald Reagan – the process went too far. Thatcher privatised natural monopolies. In America under Reagan public infrastructure was neglected to the degree that many bridges are unsafe. What requires emphasis is that in all countries – whether they already have relatively free market economies, or are in transition from central planning or are developing countries that are moving away from tight government controls and a large public enterprise sector – a significant role for government remains.

13.2   UNEMPLOYMENT IN INDUSTRIAL COUNTRIES

While inflation, along with slowing economies, were major concerns in most of Western Europe, North America and Japan in 1980, at the end of 1993 high unemployment was a serious preoccupation. The countries that had moved first into recession in 1990 – the United States, Canada and Britain – were expanding again but not vigorously enough to have eliminated the high level of joblessness. The US unemployment rate came down to 6.4 per cent at the end of 1993 from a peak of 7.7 per cent in June 1992, but many American companies were continuing to announce lay-offs. Most of Western Europe was still depressed, with no sure signs of economic upturn and unemployment was at the highest level since World War II. Japan was suffering from its worst post-war recession while struggling to reform its political arrangements. Although its measured unemployment rate was below 3 per cent, overtime work and new recruitment were being reduced.

Unemployment in the European Community (which became the European Union, EU, with the coming into force of the Maastricht Treaty in late 1993) was causing grave concern, having brought on the crushing defeat of the Socialist Party in the French elections of March 1993, having lowered Helmut Kohl's political standing and having made John Major the most unpopular British prime minister since such public opinion polls started in the late 1930s.

The unemployment problem provides a sharp contrast between Europe and the United States. Although the two areas, the EU and the United States, grew at equal rates from 1980 to 1992 – 2.1 per cent per year – US unemployment was about the same in 1992 as in 1980, and much lower in late 1993. In the EU, on the other hand, unemployment rose from 6.3 per cent in 1980 to 10.3 per cent in 1992 and above 11 per cent in 1993. The contrast is even stronger when account is taken of the fact that participation in the labour force is significantly lower in the EU than in the United States (66.8 compared with 76.0 per cent of the adult population in 1992) and that it increased 7 per cent in the United States (solely because of rising female participation) but only 1.7 per cent in Europe from 1980 to 1992.

The US economy created many more jobs than did Europe, not only since 1980 but in the 1970s as well. By the same token productivity rose faster in Europe. From 1980 to 1991, output per employed person in the business sector rose on average by 0.8 per cent per year in the United States and 2.0 per cent in Europe. But, as noted in Chapter 4, American productivity growth picked up in 1992 and 1993. Whether that was just a normal cyclical recovery cannot be determined with certainty yet but there are indications that more is happening than that.

Once again, as in the first half of the 1980s when Germany was thought to be afflicted with 'Eurosclerosis', blame was being placed on structural impediments such as high labour and other social costs, labour immobility and lack of proper skills.[1] There was also much talk of lowering the length of the work week to four days so as to spread available jobs more widely.

The structural obstacles to increased employment are no doubt real but it is also true that scope exists for the European economies to move closer to full capacity. The OECD estimates output gaps – the difference between actual and potential GDP – ranging in 1993 from 5.5 per cent in France and the United Kingdom to 0.6 per cent in Germany (but the IMF projects the gap in Germany at about 3 per cent in 1994). There is some leeway therefore for aggregate demand to be boosted by macroeconomic policies.

It is noteworthy that hardly any of the industrial countries are using fiscal policy to reduce unemployment and move their economies out of recession. In fact, several of them, including Germany, have acted recently to reduce their budget deficits. The overriding reason is that most of these countries already have budget deficits that are too large to be sustainable. Even apart from the effects of recession, the structural budget deficit averaged 5 per cent of GDP in Europe in 1993 and 3.3 per cent in the United States. Japan was the exception, with a structural budget surplus of 0.7 per cent of GDP. In the United States and most European nations the ratio of government debt to GDP has risen steadily since 1980, if not earlier. That is what makes the deficits unsustainable. Thus a determination exists to reduce deficits, even in the face of depressed economies. Another reason for the disinclination to use fiscal stimulus in the EU can be traced to the limits on government deficits and debt embodied in the convergence criteria of the Maastricht Treaty, as noted in Chapter 6.

It could well be therefore that while 1980–93 was an era of tax reduction in many industrial countries, the period ahead will be one of tax increases. That already happened in 1993 in the United States under President Clinton's medium-term budget reduction plan. The end of the Cold War, if it remains over, and the consequent ability of governments to cut military expenditures should help. The IMF projects a drop of such spending in industrial countries from 3.1 per cent of GDP in 1992 to 2.3 per cent in 1998.

In the United States monetary policy was actively used to encourage revival of the economy but fiscal policy was tightened by both the Bush and Clinton administrations. In Europe the Bundesbank sets the tone for monetary policy and its interest rates were still rather high at the end of 1993. One of the lessons to be drawn from the 1980s and early 1990s is that a second instrument of macroeconomic policy is needed in most industrial countries – in other words, a revival of fiscal policy. That is all the more true when monetary policies are immobilised as economic stabilisation instruments because they are devoted to keeping exchange rates in line. But fiscal deficits will have to be brought down before that can be expected to happen. Thus the European nations are in a Catch-22 dilemma with respect to fiscal policy. They need to reduce budget deficits before they can use it to stimulate their economies but the very process of cutting deficits can depress their economies further.

The upshot of these considerations is that the European countries may face a slow recovery and a continuation of high levels of unemployment. The political repercussions of this outlook cannot be predicted, at least by me, but they are likely to be significant.

Although the Maastricht Treaty is in effect and the European Monetary Institute, a forerunner of the proposed European central bank, has been set up, the outlook for creation of European Monetary Union did not look especially bright as 1993 ended. The exchange-rate mechanism (ERM) of the EMS had run into serious trouble in the autumn of 1992 and again in the summer of 1993. The unemployment problem was a much greater current preoccupation than eventual union. That could, of course, change as the end of the decade approaches. Another question has to do with the priorities as between widening and deepening the EU; that is, between admitting new members – Austria, Scandinavian countries, and eventually some Eastern European nations – and tightening the bonds among the present members.

13.3   BALANCE-OF-PAYMENTS DEFICITS

While unemployment has become a matter of greater concern in most industrial countries, worry about balance-of-payments problems has receded. In 1980 most oil-importing countries were in current-account deficit, including all industrial countries except oil-producing Norway, United Kingdom and the United States. The EC as a group moved into surplus in the mid-1980s, as did Japan. The United States current account shifted into large deficit. By 1993 the EC was near balance, the American deficit was smaller and Japan was in large surplus. These imbalances were easily financed by private capital flows with very little attention from the general public, the financial community or governments, given the heightened mobility of capital that has been a feature of our period.

That does not mean that persistent current-account deficits should *not* be a matter for concern. If they are not matched by increased domestic investment and therefore higher growth, they can be a burden on future generations.

13.4   THE NEED FOR POLICY CO-ORDINATION

The growing interdependence among the nations of the world has been stressed. It shows up in the growth of international trade relative to output and in the much greater mobility of capital across national borders. A result of this enlarged interdependence is that countries have a bigger impact on each other than in the past. A policy change in any one country has greater significance for its neighbours than before, even when those neighbours are separated by oceans.

The obvious implication of these facts is that policymakers should take account of these linkages among their economies when making their decisions. A process of policy co-ordination was implemented in the 1980s among nations of the Group of Seven. That process need not be continuous. Only from time to time is co-ordinated action needed or possible. The process has been compared with the function of firefighters sitting idly in the firestation apparently wasting taxpayers' funds. Only when a fire breaks out does their usefulness to society become evident. A case can be made for nurturing that co-ordination process and widening it beyond the Group of Seven.[2]

13.5   THE PAINFUL TRANSITION IN EASTERN EUROPE AND RUSSIA

There is very little to add here to what has been written in earlier chapters. The latest data for Eastern Europe show smaller declines in output than in 1992 and positive growth in the Czech Republic and Poland. Inflation ranged from 21 per cent in the Czech Republic to 250 per cent in Romania. In Russia, output is estimated to have fallen by another 11.5 per cent in 1993. While prices rose almost 900 per cent in 1993 – down from earlier levels – inflation decelerated in early 1994. As loss-making state enterprises the restructured unemployment could become a serious problem.

As has been said so often, the transition from central planning to a market economy is a long painful process. The danger, as is evident in Russia, is that people will lose patience and the political centre of gravity will swing away from democracy and a market economy to a less desirable system.

What can be done? The problems are complex, as should be clear from Chapters 7 and 8. But the difficulties inherent in the transition are being aggravated by balance-of-payments constraints. Recession and the restriction of some imports by EU countries have affected the exports of the Eastern European countries. In addition some of their foreign exchange earnings are being dissipated in capital flight and therefore are not available to finance imports. In technical terms, a number of these economies are import constrained. This is also true in Russia. Whether more financial assistance from the west would be helpful is a difficult and controversial question. Harvard Professor Jeffrey Sachs, formerly an adviser to the Yeltsin government, has argued strongly for such assistance.[3] Others would say that until Russia stabilises its economy the funds would be wasted.

Actually the financial assistance promised by the west (which of course includes Japan in today's jargon) has been only partially forthcoming. The reason is that much of it was to be provided by the IMF and, until the spring of 1994, Russia was unable to meet the conditions that the Fund must necessarily attach to its credits. A good case can be made for direct assistance by western countries.[4] The Marshall Plan can be cited as a historical precedent. Russia needs foreign exchange to finance imports so that more can be spent on restructuring inefficient enterprises and on supporting those who inevitably become unemployed in that process. In other words, a social safety net is a necessary complement to economic restructuring of centrally planned economies. While Russia can create rubles to finance such outlays, that would aggravate inflation without the availability of additional imports. And, it may be added, those imports would represent a welcome addition to the exports of those industrial countries suffering from high unemployment. The familiar obstacle is that most of the latter countries are in a budgetary bind.

13.6 MIGRATION

Meanwhile economic dislocation in Eastern Europe, ethnic cleansing in the former Yugoslavia and strife elsewhere have led to a mass migration into Western Europe from countries to the east and south. It is estimated that immigrants to Western Europe from Eastern Europe and North Africa numbered 3 million in 1992.[5] As was noted in Chapter 5, western Germany was one of the principal destinations, until a change in the law on asylum took effect on 1 July, 1993 under which 'Germany's immigration policy became one of the most restrictive in Europe'.[6] France also tightened its immigration policy and treatment of immigrants in a law that became effective at the beginning of 1994.

It is ironical that the disappearance of the Berlin Wall has been followed by the erection of less visible barriers to migration in Western Europe. Moreover, while unemployment is currently high, the demographic trends portend a future shortage of young people and new entrants to the labour force. Who will pay the taxes to support the pensions of the ageing population if immigration does not continue?

13.7   NATIONALISM AND FUNDAMENTALISM

The barbarism in what was Yugoslavia is the most flagrant expression of revived nationalism. Nationalism is in evidence elsewhere too: in some of the states of the former Soviet Union, in parts of Africa, in Turkey and Iraq and in attitudes and actions towards immigrants or long-resident foreign nationals in some European countries. A similar concern is the rise of militant religious fundamentalism evident from Iran westward through parts of the Middle East and North Africa. In some places the two tendencies are combined in religious nationalism. There is little I can say about these worrying tendencies except to record their existence here as problems for the future.

13.8   THE CHANGING STATUS OF DEVELOPING COUNTRIES

This narrative begins and ends with recessions in industrial countries. But a striking difference appears between the performance of the world economy in the early 1980s and the early 1990s. In 1982 growth of world output slowed to 0.5 per cent as the GDP of industrial countries fell slightly and developing countries in all areas of the world except Asia experienced slowdowns in their growth rates. In 1991 world output grew only 0.6 per cent as GDP fell sharply in Eastern Europe and Russia and rose only 0.5 per cent in industrial countries. But the combined output of developing countries rose by 4.5 per cent in 1991 and accelerated to an estimated 6.1 per cent in 1993; only Africa failed to share in the strong expansion in the early 1990s.

It turned out that much of the developing world, far from being dependent on what happened to the economies of industrial countries, was acting as a locomotive for the industrial countries in the early 1990s. The volume of imports of all developing countries as a group increased on average by 8.9 per cent per year in 1990–93, whereas those imports had fallen by 4.2 per cent in 1982. This reversal in dependency appears even more dramatic when viewed in terms of current-account positions. The combined current-account deficit of all industrial countries decreased from about $110 billion in 1990 to near balance in 1993. Much of the counterpart of that deficit reduction shows up in the enlarged deficit of LDCs, which rose from $12 billion in 1990 to about $105 billion in 1993. Unemployment in the industrial countries would have been higher without this increase in demand from the developing world.

Part of the explanation for the sharp difference in the economic performance of developing countries between the early 1980s and ten years later has to do with the very large increase in capital flows to them in recent years, as is shown in Table 13.1. Despite the sizeable but understandable fall-off in loans by commercial banks, total flows almost doubled. Most of the capital in the recent period went to Asia and Latin America.

Lawrence Summers, then Chief Economist at the World Bank, wrote in 1992 about the 'linkage between industrialized country economic performance and developing country economic performance', stating that 'it appears that each 1 percentage point of growth in the industrialized world translates into an additional 4 percentage point of

Table 13.1   Capital flows to developing countries*

	1977–81[†]	1992
Foreign direct investment	9.4	39.3
Portfolio equity	0.0	12.7
Bonds	2.8	22.3
Commercial bank loans	48.0	21.0
Official loans	29.3	63.1
Other	21.4	60.0
Total	110.9	218.4

*Excludes short-term loans. [†]Annual averages.

Source: Adapted from IMF, *World Economic Outlook*, October 1993, p. 77.

growth in the developing world'.[7] From the experience of recent years, that link may now have been broken.

More broadly, the philosophy of *dependencia* has been shown to be irrelevant and that should encourage further reforms along the lines of what we have observed in Mexico, among others.

Meanwhile the debt burden of developing countries in all regions has come down. Interest payments as a proportion of exports of goods and services fell from a peak of 12.4 per cent in 1986 to 6.7 per cent in 1993. In Latin America the interest burden is lower than in the mid-1980s but it rose again in 1991–3. Thus one has to ask whether another debt crisis could occur. Is Latin America taking on too much debt again, even if in different forms? Some encouragement can be derived from the fact that the recession of the early 1990s in the industrial countries did not trigger another debt problem. The IMF projects a decline in the interest burden of Latin America from 19 per cent of exports in 1993 to 13.9 per cent in 1994. Another positive sign is that not all of the capital inflow has been spent. Latin America's foreign exchange reserve more than doubled in 1990–93. On the other hand, the capital inflow could well taper off and decline as interest rates rise in the United States and other industrial countries.

While many LDCs are enjoying an improved economic performance and much less of a balance-of-payments constraint, if any, the countries of Sub-Saharan Africa are still in a sad state, as is brought out in Chapter 11. How to deal with that serious problem is beyond the scope of this book for the simple reason that it is beyond my knowledge and capacity, but not beyond my sympathy.

13.9 THE BASIS FOR FUTURE PROSPERITY

One of the fundamental truths of economic life – self-evident though it may be – is that rising living standards depend on advancing productivity. Growth in output per person employed and per unit of capital equipment has been the explanation for the enormous increase in economic well-being in the world since the industrial revolution began in England. Output per person of a country can also rise if a greater proportion of the popu- lation is working. But there are limits to the extent to which that ratio can be increased. Basically we come back to productivity.

There is everything to be said therefore in favour of policies that enhance competition. The significant improvement in the attractiveness of American automobiles to consumers and the productivity of their producers can be attributed to the competition from Japanese cars. The striking economic progress that we have observed in numerous developing countries is based in part on the productivity-enhancing effects of competition from imports.

While we face a future fraught with uncertainties, it is well to remember that the good society is one in which economic and political freedom are maximised. The economic transformations since 1980 have improved well-being in most countries where they have occurred. The lesson is that economic and political freedom enhance welfare but that governments still have important roles to play.

Notes

1 Introduction

1. S.V. Zhukov and A.Y. Vorobyov, 'Reforming the Soviet Union: Lessons from Structural Experience' , in *Wider Working Papers* (Helsinki: World Institute for Development Economic Research of the United Nations University, Nov. 1991) p. 3.
2. 'Chinese Feel the Strain of a New Society', *The Washington Post*, 17 June 1993, p. A1.
3. *The New York Times*, 1 April 1993, Sec. 4, p. 1.
4. I. Berlin, 'The Hedgehog and the Fox', *Russian Thinkers* (New York: The Viking Press, 1978) pp. 22–81.
5. I. Berlin, *Personal Impressions* (New York: The Viking Press, 1980) pp. 27–8.

3 Changing Philosophies of Economic Policy

1. N. Lawson, *The View from No. 11: Memoirs of a Tory Radical* (London: Bantam Press, 1992) pp. 946–7.
2. J. Newhouse, 'The Gamefish', *The New Yorker* (10 February 1986).
3. 'Economic Policy: The Task Ahead', Mr James Callaghan, Prime Minister, at Blackpool, England, 28 September , 1976, *British Information Services*.
4. A. Walters, *Britain's Economic Renaissance* (Oxford University Press, 1986) p. 4.
5. 'The State of the Union Address', Address delivered before a Joint Session of the Congress, 19 January 1978.
6. D.T. Regan, *For the Record: From Wall Street to Washington* (New York: Harcourt Brace Jovanovich, 1988) pp. 142ff.
7. D. Stockman, *The Triumph of Politics: How the Reagan Revolution Failed* (New York: Harper & Row, 1986) p. 76.
8. G. Gilder, *Wealth and Poverty* (New York: Basic Books, 1981).
9. R.L. Bartley, *The Seven Fat Years* (New York: The Free Press, 1992).
10. P.C. Roberts, 'The Keynesian Attack on Mr Reagan', *The Wall Street Journal* (19 March 1981).
11. P.C. Roberts, *The Supply-Side Revolution* (Cambridge: Harvard University Press, 1984).
12. O.J. Blanchard, 'Reaganomics', *Economic Policy* 2 (October 1987) pp. 17–48.
13. Remarks at the New York Financial Writers Dinner, 14 April 1981, *Department of the Treasury News*.
14. Letter to *The New York Times* (5 June 1991).
15. Bartley, *The Seven Fat Years*, p. 6.

16. B. Bosworth and G. Burtless, 'Effects of Tax Reform on Factor Supply, Investment, and Saving', *Journal of Economic Perspectives* 6 (Winter 1992) pp. 3–25; M.A. Akhtar and E.S. Harris, 'The Supply-Side Consequences of U.S. Fiscal Policy in the 1980s', *Quarterly Review*, Federal Reserve Bank of New York 17 (Spring 1992) pp. 1–20.

17. Statement of the Honorable Beryl W. Sprinkel, Under Secretary for Monetary Affairs, Before the Joint Economic Committee, 4 May 1981, *Department of the Treasury News*

18. *The Washington Post*, 17 October 1992, p. A1.

19. P. Favier and M. Martin-Roland, *La Décennie Mitterrand* (Paris: Editions du Seuil, vol. 1, 1991) p. 41. I draw on this valuable work and on volume 2 (1991) for the story of developments in France.

20. M. Hellwig and M. Neumann, 'Germany under Kohl', *Economic Policy* 5 (October 1987) pp. 113–14.

4   Reaganomics and Thatcherism

1. P. Volcker and T. Gyohten, *Changing Fortunes* (New York: Times Books, 1992) Chapter 6.

2. M.N. Baily, G. Burtless and R.E. Litan, *Growth with Equity: Economic Policymaking for the Next Century* (Washington: The Brookings Institution, 1993) Chapter 3.

3. P. Kennedy, *The Rise and Fall of the Great Powers* (New York: Random House, 1987).

4. W.J. Baumol and others, *Productivity and American Leadership: The Long View* (MIT Press, 1989) Chapter 5.

5. J.S. Nye, Jr., *Bound to Lead* (New York: Basic Books, 1990); H.R. Nau, *The Myth of America's Decline* (New York: Oxford University Press, 1990).

6. K.E. House, 'Though Rich, Japan is Poor in Many Elements of Global Leadership', *The Wall Street Journal*, 30 January 1989, p. A1.

7. N. Lawson, *The View From No. 11: Memoirs of a Tory Radical* (London: Bantam Books, 1992) pp. 64–5.

8. Ibid., p. 415.

9. Ibid., p. 70.

10. C. Johnson, *The Economy Under Mrs. Thatcher, 1979–90* (London: Penguin Books, 1991) p. 41.

11. *The Journal of Commerce*, 24 March 1981, p. 4.

12. Lawson, *The View from No 11*, pp. 88–9.

13. K. Matthews and P. Minford, 'Mrs. Thatcher's Economic Policies, 1979–1987', *Economic Policy* 5 (October 1987) pp. 62–3.

14. A. Walters, *Britain's Economic Renaissance* (New York: Oxford University Press, 1986) pp. 140–41.

15. Lawson, *The View from No 11*, p. 652.

16. M. Thatcher, *The Downing Street Years* (New York: Harper Collins, 1993) p. 701.

17. M. Wolf, 'From Delusion to Devaluation', *Financial Times*, 30 September 1992, p. 14.
18. Lawson, *The View from No 11*, p. 835.
19. Thatcher, *The Downing Street Years*, pp. 715–18.
20. Lawson, *The View from No 11*, pp. 867–73. He put this proposal in a memorandum to the Prime Minister in November 1988.
21. *The Economist*, 16 September 1989, pp. 15–16.
22. Ibid., 7 October 1989, pp. 13–14.
23. D. Healey, *The Time of My Life* (New York: W.W. Norton, 1989) p. 150.
24. *The New York Times*, 28 February 1993, p. 9.

5 Adjusting to Shocks in France, Germany and Japan

1. D. Singer, *Is Socialism Doomed?: The Meaning of Mitterrand* (New York: Oxford University Press, 1988) pp. 78–92.
2. P. Favier and M. Martin-Roland, *La Décennie Mitterrand* (Paris: Editions Du Seuil, 1991) vol. 2, p. 389.
3. *Financial Times*, 31 December 1993, p. 11.
4. C. Imbert, 'The End of French Exceptionalism', *Foreign Affairs*, 68 (Fall 1989), pp. 48–60.
5. *The Washington Post*, 26 September 1993, p. H1.
6. *The Financial Times*, 14 October 1993, p. 13.
7. M. Kreile, 'The Political Economy of the New Germany', in P.B. Stares, (ed.), *The New Germany and the New Europe* (Washington: The Brookings Institution, 1992) p. 55.
8. Interview in *The New York Times*, 29 December 1992, p. C11.
9. In a preface to A. Stead, *Great Japan: A Study in National Efficiency*, cited in C. Wood, *The Bubble Economy* (The Atlantic Monthly Press, 1992) pp. 14–15.
10. A detailed presentation of financial market liberalization may be found in *OECD Economic Surveys: Japan 1990–1991* (Paris: Organization for Economic Cooperation and Development, 1991) pp. 137–47.
11. C. Wood, *The Bubble Economy* (New York: The Atlantic Monthly Press, 1992) p. 50.
12. Ibid., p. 60.
13. *The Wall Street Journal*, 14 January 1994, p. A4.
14. *The New York Times*, 9 November 1993, p. A7.

6 Economic Interactions and Economic Integration

1. This point is made in the Background Paper by Robert Solomon in *Partners in Prosperity*, The Report of the Twentieth Century Fund Task Force on the International Coordination of National Economic Policies (New York: Priority Press Publications, 1991) pp. 60–61.

2. M. Feldstein and C. Horioka, 'Domestic Saving and International Capital Flows', *Economic Journal* 90 (1980) pp. 314–29.

3. A. Dean, M. Durand, J. Fallon and P. Hoeller, 'Saving Trends and Behavior in OECD Countries', *OECD Economic Studies* 14 (Spring 1990), pp. 8–58.

4. R. Solomon, 'The United States as a Debtor in the 19th Century', *Brookings Discussion Papers in International Economics*, No. 28, May 1985 and in 'Endettement, Flexibilité, et Regulation des Financiers', in *Économies et Sociétés*, Cahiers de l'Institut de Sciences Mathématiques et Économiques Appliquées, XIX (September 1985).

5. R. O'Brien, *Global Financial Integration: The End of Geography* (New York: Royal Institute of International Affairs, Council on Foreign Relations, 1992) p. 48.

6. N. Lawson, *The View From No. 11: Memoirs of a Tory Radical* (London: Bantam Press, 1992) p. 538.

7. D.T. Regan, *For the Record* (New York: Harcourt Brace Jovanovich, 1988).

8. For this and a detailed inside story on exchange-rate negotiations see Y. Funabashi, *Managing the Dollar: From the Plaza to the Louvre* (Washington: Institute for International Economics, 1988).

9. P. Volcker and T. Gyohten, *Changing Fortunes* (New York: Times Books, 1992) p. 279.

10. Ibid., p. 268.

11. E. Hoffmeyer, *The International Monetary System: An Essay in Interpretation* (Amsterdam: North-Holland, 1992) p. 215.

12. S. Marris, *Deficits and the Dollar: The World Economy at Risk* (Washington: Institute for International Economics, 1985).

13. M. Dealtry and J. Van't dack, 'The US External Deficit and Associated Shifts in International Portfolios', *BIS Economic Papers*, no. 25, September 1989.

14. Speech by the Rt. Hon. Baroness Thatcher, OM, FRS to the CNN World Economic Development Congress on Saturday, 19 September 1992, Washington, DC.

15. P. Cecchini, *The European Challenge: 1992* (Aldershot: Gower, 1988).

16. R. Baldwin, 'On the growth effects of 1992', *National Bureau of Economic Research Working Paper Series*, Working Paper No. 3119, September 1989.

17. André Szasz, 'Towards a Single European Currency: Ecu, Franc-Fort, Question-Mark', in O.E. Fair and R. Raymand (eds), *The New Europe: Evolving Economic and Financial Systems in East and West* (Dordrecht: Kluwer Academic Publishers, 1993) p. 221.

18. See, for example, P.B. Kenen, *EMU After Maastricht* (Washington: Group of Thirty, 1992); C.R. Bean, 'Economic and Monetary Union in Europe', *Centre for Economic Policy Research Discussion Paper Series, No. 722* (Oct. 1992); and W.H. Buiter, G. Corsetti, and N. Roubini, ' "Excessive Deficits": Sense and Nonsense in the Treaty of Maastricht', *Centre for Economic Policy Research Discussion Paper Series No. 750* (December 1992).

19. Group of Ten, *International Capital Movements and Foreign Exchange Markets*, A Report to the Ministers and Governors by the Group of Deputies, April 1993, p. 37.
20. Kenen, *EMU After Manstricht*, pp. 66–7.
21. Bean, 'Economic and Monetary Union in Europe', p. 35.
22. G. Hufbauer and J.J. Schott, *NAFTA: An Assessment* (Washington: Institute for International Economics, February 1993) p. 1.

7 The Elements of Economic Reform: Eastern Europe

1. A. Maddison, *The World Economy in the Twentieth Century* (Paris: Development Centre of the Organization for Economic Cooperation and Development, 1989) pp. 38, 126.
2. S. Fischer, *Russia and the Soviet Union: Then and Now*, National Bureau of Economic Research, Working Paper No. 4077 (May 1992) pp. 17–18.
3. R. East, *Revolutions in Eastern Europe* (Pinter Publishers, 1992) pp. 96–7.
4. D. Lipton and J. Sachs, 'Creating a Market Economy in Eastern Europe: The Case of Poland', *Brookings Papers on Economic Activity* (1:1990) p. 78.
5. Quoted in S. Fischer and A. Gelb, 'The Process of Socialist Economic Transformation', *Journal of Economic Perspectives*, 5 (Feb. 1991) p. 91.
6. L. Balcerowicz, 'Common fallacies in the debate on the economic transition in central and eastern Europe', European Bank for Reconstruction and Development, *Working Papers* No. 11 (October 1993) p. 3.
7. M. Bruno, 'Stabilization and Reform in Eastern Europe', *Staff Papers*, International Monetary Fund, 39 (Dec. 1992) p. 761.
8. International Monetary Fund, *World Economic Outlook*, October 1992, pp. 45–6,
9. S. Thomas, 'The Politics and Economics of Privatization in Central and Eastern Europe', *The Columbia Journal of World Business*, XXVIII, (Spring 1993) p. 169.
10. *Financial Times*, 6 April 1993, p. 2.
11. A. Robinson, *Financial Times*, 3 July 1992, Section III, p. I
12. For a good general discussion of these points see J. Nellis and S. Kikeri, 'The Privatization of Public Enterprises', in S. El-Naggar, *Privatization and Structural Adjustment in the Arab Countries* (Washington: International Monetary Fund, 1989) pp. 50–80 and European Bank for Reconstruction and Development (EBRD), *Annual Economic Outlook*, September 1993.
13. A. Ewing, B. Lee, and R. Leeds, 'Accelerating Privatization in Ex-Socialist Economies', *The Columbia Journal of World Business*, XXVIII (Spring 1993) p. 160.
14. EBRD, p. 64.
15. *The Economist*, Survey, 13 March 1993, p. 15
16. *OECD Economic Outlook*, December 1993, p. 1178.

8   Chaos and Reform in the Soviet Union and Russia

1. E.A. Hewett, *Reforming the Soviet Economy: Equity versus Efficiency* (Washington: The Brookings Institution, 1988) pp. 37–8.
2. M. Gorbachev, *Perestroika: New Thinking for Our Country and the World* (New York: Harper & Row, 1987) pp. 18–19.
3. *A Study of the Soviet Economy* (International Monetary Fund, World Bank, Organization for Economic Cooperation and Development, European Bank for Reconstruction and Development, Feb. 1991) vol. 1, p. 12.
4. A. Maddison, *The World Economy in the 20th Century* (Paris: Development Centre of the Organization for Economic Cooperation and Development, 1989) pp. 81, 91.
5. K. Tidmarsh, 'Russia's Work Ethic', *Foreign Affairs*, 72 (Spring 1993) pp. 67–77.
6 Hewett, *Reforming the Soviet Economy*, p. 81.
7. D.C. Diller (ed.), *Russia and the Independent States* (Washington: Congressional Quarterly, 1993) p. 108.
8. E.A. Hewett with C.A. Gaddy, *Open for Business: Russia's Return to the Global Economy* (Washington: The Brookings Institution, 1992) p. 96.
9. Hewett, *Reforming the Soviet Economy*, pp. 390–91.
10. *The Economist*, 8 May 1993, p. 79.
11. D. Remnick, *Lenin's Tomb: The Last Days of the Soviet Empire* (New York: Random House, 1993) p. 477.
12. G. Arbatov, *The System* (New York: Times Books, 1992) pp. 345–6.
13. Remnick, *Lenin's Tomb*, p. 500.
14. G.W. Breslauer, 'Evaluating Gorbachev as Leader', in E.A. Hewitt and V.H. Winston (eds), *Milestones in Glasnost and Perestroika*, vol. 2, *Politics and People* (Washington: The Brookings Institution, 1991) pp. 390–430.
15. *Russia and the Independent States*, p. 306.
16. *Financial Times*, 27 May 1993, 'Survey of Russia', p. I.
17. V. Koen and S. Phillips, *Price Liberalization in Russia* (Washington: International Monetary Fund, Occasional Paper 104, 1993) p. 36.
18. S. Fischer, 'Socialist Economy Reform: Lessons of the First Three Years', *American Economic Review*, 83 (May 1993) p. 394.
19. J.S. Berliner, 'The Gains From Privatization' in *The Former Soviet Union in Transition*, vol. 1 (US Congress, Joint Economic Committee, 1993) Feb. 1983, pp. 240–55.
20. *The New York Times*, 21 January 1994, p. A1.

9   From Mao to Deng: Economic Reform in China

1. *The Economist*, A Survey of China (28 November 1992) p. 6.
2. J.K. Fairbank, *China: A New History* (Cambridge: Harvard University Press, 1992) p. 385. I rely on this valuable work for descriptions of the Great Leap Forward and the Cultural Revolution.

3   Ibid., pp. 402–3.
4   Ibid., p. 410.
5.   H. Harding, *China's Second Revolution* (Washington: The Brookings Institution, 1987) p. 30. For the period up to 1987 I rely heavily on this valuable book.
6.   M. Bell and K. Kochhar, 'China: An Evolving Market Economy – A Review of Reform Experience', *IMF Working Paper* 92/89 (November 1992) p. 7.
7.   A. Hussein and N. Stern, 'Effective Demand, Enterprise Reforms and Public Finance in China', *Economic Policy*, 12 (April 1991) p. 145.
8.   Fairbank, *China*, p. 412.
9.   *Financial Times*, Survey, 16 June 1992, p. VI.
10. M.W. Bell, H.E. Khor and K. Kochhar, 'China at the Threshold of a Market Economy' (Washington: International Monetary Fund, Occasional Paper 107, Sept. 1993) pp. 27, 60.
11. Ibid., pp. 3–4.
12. *The New York Times*, 15 August 1993, Sec. 1, p. 7.
13. N.R. Lardy, 'China as a NIC', *International Economic Insights*, IV, (May/June 1993) p. 5.
14. *Financial Times*, 20 January 1994, p. 4.
15. R.S. Jones, R.E. King and M. Klein, 'Economic Integration Between Hong Kong, Taiwan, and the Coastal Provinces of China', *OECD Economic Studies*, 20, Spring 1993, p. 119.
16. The Economist, A Survey of China, 28 November 1992, p. 4.
17. *The Wall Street Journal*, 3 September 1993, p. A6.
18. *The New York Times*, 11 April 1993, Sec. 1, p. 1.
19. *The New York Times*, 6 September 1993, p. A1.
20. L. Summers, 'The Rise of China', *International Economic Insights*, III (May/June 1992) p. 17.

10   Other Asia: Dragons, Tigers and an Elephant

1.   The World Bank, *The East Asian Miracle* (New York: Oxford University Press, 1993) p. 133.
2.   E.F. Vogel, *The Four Little Dragons: The Spread of Industrialization in East Asia* (Cambridge: Harvard University Press, 1991) p. 50.
3.   Ibid., p. 61.
4.   I. SaKong, *Korea in the World Economy* (Washington: Institute for International Economics, January 1993) p. 61.
5.   B. Aghevli and J. Marquez-Ruarte, 'A Case of Successful Adjustment in a Developing Country: Korea's Experience During 1980–84', in Sir F. Holmes (ed.), *Economic Adjustment: Policies and Problems* (Washington: International Monetary Fund, 1987) pp. 100–1.
6.   *The East Asian Miracle*, p. 130.
7.   United Nations Conference on Trade and Development (UNCTAD), *Trade and Development Report, 1993* (New York: United Nations, 1993) p. 128.

8. *Financial Times*, Survey, 31 August 1992, p. III.
9. *The East Asian Miracle*, pp. 136–9.
10. See, for example, *The Economist*, 2 October 1993, pp. 18–20, 41–2 and *Financial Times*, 27 September 1993, pp. 3, 27.
11. *The East Asian Miracle*, pp. 5–6.
12. Ibid., p. 354.
13. J. Eccheverri-Gent, 'Economic Reform in India: A Long and Winding Road', in *Economic Reform in Three Giants*, U.S.–Third World Policies Perspectives, No. 11, Overseas Development Council (New Brunswick, New Jersey: Transaction Books, 1990) p. 104.
14. J. Bhagwati, *India in Transition: Freeing the Economy* (Oxford: Clarendon Press, 1993) pp. 49–50.
15. Ibid., pp. 46–7.
16. Ibid., p. 79.
17. Ibid., p. 80.
18. Ibid., p. 69.
19. J. Bhagwati and T. N. Srinivasan, *India's Economic Reforms* (New Delhi: Ministry of Finance, July 1993). A report prepared at the invitation of Finance Minister Manmohan Singh.
20. *Financial Times*, Survey, 3 September 1993, p. x.
21. Bhagwati and Srinivasan, *India's Economic Reforms*, pp. 48–52.

11 Middle East and Africa: Oil, Wealth and Poverty

1. E.R. Fried and P.H. Trezise, *Oil Security: Retrospect and Prospect* (Washington: The Brookings Institution, 1993) p. 10.
2. D. Yergin, *The Prize: The Epic Quest for Oil, Money, and Power* (New York: Simon & Schuster, 1991) p. 721.
3. A. Richards and J. Waterbury, *A Political Economy of the Middle East* (Boulder, Colorado: Westview Press, 1990) p. 247.
4. Ibid., p. 248.
5. F. Al-Farsy, *Modernity and Tradition: The Saudi Equation* (London: Kegan Paul International, 1990) p. XXII.
6. The *Economist*, Survey, 13 February 1982, p. 4.
7. *The New York Times*, 3 January 1994, p. A3.
8. *Financial Times*, Survey, 5 May 1981, p. x.
9. *The Washington Post*, 13 December 1993, p. A1.
10. Data from World Bank, *World Development Report* (New York: Oxford University Press, various issues)
11. S. El-Naggar, 'Investment Policies in the Arab Countries: The Basic Issues', in S. El-Naggar (ed.), *Investment Policies in the Arab Countries* (Washington: International Monetary Fund, 1990) p. 8.
12. UN Economic Commission for Africa, *Economic Report on Africa 1993* (undated) pp. 47–8.

12 Democratisation and Reform in Latin America

1. *World Debt Tables, 1989–90* (The World Bank, 1989) p. 94.
2. R. Solomon, 'The Debt of Developing Countries: Another Look', *Brookings Papers on Economic Activity* (2:1981) pp. 602, 605.
3. The details of the Mexican crisis and how it was handled are graphically set forth in J. Kraft, *The Mexican Rescue* (Group of Thirty, 1984).
4. R. Solomon, 'An Overview of the International Debt Crisis', in H. Scholl (ed.), *International Finance and Financial Policy* (Westport, Connecticut: Quorum Books, 1990) p. 136.
5. N. Lustig, *Mexico: The Remaking of an Economy* (Washington: The Brookings Institution, 1992) p. 46.
6. P. Aspe, *Economic Transformation: The Mexican Way* (Cambridge: MIT Press, 1993) p. 147.
7. *Private Market Financing for Developing Countries* (International Monetary Fund, December 1993) p. 22.
8. *Financial Times*, Survey (29 March 1993) p. II.
9. B. Larre, 'Mexico', *The OECD Observer* 178 (November 1992) p. 40.
10. M.J. Francis, 'Dependency: Ideology, Fad, and Fact', in M. Novak and M.P. Jackson (eds), *Latin America: Dependency or Interdependence?* (Washington: American Enterprise Institute for Public Policy Research, 1985) pp. 88–105.
11. Aspe, *Economic Transformation*, p. 224.
12. Lustig, *Mexico*, p. 152, fn 38.
13. Volcker and Gyohten, *Changing Fortunes*, p. 199.
14. See Lustig, *Mexico* pp. 26–8.
15. Ibid., p. 39.
16. Aspe, *Economic Transformation*, pp. 22–4.
17. The complex details of the arrangement may be found in *World Debt Tables 1990–91* (The World Bank, 1990) pp. 58–9.
18. Solomon, 'An Overview of the International Debt Crisis', p. 154.
19. 'Mexico's Economic Performance Strengthens Adjustment and Reforms Continue', IMF *Survey* (23 August 1993) pp. 269–70.
20. C. Loser and E. Kalter (eds), *Mexico: The Strategy to Achieve Sustained Economic Growth*, Occasional Paper 99 (International Monetary Fund, September 1992) p. 7.
21. Aspe, *Economic Transformation*, p. 31.
22. P. Aspe, 'The Recent Experience of the Mexican Policymakers', in *Sea Changes in Latin America* (Washington: Group of Thirty, 1992) p. 5.
23. Lustig, *Mexico*, p. 109.
24. Larre, 'Mexico', pp. 40–41.
25. Lustig, *Mexico*, pp. 115–16, 121–2.
26. *The Wall Street Journal*, 15 June 1993, p. A15.
27. *World Tables 1993* (published for The World Bank, Baltimore: Johns Hopkins University Press, 1993) pp. 416–17.

28. *Financial Times*, Survey, 14 May 1992, p. IV.
29. A. Maddison, *The World Economy in the 20th Century* (OECD, 1989) p. 19.
30. *The Wall Street Journal*, 29 June 1993, p. A15.
31. *Financial Times*, Survey, 27 May 1993, p. 4.
32. *The Economist*, 18 April 1992, p. 20.
33. P. Meller, 'Chile', in J. Williamson (ed.), *Latin American Adjustment: How Much Has Happened?* (Washington: Institute for International Economics, April 1990), p. 54.
34. J. Williamson, *The Progress of Policy Reform in Latin America* (Washington: Institute for International Economics, Jan. 1990) p. 37.
35. Meller, 'Chile', pp. 80–84.
36. A. Bianchi, 'Chile: Economic Policies and Ideology during the Transition to Democracy', in *Sea Changes in Latin America* (Group of Thirty, 1992) p. 19.
37. S. Mainwaring, 'Democratic Governance and Political Institutions in Brazil', in *Brazil in a New World* (Report of the Inter-American Dialogue Workshop on Brazil, The Aspen Institute, June 1993) pp. 13–20.

13 Problems and Promises of an Uncertain Future

1. Commission of the European Communities, *Growth, Competitiveness, Employment – The Challenges and Ways Forward into the 21st Century (White Paper)* (Luxembourg: Office for Official Publications of the European Communities, 1993).
2. These propositions are spelled out in *Partners in Prosperity: The Report of the Twentieth Century Fund Task Force on the International Coordination of National Economic Policies* (New York: Priority Press Publications, 1991).
3. For example in the *Financial Times*, 11 January 1994, p. 19.
4. As recommended by *The Economist*, 15 January 1994, p. 16.
5. *The Washington Post*, 11 July 1993, p. A1.
6. *The New York Times*, 10 August 1993, p. A1.
7. L. Summers, 'Back to the Future', *The American Economy*, July/August 1992, p. 41.

Glossary

Current account balance Exports minus imports of goods, services, investment income and remittances.

Gross domestic product (GDP) The total value of the goods and services produced within the territory of the economy – that is, the economy's output. It is equal to expenditures by consumers, by businesses for investment goods and inventories, by governments and by foreigners for the country's exports minus expenditures for imports (which are included in the other spending categories). Real GDP values the output in the prices of a single year so as to measure physical output unaffected by price changes.

Gross national product (GNP) The total value of the output of the nationals of the country – GDP plus their income from economic activity abroad minus income earned in the country by foreign nationals.

Productivity Output per hour of work (labour productivity) or output per unit of capital equipment (capital productivity).

Real interest rates Nominal interest rates minus the change in prices during the period in which the interest rates prevailed.

Structural budget balance The budget surplus or deficit adjusted for the effects of the business cycle on the budget – that is, the surplus or deficit that would prevail if the economy were at high employment and full capacity.

Unit labor costs Wage and salary costs per unit of output (equal to wage rate divided by productivity).

Value added The value of output in a firm or sector or economy minus the value of materials bought from other firms, sectors or economies.

Index